Turkey facing east

Manchester University Press

Turkey facing east
Islam, modernity and foreign policy

Ayla Göl

Manchester University Press

Published by Manchester University Press
Altrincham Street, Manchester M1 7JA, UK
www.manchesteruniversitypress.co.uk

British Library Cataloguing-in-Publication Data is available

ISBN 978 1 5261 0748 0 *paperback*

First published by Manchester University Press in hardback 2013

This edition first published 2017

Printed by Lightning Source

Contents

Maps

Preface

This book is, first of all, a result of my intellectual curiosity about the relationship between Islam, modernity and foreign policy in Turkey. Both the *complexity* of the relationship between Islam and modernity, and the *necessary* conditions of the Turkish transformation from an Islamic empire to a modern state are usually *ahistorically* defined and poorly understood in the existing literature. Furthermore, despite Turkey's geo-political and geo-cultural existence 'in-between' the West and the East, the majority of works tend to focus almost exclusively on Turkey's engagement with the West in the process of its transition to a secular nation-state. I wanted to write a book which offers a critical analysis of the Turkish state transformation with reference to the complex interplay between Islam, modernity and foreign policy.

In doing so, this book makes three claims. First, it offers a new historical account of the Turkish state transformation, which highlights the importance of Eastern affairs during Turkey's transition from an Islamic empire to a modern nation-state. Existing studies have tended to focus almost exclusively on Turkey's engagement with Europe, and its subsequent pro-Western orientation and foreign policies in the early twentieth century. These studies, however, are somewhat blind to the important role played by Turkish nationalists' interactions with its Eastern neighbours – Armenia, Azerbaijan, Georgia and the Soviet Union – in establishing and legitimising the transitional regimes' existence in the European-dominated international system; they also fail to properly analyse the crucial role of Kemalist–Leninist engagement in the making of Turkey as a modern state. This book advances a new interpretation of this crucial historical juncture by arguing that the Turkish nationalists under Atatürk successfully resolved Turkey's nationalist disputes with their Eastern neighbours to cement their claims to sovereign authority over clearly demarcated territorial borders, thus legitimising their claims between 1918 and 1921 to modern statehood. Furthermore, by attaining the recognition of Turkish sovereignty from its neighbours in the East – as opposed to the West – they overrode Armenian territorial claims to Eastern Anatolia. Such an unorthodox reading of Turkish history highlights the long-neglected origins of Turkey's Eastern orientation as a response to changing geopolitics and balances of power at the beginning of the twentieth century.

Second, this book turns the spotlight on the historical origins of the ethno-nationalist tensions between Turks, Armenians and Kurds, which continues to haunt Turkish politics to the present day. Existing studies have tended to look at this issue in an ahistorical manner, preferring to concentrate on the highly politicised debate over whether or not the mass killings of Armenians took place. While this issue is important, focusing solely on this particular aspect of Turkish politics does not help us understand the historical origins of this ongoing dispute, which can be seen as one of the key obstacles to Turkey's European Union (EU) membership. This book therefore makes an important contribution by examining the process by which on-going competition between different nationalisms emerged among the successor states of the Ottoman Empire in the Middle East and the South Caucasus.

Third, this book highlights important historical continuities in Turkey's engagement with its Eastern neighbours. Turkey has long denied its cultural and Islamic connections in the East and relied on its relations with the West in international politics. However, at the beginning of the twenty-first century, the current pro-Islamic AKP (*Adalet ve Kalkinma Partisi* – the Justice and Development Party) government has shifted its foreign policy towards the Middle East by emphasising its cultural and historical 'soft' power. Conventional studies, which tend to overemphasise the importance of the West to Turkish foreign policy, cannot offer nuanced historical insights into Ankara's 'turn to the East', and treat it as if it was an entirely new and unexpected development. This book thus challenges many of the predominant assumptions about Turkey's unconditional pro-Western alignment by showing how Turkish foreign policy has historically oscillated between the West and the East. Furthermore, it emphasises the importance of the interplay between domestic and foreign relations during the creation of the modern state in a Muslim context based on European modernity. As such, it is better placed to analyse the historical continuities and changes in Turkey's Eastern engagement. Moreover, it highlights the relevance of Turkey's unique experience for Arab successor states of the Ottoman Empire in the contemporary Middle East. It warns the reader to be cautious about some premature conclusions in relation to the outcome of the Arab Spring. The findings prove that transition from authoritarian rule to a democratic and secular nation-state is possible in a Muslim society, but it is a long and complex historical process.

Acknowledgements

This is a long overdue book. At last, I am delighted to be able to thank many institutions, colleagues and friends who have been part of an intellectual journey stretching from Australia, England and Turkey to Wales. At the London School of Economics (LSE), Christopher Hill, who is now based at Cambridge University, was a great source of wisdom that guided me along the way to combining theory and history in the analysis of foreign policy. Fred Halliday offered the most valuable criticisms that made me aware of the importance of historical understanding of the international relations of the Middle East and strongly recommended the publication of this book. I was deeply saddened by his premature death.

While I had benefited enormously from the challenging intellectual tradition at the LSE, the strong research culture in Aberystwyth has been just as valuable in my transition from a research student to a lecturer. As a visiting fellow, I was lucky enough to take a break from teaching and be part of world-class research environments at the Research School of Pacific and Asian Studies, Australian National University in Canberra, and the Centre for Islamic Studies in Cambridge. It is a great pleasure to express my gratitude to the following people, who have all given me guidance and support whenever I needed at different stages of this journey: Ken Booth, Marie Breen-Smyth, Christopher Coker, Jenny Edkins, Lorraine Elliot, Mike Foley, Greg Fry, Richard Jackson, Paul Keal, Margot Light, Andrew Linklater, Jenny Mathers, Heather Rae, Chris Reus-Smit, Hidemi Sugunami, Yasir Suleiman, and Nicholas Wheeler. They all showed me the meaning of a true scholar. I know there is still a long way to go.

I should also like to acknowledge the help provided by the staff of the Public Record Office, Kew, the British Library, the National Library of Wales and the libraries of the LSE, the School of Oriental and African Studies, London University and Aberystwyth University; and also that of *Siyasal Bilgiler Fakültesi Kütüphanesi, Milli Kütüphane, TBMM Kütüphanesi* and *Başbakanlık Cumhuriyet Arşivi* in Ankara.

As usual, I would like to thank my family and friends who provided emotional support, encouragement and friendship over the years. In particular, I thank Gail Birkett, Hilaire Goodson, Megan de Messieres, Razmik Panossian, Herman

Salton, Aylin Ozet Siyahhan, Shogo Suzuki and Gül Tokay for being real friends. My deepest thanks also go to Kevin Williams for his unrivalled editorial skills and going well beyond the call of duty in helping me complete the final manuscript on time. My greatest debt is, however, particularly to my mother Perihan, who has supported me like no other throughout my career. I would not be where I am today without her support and encouragement, and I could not have achieved her unfulfilled dream of being a learned woman in a patriarchal society. My sister Nurcan and my brother Murat have always been there with their enthusiastic encouragement. Unfortunately, my father, Ismail Göl, did not live long enough to see the completion of this book. However, I have always derived inspiration from his strong belief in the progressive role of educated women in Turkish society.

I particularly wish to thank the students who I have had the great privilege of supervising and teaching at both postgraduate and undergraduate levels at the Department of Internationals at the LSE and the Department of International Politics in Aberystwyth University over the last couple of years. Finally, special thanks to Alexander James Dauncey for bringing the manuscript closer to immaculately proofread and the most efficient publishing team at the Manchester University Press as well as the two anonymous readers who strongly supported the project for yet another book on Turkey.

In short, it has been a long journey but which ended with self-discovery and the confidence that I have a voice to be heard, as Edward Said criticised with reference to Flaubert's description of 'Kuchuk Hanem' in *Orientalism, Western Conceptions of the Orient*. Of course, I am not only responsible for all mistakes and misconceptions but also sorry if I have forgotten to thank anyone here.

Aberystwyth, October 2012

Abbreviations

AKP	*Adalet ve Kalkınma Partisi*
AKSY	*Atatürk'ün Kurtuluş Savaşı Yazışmaları*
AMDP	*Atatürk'un Milli Dış Politikası*
ATTB	*Atatürk'ün Tamim, Telgraf ve Beyannameleri*
BBCumA	*Başbakanlık Cumhuriyet Arşivi*
BDA	British Documents on Atatürk
BDFA	British Documents on Foreign Affairs
BDHK	*Birinci Doğu Halkları Kurultayı*
CFP	Comparative Foreign Policy
CUP	Committee of Union and Progress
DBFP	Documents on British Foreign Policy
FO	Foreign Office
FPA	Foreign Policy Analysis
GNA	Grand National Assembly
IR	International Relations
NATO	North Atlantic Treaty Organisation
NEP	New Economic Policy
PRFRUS	Papers Relating to the Foreign Relations of the United States
TBMM	*Türkiye Büyük Millet Meclisi*
TKP	*Türk Komünist Partisi*
USSR	Union of Soviet Socialist Republics

1
Foreign policy analysis and transitional states

Turkey between 1918 and 1921 is identified as a transitional state, which had gone through a transformation from an Islamic empire to a modern nation-state. Turkey was the first historical example of a secular, nation-state in the Islamic world. However, such a complex process of transformation is usually explained as a 'one-man revolution', and its foreign relations as 'Kemalist' foreign policy in orthodox Turkish historiography.[1] The emergence of Turkish nationalism under the leadership of Mustafa Kemal Atatürk and foreign relations between the Turkish nationalists and Western Allies after the First World War became the dominant point of departure in understanding the making of modern Turkey.[2] This explanation overlooks one important fact: such a transformation is a product of complex socio-historical conditions, which cannot be reduced either to a single leader or to domestic conditions at a certain point in time. The existing literature also overlooks the role of the Turkish–Bolshevik rapprochement in the East during the making of a modern state in Turkey. Specifically, to understand the causes and consequences of the unique rapprochement between Turkish nationalists and the Russian Bolsheviks, after the collapse of the Ottoman and Russian empires, requires engagement beyond the mono-causal explanation of their common struggle against Western imperialism.

A new interdisciplinary theoretical framework is necessary in order to explain the complexity of state transformation and foreign policy-making when understanding a Muslim country's engagement with European modernity. After pointing out the insufficiency of studying domestic politics and/or the leadership only, the proposed theoretical approach here offers an analysis within a wider historical structure and specific context from a multi-causal and multi-disciplinary perspective. An attempt is made to base this new framework on three pillars: the study of foreign policy, transition to modernity and the ideology of nationalism. Alone, neither foreign policy nor modernity nor nationalism can explain Turkish state transformation and its influence on foreign policy-making. Together, each pillar is analysed, taking into consideration the implications of each analysis for the others, in order to present a novel understanding of Turkish foreign policy towards its eastern neighbours in the South Caucasus.

Bringing foreign policy back to international relations

As Hill argues 'foreign policy is a central part of our understanding of international relations, even if it is far from being the whole story. It is currently neglected, for some good reasons, but many bad, and it needs bringing back into focus.'[3] This need has become evident in the context of better understanding Muslim societies in the aftermath of 9/11 terrorist attacks in 2001 and the Arab Spring of 2011. The unprecedented events in international politics made us re-think the meaning of foreign policy in relation to who decides for whom, and who is affected by foreign policy decisions and actions at the international level. Therefore, the study of Foreign Policy Analysis (FPA) is chosen as the departing point for two main reasons: it is a 'bridging discipline',[4] and, more importantly, it translates 'abstract theory into concrete problems'.[5] Furthermore, FPA's interdisciplinary character creates the possibility of breaking down boundaries among the disciplines of social sciences in general, sociology in particular and International relations (IR). According to Rengger and Hoffman:[6]

> there were previous attempts in the late nineteenth century to identify international relations as an aspect of the developing discipline of sociology, thus firmly placing it within the history of the social sciences. These attempts to define the study of the international system as the sociology of world politics were unsuccessful in overturning the intellectual grip of international law. It is only within the last decade that there have been concerted efforts to try and reformulate the study of international relations in an historical sociological framework. This approach is exemplified, for example, in the works of Skocpol, Tilly, Barrington Moore, Halliday, Gellner and Hall.

Since the mid-1990s, there has also been a new trend to break down the boundaries among disciplines in order to understand the various aspects of global politics that scholars deal with under separate sub-fields in IR and FPA.[7] Based on this trend, this book proposes 'an interdisciplinary approach' to the analysis of the foreign policy of a state in transition by offering a new conceptual and theoretical framework and bringing history, sociology and FPA together.[8] The first part of the book, consisting of three chapters, proposes a new approach to the study of the foreign policy of a state, which aims to transform itself from an empire into a modern nation-state. The proposed interdisciplinary approach based on the triangle of foreign policy, modernity and nationalism which together represent a powerful explanation of the relationship between Turkish state-transformation and foreign policy-making. The second part of the book, consisting of four chapters, draws on a case-study in order to apply the new conceptual framework to the systematic empirical investigations of Turkish foreign policy towards the South Caucasus between 1918 and 1921. By combining conceptual framework with empirical study, it offers a theoretically informed analysis of history that explains the origins of Turkey's engagement in Eastern affairs from an interdisciplinary and critical perspective.

For methodological clarity, this chapter begins by evaluating the orthodox studies of FPA in the next section; it will assess the evolution of foreign policy analysis to demonstrate why a new theoretical approach to the foreign policies of transitional states is proposed here. The rest of the chapter will identify the main dimensions of the foreign policies of transitional states by differentiating them from those of traditional and modern states.

An evaluation of orthodox foreign policy analysis

In the age of globalisation and post-9/11 era, we witnessed the rise of new challenges to international security and the discourses of the global 'war on terror'. Meanwhile, the notions of modernity such as statehood, sovereignty, national identity and the foreign policy of states have become increasingly contested in the study of international relations. In general, the concept of foreign policy has been by-passed in the main theories of IR.[9] In particular, the increasing meta-theoretical interests in the studies of global politics 'have only occasionally collided with what has by now become the orthodoxy of a decision-making approach' in FPA.[10] However, the study of foreign policy is not only limited to the analysis of the decision-making process. As Hudson argues, FPA among all subfields of IR is the 'most radically *integrative* theoretical enterprise', which brings a broad variety of information from numerous disciplines of human knowledge through different levels of analysis.[11] This is why it is the departing point of an interdisciplinary approach to foreign policy, which sets up a new conceptual framework to explain a complex process of transformation from an Islamic empire to a modern nation-state in Turkey.

One minimalist definition of foreign policy is that it is 'the sum of official external relations conducted by an independent actor (usually a state) in international relations'.[12] The analysis of foreign policy is the ground of IR, which arguably could not exist as a discipline without FPA.[13] In this sense, FPA is the study of transactions between different units as independent actors; 'the domestic circumstances that produce them, the effect on them of the system and its structures and their influence on the system'.[14] Furthermore, as Smith argues, the disciplinary concerns of FPA overlap with four main epistemological, methodological and even ontological difficulties that are part of the general studies of IR.[15]

The first problem is about the theoretical concern: is there a general theory of international behaviour?[16] The second problem concerns the impact of the international system on the behaviour of states. The relationship between the state and the international system is double-edged. On the one hand, the international system determines the behaviour of states; on the other, the state becomes an independent agent. The third problem is on the role of human agencies/individuals given the fact that the main actors of foreign policy have been accepted as the decision-makers of states. But the impact of structures and processes on the behaviour of decision-makers cannot be denied by the theories of foreign policy.[17] And finally, the emphasis on the nation-state and the decision-making process has been particularly problematic for FPA.[18] However, despite the main criticism that FPA is state-centric foreign policy, analysts managed to move away from the state as the main actor and its policy-procedures.[19] Therefore, it is useful to begin with the self-criticism of foreign policy analysts but keeping in mind these major problems of IR.

The origins of traditional FPA can be divided into three main categories: the domestic politics perspective, middle-range theories and comparative foreign policy (CFP).[20] The first perspective sought to generalise about the sources of state behaviour by focusing on the decision-making process of the formal state apparatus.[21] Within this approach, the 'bureaucratic politics', 'rational actor' and 'organisation process' models became the most well-known explanations of how foreign policy decisions were made.[22] Thus, the study of decision-making occupied a central part of FPA.[23] The second approach, middle-range theories under the influence of behaviouralist methods, moved the focus to the concepts of perception/misperception, the personality of individual leaders and the effect of the psychology of groups on foreign policy.[24] Finally, the CFP approach, which is rooted in the neo-positivist vision of science, was a search for a theory via comparisons of a cross-national data analysis.[25]

Despite these developments, the increased importance of economic factors in international relations also led to a questioning of the role of state and the centrality of its decision-makers. Not only was the distinction between foreign and domestic policy seen as blurred because of interdependence between the developed and the developing worlds, but it was also recognised that a general theory of foreign policy behaviour was not going to emerge. Since the early 1970s, there has been a decline of CFP-type analysis and a resurgence of interest in an analytical focus on single-country theories.[26] Moreover, foreign policy analysts realised that FPA could afford to ignore neither the norms of external environment nor the structure of the international system.

Three main criticisms against 'classic FPA scholarship' will be summarised here.[27] As classified by Light, the first complaint is about the methodology of subject:

> 'grand' theorists maintain that FPA is devoid of theory; it is simply diplomatic history. Both diplomatic historians and IR traditionalists disagree, complaining that foreign policy analysts concentrate on political process at the expense of policy outcome and accusing them of 'scientism'. Methodological purists, on the other hand, believe that FPA methodology is insufficiently rigorous, while international system theorists argue that by focusing on the inner workings of the state, foreign policy analysts get the level of analysis wrong and study politics, not international relations.[28]

While the second complaint is a result of general disappointment that the empirical data of FPA relies heavily on US foreign policy, the third complaint was raised among foreign policy analysts themselves. Despite the early proponents' hopes, opening the 'black box' or 'billiard ball' did not lead the subject to produce the all-encompassing IR theory. More importantly, many analysts agree that FPA overemphasised processes taking place within states and, hence, understated systemic forces that might constrain the autonomy of policy-makers.[29] However, to accept these criticisms without giving counter arguments would be unfair to FPA.

In relation to the first complaint, one can argue that the study of foreign policy cannot be separated from the main theoretical and methodological concerns of IR. The forces of globalisation, international economy and digital revolution brought not only the state itself but also the international system into re-consideration. All these developments challenged the main concerns of foreign policy by re-questioning 'who acts, for whom and with what effects' at international level.[30] One of the main dilemmas of contemporary, and indeed of international theory, is that there is no legitimate means of allowing people to hold key policy-makers accountable for their decisions and actions at the international level.[31] Perhaps, one way of freeing international relations from this dilemma is in reconstituting the notions of agency, namely state and/or other units, with more sociological and critical explanations. In particular, it is true that the state and its decision-makers have been the major occupation of the study of foreign policy. As Fred Halliday reminds us:

> [t]he long-run implications of foreign policy analysis are such as to challenge the prevailing totality concept of the state: but much of the literature has been within a behavioural framework that ignores the relevance of sociological writing on the state, or has become restricted by a fetishism of decision-making as an end in itself.[32]

This criticism has its merits. But it unjustly misses a point; that not all foreign policy analysts neglected the sociological explanations about its main actor, namely the state, even if foreign policy has not reached the same degree of sophistication of sociology. Two major debates, which are ontologically embedded in the theoretical concerns of IR, have been taking place in FPA: the distinction between domestic and foreign, and the agency–structure debate. One the one hand, the debate over internal/external, domestic/foreign, and inside/outside in IR forced foreign policy analysts to re-consider 'the domestic sources of foreign policy' and its reverse, 'the external sources of domestic policy'.[33] On the other hand, the definition of foreign policy in the context of the agency–structure debate, and its relationship to the state has been prominent both in main debates of IR and FPA.[34]

The second complaint against FPA, that is its preoccupation with the already modernised/developed states, and in particular the United States of America, was addressed in the 1970s. Historically, a need for new theories for new states has become a subject for foreign policy analysts.[35] Most foreign policy analysts developed new models for the study of the new states' foreign policies by explaining their preoccupation with domestic politics and the role of interdependence within Third World literature. With the emergence of new states outside the European continent a new mode of thought had to take shape after the 1970s. There were various alternatives available:

(1) applying to new states the models constructed during the study of the already modernised countries, even though the concepts concerned may be culture-bound;

(2) employing a special frame of reference which focuses exclusively on the behaviour of young states with little experience or weight in international politics, and as yet only small industrial sectors;

(3) effectively combining the first two approaches by treating different types of
     state within the same set of concepts, but within a wider set than that gener-
     ally used in the US-based school of FPA.[36]

In the late 1970s, foreign policy analysts changed their attention to different independent variables and various types of states to investigate their foreign policies.
It was evident that to make any clear-cut generalisations about the sources of
foreign policy was difficult since there were so many various kinds of states, with
such diverse socio-economic backgrounds, cultural characteristics, geographic
locations and types of leadership.[37] Clearly, these attempts provided a departing
point from which to establish different approaches for the foreign policy of new
states. The question of developing a different understanding for the foreign policy
of new states was tackled within Third World studies by emphasising their interdependence within the world capitalist system in the 1980s.

The third criticism, that is that FPA did not produce the all-encompassing IR
theory, is itself contested. Since the 1980s, there have been five main approaches to
FPA.[38] The first approach is neo-realism, as represented by Kenneth Waltz's analysis. The second approach is the world economy perspective, which is popularised
by Immanuel Wallerstein and the world-system theorists. The third approach
can be labelled the quantification approach that is essentially the residual of CFP.
For this approach, the regularities of foreign policy behaviour can be discovered
through the gathering of empirical data. The fourth approach emphasises the use
of middle-range theories. The final, and most popular, approach involves a return
to single-country case studies, as used in this book.

Although the first two approaches did not actually analyse the foreign policy
of states, they made two important contributions to FPA: on the one hand, neo-
realism emphasised the centrality of the structure of the international system in
determining state behaviour; on the other, the world-system theorists brought
attention to the international economy as the main determinant of the foreign
policy behaviour of states.[39] Consequently, FPA has always produced many
competing approaches to the study of foreign policy rather than setting out to
provide an overarching single theory for IR, which has never been possible or
desirable.

In accordance with the progress of social sciences as a response to new challenges in the post-Cold War era, foreign policy analysts added further discussions
to FPA as a 'bridging discipline' in the changing politics of international relations.
This new trend has offered various alternative approaches to the study of foreign
policy by expanding the scope of the field into post-positivism.[40] In particular,
since Samuel P. Huntington's 'clash of civilisations' thesis, 'the study of culture
and identity' has been explicitly included in the different schools of IR, stretching
from constructivism and security studies to FPA.[41] In general, constructivists in
IR view international politics as a social interaction and put the emphasis on the
common system of values and ideas – culture, religion and identity.[42] Identity of
states, which is one of the main interests of constructivists, cannot be taken as
given, as the dominant theories of IR and the US-based school of FPA do, but

they are 'shaped through an interactive process between the choices of the state, the choices of other states and the impact of international society'.[43] However, constructivists have also been largely criticised by not taking 'domestic politics' and 'material interests' into account as seriously as mainstream approaches to IR and FPA might expect.[44]

By keeping these concerns in mind and as part of continuing regeneration that characterises FPA, I propose an interdisciplinary approach to the foreign policy of transitional states here so as to understand a single country case-study: the transformation of Turkey, which is in constant search for identity 'in-between' Islamic and Western civilisations. Hence, the study of identity is explicitly included in the analysis of the foreign policy of Turkey in transition from an Islamic empire to a modern nation-state. Furthermore, I argue that the 'transition to modernity', with its institutional clusters of nation and state, indicates a complex process of historical, social and political changes. Therefore, foreign policy behaviour of a state during transformation, as in the case of Turkey at the end of the First World War, must be considered within a wider framework by exploring the forces of socio-historical and political change. While constructivists generally acknowledge the influence of identity on foreign policy, they do not engage with the impact of any change in domestic politics. This is where an interdisciplinary approach to foreign policy turns to a Frankfurt School-inspired critical theory to question the process of socio-historical change.

In the sense that Robert Cox describes it, critical theory 'stands apart from the prevailing order of the world and asks how that came about'. Like constructivism, critical theory 'does not take institutions and social and power relations for granted but calls them into question concerning itself with their origins and how and whether they might be in the process of changing'.[45] Hence, it is important to highlight here that '[c]ritical theory is a theory of history in the sense of being concerned not just with the past but with a continuing process of historical change'.[46] Based on this notion of critical theory, a critical approach to foreign policy is concerned with 'the social and political complex as a whole' when analysing the foreign policy behaviour of a state going through an historical process of radical change. Furthermore, as emphasised by post-modernist critical theory, a critical approach to foreign policy of transitional states is explicitly concerned with 'historical and cultural contexts'.[47] Hence, it is not only engaged with critiquing 'traditional' FPA, but also engages with a 'changing reality' of foreign policy-making by continually adjusting 'its concepts to the changing object it seeks to understand and explain'.[48] In transitional states, the formulation and implementation of foreign policy are in flux due to the forces of socio-historical change and continually in search of ways to adjust to changing internal and external politics. Consequently, the foreign policy of transitional states is identified by five dimensions: the elements of historical continuity and change in policy-making; the dialectical relationship between historical structure and human agency; the role of the charismatic leader; the breakdown of the domestic-foreign policy distinction; and the social construction of national identity.

Five dimensions of the foreign policies of transitional states

The different disciplines of social sciences defined societies using 'binary oppositions' such as 'modern or backward, Western or non-Western, civilised or barbarian, and democratic or despotic'.[49] The differentiation between 'modernised or new states' and 'Western/developed or Third World' has been particularly influential in FPA literature. This is precisely the point at which the new theoretical framework of this book departs: in some societies there was a transitional period that placed them between these two opposed types, traditional and modern. The state in transition from one mode of organisation to another one bears the characteristics of these two different modes during the transformation process. Moreover, the transition to modernity is accepted as a continuing historical process that does not occur with a clear break between past and present. On the contrary, it is a historical process that can be interpreted as a dialogue between past and present. Therefore, states in transition have the characteristics of both 'traditional/pre-modern' and 'modern/developed' states. The influence of the Third World and/or new states discourse in FPA literature in the 1970s will be examined here first for two reasons: to understand how the foreign policy of new states is analysed; and to propose how this framework can be helpful, given the fact that the aim of a transitional state is to be a new state in the international system. The five dimensions of the foreign policies of transitional states will then be explained.

Generally, IR scholars dealing with new states begin with the liberation movements of the colonised states. For example, Robert Good accepts the modern state as a territorial one within the geographical framework of the old colony.[50] He argues that every new state tries to become a nation. In their struggle to gain nationhood against a colonial past, they face the task of effective and responsible government. During this process, foreign policy can be useful in four ways: first, as a continuation of the 'revolution' against colonial rule; second, as an attempt to establish the identity and integrity of the new state; third, as a means of keeping an in-group in power; fourth, as a means of reducing foreign influence at home.[51] In sum, his analysis emphasises the preoccupation of the new states with domestic politics.

Joel Migdal begins his analysis by showing the insufficiency of the main foreign policy models, namely the geopolitical, the organisational process and the bargaining models, to and understanding of the foreign policy orientations of the Third World states. He emphasises the lack of a unitary actor in these states and continues that in foreign policy there is a much greater stress on the concept of statesmanship than either a geopolitical, organisational process or bargaining model would allow.[52] Migdal suggests that analysts of the foreign policy-making of new states would do best to focus on the top leadership and would also benefit from the rational decision-making model. But he also emphasises that the rational actor model bears the specific limitations, which can be identified as non-human factors: the problem of information, international systemic constraints and ideology.[53] Thus, Migdal's conclusion is that when the foreign policy-making of new states is being studied, it is necessary though not satisfactory to focus on leadership.

In this case, to focus on leadership and to be preoccupied with domestic politics has become a general tendency when studying the foreign policies of these states. However, I argue that an interdisciplinary approach to the foreign policies of transitional states must be developed within a wider framework without associating it with either the level of the individual leader or domestic politics. While establishing a new theoretical framework, the explanations of different disciplines, such as critical theory on historical change, the international political theory on nationalism and historical sociology about behaviours of states, are taken into consideration. For instance, '[o]n the empirical side, the impact of historical sociologists has both directed attention away from politics and insisted on a much longer perspective than that employed by those interested in what is done (and not done) by foreign policy-makers'.[54] In general, it is true that while nation-states are often treated as 'actors' and/or 'agents' in the literature of IR, their decision-makers become the main actors/agents of FPA. In particular, the construction of the nation-state and the role of foreign policy during this process is analysed from a critical and sociological perspective. Moreover, these debates are particularly important in understanding the current rise of political and popular interests in the transitional period between the end of an Islamic empire and the emergence of a secular Republic with reference to Turkey's place and identity in the twentieth century.[55]

Historical continuity and change in policy-making

Having stated that transitional states experience historical change as a dialogue between past and present, the past represents traditional conditions while modernity becomes the present. In order to understand how this dialogue between past and present is intertwined with the historical continuity and change in the foreign policy of Turkey as a transitional state, we must identify these pre-modern and modern conditions first.

In general, the European experience of modernity was identified with the democratic values of individual freedom, the restrained power of government and the establishment of market economies. Intellectual historians found the roots of this project in the Reformation, the eighteenth-century Enlightenment, the French Revolution and the Industrial Revolution. In particular, the British, French, Italian and German nation-state building attempts in the nineteenth century meant the imposition of common political and cultural values, 'historical identity, even language on their populations'.[56] Therefore, some scholars accepted this European experience as the 'only one main highway to the world of modern industrial society, a highway leading to capitalism and political democracy' in the past.[57] Historically, to establish a new form of society based on the European model became the main aim of different societies outside Europe. Russia, Japan and Ottoman Turkey were the first examples of such transition among non-European societies; and within this trio Turkey stands out as the only Muslim country. As William Wallace pointed out:

'Europeanisation' and 'modernisation' were synonymous for states which wished to catch up with France, Britain, and later Germany, as these three countries competed for political economic and cultural superiority. First Peter the Great's Russia, then post-Meiji restoration Japan, then Kemal Atatürk's Turkey, saw the adoption of European education and institutions, and even of European dress, manners, dancing styles, as the key to national advance. In the confident decades which preceded World War I, European history and world history seemed practically synonymous; 'the expansion of Europe' … was the march of progress.[58]

Even if calling these societies 'non-European', 'oriental despotism',[59] 'an agrarian bureaucracy or an Asian version of royal absolutism'[60] is discredited in post-modern and post-colonial studies, one cannot deny that the political systems of these non-European societies had certain characteristics different from those of their West European counterparts. In a very broad sense, their mode of imperial organisation depended on an autocratic ruler with a relatively small professional bureaucracy. Their limited sense of community was not based on national consciousness but on local and religious affiliations. While a strong military aristocracy was a significant characteristic, apolitical submissive peasants were the majority. As a result of expansion of international society in the nineteenth century, according to Barrington Moore's analysis, these societies, especially Japan, 'faced two major problems: one was to achieve a modern centralised state. The other was to create a modern industrial economy.'[61] If they wanted to survive as an independent state in the international system, these were the requirements.

Some key characteristics of traditional non-European societies, such as the lack of developed administrative co-ordination, the military strength of the ruling authorities and inefficient bureaucracy, changed little during the transition process.[62] However, as will be examined in the case of Turkey, once the political system of the nation-state was established, these characteristics had to change and adapt to European models of modernity significantly. During the transformation process three main features of modernity influenced the nature of socio-political organisation in Europe: firstly, 'the emergent social order of modernity is *capitalistic* in both its economic system and its other institutions'; secondly, 'the rapidly changing character of modern social life' derives from 'the industrial exploitation of nature'; third, '"Rationalisation", as expressed in technology and in the organisation of human activities, in the shape of bureaucracy, is the keynote.'[63] While the features of the modern political system – the nation-state – is analysed separately from discussion of the progress of either capitalism or industrialism, the emphasis will be on the rationalisation of bureaucracy in order to understand the link between the transition to modernity and the foreign policy analysis of a transitional state in the context of Turkey.[64]

If a society wanted to become modern, the great emphasis has been on goal-directed rationality.[65] Therefore, the notion of 'instrumental rationality' and the establishment of 'a large-scale professional bureaucracy' can be identified as the main difficulties facing transitional states.[66] Within this context the forces of socio-political change during the transformation process not only influence domestic policies but also create 'certain disabilities that impede rational and efficient foreign policies'.[67] As a consequence of these difficulties, the dimensions of foreign policies of transitional societies differ from those of relatively modernised and/or developed societies.[68]

First, the policy-making of modern states has been intensively 'bureaucratised', increasing the importance of a bureaucratic model while decreasing the relevance of rationality models for understanding foreign policy. Second, the analysis of modern bureaucracies not only undermines the picture of a political leader rationally pursuing explicit external goals, but also emphasises the role of interest-group politics, which involves both lateral and vertical bargaining among and/or within different administrative units. Thus, not only does the making of foreign policy become a reflection of what occurs in the bureaucracies, but also the plurality of policy channels brings home the contrast between daily decision-making in low-policy areas and 'the more unified and consistent nature of decision-making in crises and in high politics. With such increases in routine, control at the top becomes more difficult.'[69] Third, as a consequence of transition to modernity not only do the mechanised technologies of communication turn an apolitical mass into a self-aware public, but also the growth in the mass circulation of newspapers creates an influential media and public opinion.

Contrary to these features of modernised states' policy-making, no pre-modern and/or transitional 'states were able even to approach the level of administrative co-ordination developed in the nation-state'.[70] The policy-making process was dominated by a ruling group which usually had direct access to the means of violence. As Anthony Giddens recognises, this used to be 'a class of warriors'.[71] It makes perfect sense in the case of Turkey, as the leaders of the Turkish national liberation movement were the high rank soldiers of the Ottoman Empire during the First World War. Moreover, as taken for granted in the case of modern states' foreign policy-making, an effective bureaucratisation of policy-making which is based on lateral bargaining among the different administrative units cannot be found during transition. In addition, it would be naive to trace the influence of public opinion, media and pressure groups within this process. Therefore, in order to understand the foreign policies of transitional states an analytical focus on top political leaders and their domestic politics seems inevitable. Yet although these approaches are not regarded as entirely irrelevant here, the critical approach of this study is that they neglect the particular historical–structural conditions which might affect the decisions of leaders in domestic politics.

The impact of modernity on the decision-makers

As a result of the traditional characteristics of transitional states, foreign policy might be considered as a personal rather than an institutional process. In general, traditional foreign policy approaches often focus on the level of the individual leader by '[a]ssuming that the individual decision-maker, mostly a top political leader, is important, [and] approaches such as operational core or cognitive mapping are used to establish the belief system of the actor'.[72] This is even more noticeable in the case of newly emerging states since their image is based mainly on two conditions. The first is the importance of strong leaders: we accept that decisions are taken either by an individual or by a council of leaders in both domestic and foreign policy. The second is the lack of expertise in policy-making. Leaders of developing countries do not have a complex and coherent set of organisations which constrain their decisions.[73] Under these conditions in most developing states, one expected result is a 'personalised foreign policy', as in the cases of Atatürk, Castro, Nehru, Nasser, Nkrumah, Sukarno, Gaddafi and Saddam to mention but a few outstanding examples.[74] Therefore, the appearance of 'charismatic' and/or 'revolutionary' leaders in Asia, Africa, the Middle East and Latin America has been accepted as an integral part of the political readjustments and development of the Third World countries.[75] But it is still arguable whether the presence of strong leadership alone can suffice to take a country along the path to modernity or to implement a country's long-term foreign policy orientations.

After mentioning these empirical considerations, it is worth summarising how foreign policy analysts theoretically deal with the relationship between the role of the decision-makers as agency and the structure of the political sphere. There were two main debates which brought the scholars of IR and FPA together: the 'level of analysis' and the 'agent-structure' issue. In relation to the first debate, David Singer articulated two possible levels of analysis – the international system and the national state – 'to assess the relative utility of the two and attempt some general statement as to their prospective contributions to greater theoretical growth in the study of international relations'.[76] These two levels are not immediately combinable.[77] Therefore, each level stands for itself and ignores the other. In relation to the second debate, Alexander Wendt brought the 'agent-structure' issue into IR discussions. After criticising Waltz's version of structuralism and that of Immanuel Wallerstein, Wendt introduced structuration theory, which 'conceptualises agents and structures as mutually constituted or codetermined entities'.[78] In response to Wendt's attempts, Hollis and Smith demonstrated that the 'level-of-analysis' or structure/actor problem belongs to a holism versus individualism problem.[79] At this point, the debate became more problematic. Wendt criticised Hollis and Smith for conflating the level of analysis problem with the agent-structure problem. Furthermore, 'what Wendt felt Hollis and Smith importantly overlook is that, regardless of the level, the same *unit* of analysis is utilised as the dependent variable: the foreign policy of states'.[80] In order to resolve the agency-structure issue within FPA, Walter Carlsnaes suggests:

> a framework for analysing foreign policy actions in terms of a dynamic account of the ways in which such actions are continually being constrained *and* enabled by contextually defined structures, and how these in turn are affected by human agency, it follows that one must perforce jettison the practice of viewing foreign policy in terms of separate and distinct actors possessing discrete, divisible, and 'comparable' properties, whose behaviour can be encapsulated inductively in terms of discontinuous events-behaviours proceeding serially in temporal increments.[81]

Following this mode of thought, Hill argues 'a clear distinction must be made between units of analysis and modes of explanation, which proponents of the old "levels of analysis" model did not always do. Individuals, states and the international system are units of analysis; they do not necessarily explain outcomes in themselves.'[82] Hill adds a new dimension to the debate that 'the "level of analysis" approach will no longer do, except in the most basic sense of alerting newcomers to international relations of the different perspectives that may be obtained by looking at things through the perspective of the individual, the state and the international system as a whole'.[83] In order to provide an explanation of causation or prescriptions for change, the analysis must focus on sources such as 'structures, processes and interactions between units'. Hence, 'foreign policy-making is a complex process of interaction between many actors, differentially embedded in a wide range of different kinds of structure. Their interaction is a dynamic process, leading to the constant evolution of both actors and structures.'[84]

In addition, it can be argued that internal change itself and international systemic constraints within which goals and policies are chosen can be more determining than the role of the leader in certain circumstances. Clearly, the conditions of newly emerging states 'are related to world historical circumstances largely beyond the leaders' control'.[85] This book argues that one of the most important elements of these conditions is the transition to modernity via nation-state building. Although the transition to modernity is accepted as a political structure within which the foreign policy of this kind of state can be engaged, this does not imply that the political structure is the only structural source of foreign policy. As Larsen suggests, there are other structural sources, such as 'the economic structure or the social structure', which influence foreign policy.[86] Therefore, the concept of modernity contributes not only to bringing the political, economic and social dimensions together, but also to establishing a wide historical structure based on multi-causality for analysing the foreign policy of transitional states. The structural forces of the Turkish transition to modernity and its impact on the leaders are examined in Chapter 2.

Moreover, the leaders are also the products of their own historical time. The reasons for the rise and fall of one-man power must be situated within an understanding of the socio-political structure of these states. It is similarly a debatable point whether leadership in itself will produce adequate cohesion to continue in power, as we witnessed in the case of the fall of Saddam and of Gaddafi in the twenty-first century. Thus, the level of individuals should not be accepted as a *sine qua non* of socio-political transformation and foreign policy-making in non-European societies. In addition, the role of leaders still needs to be considered with care since 'personalised foreign policy' cannot only be associated with the developing countries.[87] The element of leadership is undoubtedly a key factor in the political outcomes of developing countries as well as in those of developed countries. The argument here is that in a single, low-level foreign policy decision or in a crisis situation, the role of the individual leader might be extended.

However, when it is related to the analysing of general trends in a country's foreign policy, such as Turkish policy towards the South Caucasus between 1918 and 1921, 'the individualist beliefs give way to social beliefs and those beliefs constitute a central framework within which policy-making takes place (rather than just being one variable amongst many)'.[88] In particular, the question to which an answer must be found is whether a key individual, Mustafa Kemal Atatürk in this case-study, 'can occupy a structural position which would ensure a special influence on decisions. In a broader perspective, the question is whether the individual as a result of, for example, charisma can change the dominant culture or consensus and perhaps the rules of governance.'[89] The implications of the concept of 'charisma' in FPA lead us to the investigation of the role of the charismatic leader during the transition process.

The role of the charismatic leader

Weber distinguishes three bases of legitimate authority: the rational-legal authority, the traditional authority and the charismatic authority. In addition to this differentiation, he also emphasises the transformations of these types of authority, notably the traditionalisation of rational-legal authority. According to Richard Snyder *et al.*, two aspects of Weber's discussion are relevant and noteworthy for FPA. First, Weber calls attention to the different ways in which the actor orients social structures by distinguishing the various types of authority. Second, in discussing the transformations of these types, they accept that the transformations involve the traditionalisation of the other two types of authority, namely the legal and the charismatic authorities. In Weber's definition, traditionally oriented action is determined by the automatic reaction to habitual stimuli which guide behaviour in a course which has been repeatedly followed. Thus, the organisational structure may be treated as a set of rules for the actors. But, the most important question arises: 'How does the actor interpret the rules?'[90] Snyder *et al.* continue the discussion by emphasising the institutionalisation of rationality and argue that the actor does not always act rationally in a planned social system. 'The key point is that it seems necessary to postulate that to a very high degree the orientations of the actor are independent of and vary irrespective of the characteristics of the social system of which he is a member at any given time.'[91]

Carlsnaes does not seem to agree with the analysis of Snyder *et al.* Carlsnaes calls it 'Weber's methodological individualism'. He adds that the sociologist's main task is to establish a causal explanation of the social action of individuals. He uses Ernest Gellner's encapsulation of the relationship between history and men. To some extent, as a critic of methodological individualism, Gellner says that: 'History is about chaps. It does not follow that its explanations are always in terms of chaps.'[92] Carlsnaes uses Sprouts' argument that non-human and environmental factors can directly determine or cause policies. He criticises 'methodological individualism', which 'claims that everything happens in a social system is directly the intended result of human intention, and therefore can be explained wholly in such terms. This is of course not the case at all.'[93]

It seems that Weber accepts the interdependence between leaders and the social conditions. Weber defines 'charisma' as follows:

> The term 'charisma' will be applied to certain quality of an individual personality by virtue of which he is set apart form ordinary men and treated as endowed with supernatural, superhuman, or at least specifically exceptional powers or qualities. These are

such as are not accessible to the ordinary person, but are regarded as of divine origin
or as exemplary, and on the basis of them the individual concerned is treated as a
leader. ... What is alone important is how the individual is actually regarded by those
subject to charismatic authority, by his 'followers' or 'disciples'.[94]

Weber then offers five criteria to define the relationship between the charismatic leader and the followers: First, 'It is recognition on part of those subject
to authority which is decisive for the validity of charisma.' This recognition of
motivations, psychologically, arises out of enthusiasm, or of despair and hope.
Second, the disappearance of charismatic power will occur if the leader is unsuc-
cessful in the long term, more importantly if his leadership fails to benefit his
followers. Third, an emotional form of communal relationship is the base of a cor-
porate group which is subject to charismatic authority. There is no hierarchy; no
such thing as a definite sphere of authority; no established organs. Fourth, pure
charisma refuses to deal with the everyday routine; in this sense it is specifically
foreign to economic considerations. Fifth, charisma is the greatest revolutionary
force in traditionally stereotyped periods.[95]

In the light of this mode of thought, I would like to highlight the importance
of charismatic leadership as a 'revolutionary' force and also stress the irrational
side of it. In Weber's argument, the charismatic type is an antithesis of the everyday routine control of action, unlike both rational and traditional authority. He
argues that charismatic authority is irrational in terms of being foreign to all rules.
In contrast, bureaucratic authority is specifically rational in the sense of being
bound to intellectually analysable rules. In a similar way, traditional authority is
bound to the past, and to this extent is also oriented to rules, while charismatic
leadership repudiates the past.[96]

These elements of charismatic leadership are used to understand the nature
of Turkish nationalist foreign policy towards the South Caucasus in the second
part of this book. While the Ottoman rulers represented the traditional authority which was bound to the past, the Turkish nationalist leaders repudiated the
past and became a revolutionary force in the transition to modernity. As will be
examined later, Mustafa Kemal's rise as the leader of the Turkish national movement was partly based on elements of charisma displayed in his military victories
against the Allied Powers. In general, the charismatic leader has been given an
historical role 'who by force of sheer personality can apparently bridge the gap
between the [nationalist] elites and the [mass] population, and who can serve as
the symbolic link between the ruler and the ruled'.[97] Although the case of Kemal
Atatürk is not exceptional in this sense, there is an ambiguity regarding his role.
Sometimes he is accepted as a 'charismatic leader',[98] and sometimes as a strategist
or man of organisational character. However, an interdisciplinary approach to
foreign policy does not accept the role of the individual leaders as a tailor-made
explanation for transitional states. For these states, it is understandable that an
analysis focuses on the personalised policy-making under the condition of institutional vacuums, but the role of 'the great man' cannot legitimise the exclusion
of structural, societal and international factors. To focus *a priori* on the role of

leaders does not provide satisfactory answers to the basic questions related to variable factors.[99] The level of the individual is only one 'amongst several domestic structural causes which must be taken into account in foreign policy analysis of the general foreign policy line of a state'.[100] Therefore, any challenge to the level of the individual brings out the necessity for a new theoretical framework, which explains the structural constraints on the domestic and foreign policy of a given state.

The domestic-foreign policy interrelation

In conventional IR theory, it has been accepted that the state engages separately in domestic and foreign policy. For instance, while Henry Kissinger argued that '[t]he domestic structure is taken as given; foreign policy begins where domestic policy ends',[101] F.S. Northedge emphasised 'a sharp distinction between the implementation of foreign policy and the execution of domestic policy'.[102] Thus, realist theory assumed that these two spheres of policy are different.[103] Yet, for non-realist theory, specifically the pluralists like James Rosenau and John Burton, the distinction between the two forms of policy has long been 'an artificial one'.[104] As mentioned earlier, some scholars called into question this sharp distinction by providing a middle way: foreign policy has its domestic sources, and domestic policy has its foreign influences.[105] The creation of the modern international system has involved 'the emergence of relatively strong territorially-based political units, capable of exerting control domestically, but obliged to accept the existence of similarly formed political units externally'.[106] If one follows this line of thought, foreign policy becomes a necessary activity of the modern state.[107]

The main question here is how the distinction between the domestic and foreign policy spheres relates to the modernisation process of traditional states. Edward Morse argues that, in both actual and ideal terms, the distinction between foreign and domestic policies was a characteristic of the foreign policies of non-modernised societies.[108] As a result of this clear differentiation, most analyses tend to prioritise one policy over the other. There is general agreement that while foreign policy is important for any new state, the first order of business for these states is inevitably domestic.[109] However, the preoccupation of new states with domestic politics is misleading since these states are also trying to be part of the international system, which requires interaction between the different units. As has been argued earlier, transitional states by definition bear the characteristics of both pre-modern and modernised societies. Thus, it becomes even more difficult to make a clear statement about the priorities of one policy over another while dealing with transitional states. I would like to argue that the interlinked nature of the two policies, i.e. foreign policy has its domestic sources and domestic policy has its foreign influences, is a clear indication of the transition to modernity. If a state wants to be a modern one in the interdependent international system, the linkages between the two spheres of policies are an inevitable result. However, this statement does not imply that foreign policy is analytically indistinguishable from domestic policy, it simply 'accepts that the notion of domestic is inextricably bound up with that of foreign policy'.[110] In this context, it suggests 'domestic and foreign are two ends of a continuum rather than polar opposites' under the conditions of transition to modernity.[111] Therefore, this process leads to the transformation of foreign policy of a new state, which cannot be separated from either the other aspects of domestic settings or the international system's requirements.

Moreover, the argument about the preoccupation of the newly emerging states with domestic politics can be turned on its head by emphasising how these states were able to prioritise foreign affairs. For the subject matter of this book, foreign policy had an important function in the creation of a modern Turkish state between 1918 and 1921. More precisely, the co-operation between the Turkish nationalists and the Russian Bolsheviks rather than the continuation of historical Turkish–Russian animosity was a result of each other's need to succeed in the transformation of new political identities in the regional and international context. This co-operation can also be interpreted as a sign of modernisation in these new states' foreign policies. It was clear in the case of the Turkish–Armenian border dispute that the two new regimes were concerned with the notion of statehood. The relationship between border and statehood also brings the notion of the domestic into the analysis: 'The state has a clear frontier, both literally and constitutionally. Its power, even its capacity to exercise sovereignty may often be restricted, but where its legal authority starts and finishes should always be clear.'[112] In this context, the aims of both foreign and domestic polices are influenced by the requirements of the transition from a different mode of organisation to a modern state. Consequently, the next section will argue that the foreign policies of states in transition also contribute to the construction of a modern political identity.

The role of foreign policy in the recognition of political identity

A modern state has two main aspects: it represents a national identity in international society, and it exercises power through a set of central political institutions within a clearly demarcated territory.[113] While examining the construction of modern political identity in Chapter 2, it will be seen that these two aspects of modern nation-states are closely intertwined. On the one hand, the notion of 'we' is defined within the boundaries of state, while on the other, the notion of 'other' is related to outside the boundaries. In short, '[s]tate-territorial sovereignty and an associated sense of nationhood were the necessary prerequisites for a political entity achieving modern *moral* identity'.[114] It is argued that a common feature of foreign policies of the developing countries is that priority is given to the problems of nation-building and nationalism.[115] Thus, the focus is upon establishing an identity in the 'domestic realm' and protecting the integrity of new states in accordance with the forces of 'nationalism' in the modern world.[116]

However, identity construction is not only limited to the domestic realm, but also closely related to the foreign policy sphere under the conditions of the transition to modernity. As will be examined in Chapter 2, one of the main requirements of modernity is the construction of a nation in relation to a politically defined state and that foreign policy plays a crucial role during this process in two ways. On the one hand, it becomes a means of differentiating between 'inside and outside' and 'self and other'. On the other hand, foreign policy helps to establish the new political identity in international society, through its recognition by other actors. For transitional states, therefore, foreign policy becomes an important element of constructing a new self-identity. After the establishment of this identity, the relationship between foreign policy and the national identity differs from their specific relationship during the transitional period. For already established states, foreign policy helps to differentiate between the 'national community' that the government represents abroad and 'the foreigners' with whom it deals. National identity also represents necessary myths, the sources of national pride, and the values which underpin foreign policy. More importantly, it legitimises the actions of government in defence of 'national interest'.[117] In sum, nation-states need 'a sense of identity, an image of what marks their government and their citizens from their neighbours' in the modern international system and '[f]oreign policy is partly a reflection of that search for identity'.[118] Within this context, the relationship between the construction of Turkish national identity and Turkish foreign policy towards the South Caucasus will be examined in the case-study.

In conclusion, the five main dimensions of foreign policy – the elements of historical continuity and change, the impact of modernity on decision-making, the role of the charismatic leader, the domestic-foreign inter-relation and national identity construction – all appear in a distinctive way during the process of transition to modernity. There is, however, one more aspect of foreign policy to consider which is not directly related to the early stages of transition to modernity but to its later stages. It is true that, in an age of globalisation, late developers might become part of the contemporary world economy before they participate in the international diplomatic system. The inevitable result of incorporation into the world economic system is the development of a national capitalist economy and industrialisation, which are also among the essential clusters of modernity. In short, the transition to modernity via nation-state building requires the establishment of private capitalism with its own forms of organisation, capital and technology. However, in developing societies these elements cannot be brought together with their own resources. Rather, they must be imported from the developed world until indigenous capitalism is established. Foreign investment and companies will appear or even, maybe, be formally invited during the initial stage of this process. Without going into more detail about economic development policies, we can clearly underline the importance of the foreign policy channel when deciding the terms of foreign aid between the partners. However, this dimension of transitional foreign policy is beyond the scope of this book, which is limited to the socio-historical stages of the transition to modernity.

Concluding remarks

This chapter explained why FPA – as the ground of IR – has been accepted as the first pillar of a new theoretical framework, which aims to analyse Turkish foreign policy towards the South Caucasus between 1918 and 1921. It was suggested that FPA, due to its interdisciplinary character, has become the departing point of the new approach that attempts to break the boundaries between the disciplines of social sciences. In particular, this chapter identified five main dimensions of foreign policy as a consequence of the transition to modernity in non-European societies: historical continuity and change in policy-making, the impact of modernity on the decision-makers, the role of charismatic leader, breakdown of the domestic-foreign distinction and the national identity construction. The main concern was to explain that the foreign policy of a transitional state must be developed within a wider historical and socio-political context.

Having evaluated the progress of foreign policy analysis, it was concluded that it is inevitable, though not satisfactory to focus on leadership and the domestic realm when the foreign policy of a state in transition is being studied. It was also stated that the transition to modernity is a consequence of a dialogue between past and present and also that the transitional states, by definition, bear the characteristics of both traditional and modern societies. While the nation-state is accepted as the most prominent social form of modernity, the transition to a modern nation-state is regarded as a particular historical structure, which influences the foreign policies of such states. Under the conditions of transition to modernity, domestic structural change itself and the international systemic constraints within which foreign policy goals are chosen can be more determining than the role of the leader. Therefore, Chapter 2 will explain why the concept of modernity has become the second pillar of an interdisciplinary approach to foreign policy of transitional states while bridging the gap between FPA and historical sociology.

Notes

1 See Patrick Kinross, *Atatürk: The Rebirth of a Nation*, London, Weidenfeld, 1993; Ahmet Taner Kışlalı, *Kemalizm, Laiklik ve Demokrasi*, Ankara, İmge, 1994; Suna Kili, *Atatürk Devrimi: Bir Çağdaşlaşma Modeli*, Ankara, 1995; Levent Köker, *Modernleşme, Kemalizm ve Demokrasi*, İstanbul, İletişim, 1995; Emin Türk Eliçin, *Kemalist Devrim İdeolojisi*, İstanbul, Sarmal Yayınevi, 1996; Menter Şahinler, *Atatürkçülüğün Kökeni, Etkisi ve Güncelliği*, İstanbul, Çağdaş Yayınları, 1998; Robert Mantran, 'Mustafa Kemal Atatürk', in Olivier Roy, ed., *Turkey Today: A European Country?*, London, Anthem Press, 2004, pp. 119–130.

2 Bernard Lewis, *The Emergence of Modern Turkey*, London, Oxford University Press, 1968; Feroz Ahmad, *The Making of Modern Turkey*, London, Routledge, 1993; Erik Jan Zürcher, *Turkey: A Modern History*, London, I.B. Tauris Publishers, 1995; Serif Mardin, *Religion, Society and Modernity in Turkey*, Syracuse University Press, 2006; Dietrich Jung and Wolfango Piccoli, *Turkey at the Crossroads: Ottoman Legacies and a Greater Middle East*, London: Zed Books, 2001; Roy, ed., *Turkey Today*; Ersin Kalaycioglu, *Turkish Dynamics: Bridge across Troubled Lands*, London, Palgrave Macmillan, 2005, pp. 35–38; Roy, ed., *Turkey Today*.

3 Christopher Hill, *The Changing Politics of Foreign Policy*, London, Palgrave Macmillan, 2003, p. 23.

4 James N. Rosenau, 'Introduction: New Directions and Recurrent Questions in the Comparative Study of Foreign Policy', in C.F. Hermann, C. Kegley, W. Charles and

J.N. Rosenau, eds, *New Directions in the Study of Foreign Policy*, London, George Allen & Unwin, 1987, p. 1.

5 Margot Light, 'Foreign Policy Analysis', in A.J.R. Groom and Margot Light, eds, *Contemporary International Theories: A Guide to Theory*, London, Pinter Publishers, 1994, p. 94.

6 Nick Rengger and Mark Hoffman, 'Modernity, Postmodernism and International Relations', in J. Doherty, E. Graham and M. Malek, eds, *Post-Modernism in the Social Sciences*, Houndmills, Basingstoke, Macmillan, 1992, p. 144, fn. 5.

7 See, for example, Fred Halliday, *Rethinking International Relations*, London, Macmillan, 1994; Justin Rosenberg, *The Empire of Civil Society: A Critique of the Realist Theory of International Relations*, London, Verso, 1994; Stephen Hobden, *International Relations and Historical Sociology: Breaking Down Boundaries*, London, Routledge, 1998; Valerie M. Hudson, 'Foreign Policy Analysis: Actor-specific Theory and the Ground of International Relations', *Foreign Policy Analysis*, 1:1 (2005), pp. 1–30; Jeffrey Haynes, *An Introduction to International Relations and Religion*, Harlow: Pearson, 2007; Carolyn M. Warner and Stephen G. Walker, 'Thinking about the Role of Religion in Foreign Policy: A Framework for Analysis', *Foreign Policy Analysis*, 7:1 (2011), pp. 113–135.

8 Peter van den Besselaar and Gaston Heimeriks, 'Disciplinary, Multidisciplinary, Interdisciplinary – Concepts and Indicators', paper presented for the 8th Conference on Scientometrics and Informetrics, Sydney, Australia, 2001, p. 2.

9 See Scott Burchill, Andrew Linklater *et al.*, *Theories of International Relations*, London, Palgrave Macmillan, 2012.

10 Christopher J. Hill, 'What is Left of the Domestic?: A Reverse Angle View of Foreign Policy', in Michi Ebata and Beverly Neufeld, eds, *Confronting the Political in International Relations*, London, Macmillan, 2000, p. 151.

11 Hudson, 'Foreign Policy Analysis', p. 2.

12 Hill, *The Changing Politics of Foreign Policy*, p. 3.

13 Hudson, 'Foreign Policy Analysis', p. 2.

14 In this line of thought, the unit is 'an independent actor' so as to allow the inclusion of all parts of the governing mechanisms of the state and/or non-state enterprises. Hill, *The Changing Politics of Foreign Policy*; Light, 'Foreign Policy Analysis', p. 94.

15 Steve Smith, 'Theories of Foreign Policy: An Historical Overview', *Review of International Studies*, 12:1 (1986), p. 24.

16 Martin Wight, 'Why is There no International Theory?', in James Der Derian, ed., *International Theory: Critical Investigations*, London, Macmillan, 1995, p. 15.

17 Walter Carlsnaes, 'The Agency-Structure Problem in Foreign Policy Analysis', *International Studies Quarterly*, 36:3 (1992), p. 245.

18 Smith, 'Theories of Foreign Policy', p. 25.

19 Christopher J. Hill, 'The Credentials of Foreign Policy Analysis', *Millennium: Journal of International Studies*, 3:2 (1974), 158.

20 Light, 'Foreign Policy Analysis', p. 93.

21 Steve Smith, 'Foreign Policy Analysis and International Relations', in Hugh C. Dyer and Leon Mangasarian, eds, *The Study of International Relations*, London, Macmillan, 1989, p. 376.

22 Graham T. Allison, *Essence of Decision*, Boston, Little, Brown, 1971, *passim*.

23 Christopher J. Hill and Margot Light, 'Foreign Policy Analysis', in Margot Light and A.J.R Groom, eds, *International Relations: A Handbook of Current Theory*, London, Frances Pinter, 1985, p. 157.

24 The best examples are Steve Chan and Donald A. Sylvan, *Foreign Policy Decision Making: Perception, Cognition, and Artificial Intelligence*, New York, Praeger, 1984; Eric Singer and Valerie Hudson, eds, *Political Psychology and Foreign Policy*, Boulder, CO and Oxford, Westview Press, 1992.

25 Charles F. Hermann and Gregory Peacock, 'The Evolution and Future of Theoretical Research in the Comparative Study of Foreign Policy', in C.F. Hermann *et al.*, eds, *New Directions in the Study of Foreign Policy*, London, George Allen & Unwin, 1987, pp. 17–18.

26 James N. Rosenau, 'Toward Single-Country Theories of Foreign Policy: The Case of the USSR', in Herman *et al.*, eds, *New Directions in the Study of Foreign Policy*, pp. 53–54.

27 Hudson, 'Foreign Policy Analysis', p. 13.

28 Light, 'Foreign Policy Analysis', p. 94.

29 Ibid.

30 Hill, *The Changing Politics of Foreign Policy*, p. 2.

31 Hill, 'What is Left of the Domestic?', p. 163.

32 Fred Halliday, 'State and Society in International Relations: A Second Agenda', *Millennium: Journal of International Studies*, London, 16:2 (Summer 1987), p. 228, fn.12.

33 As Hill reminds us, James Rosenau was the first to use the term 'the domestic sources of foreign policy' in his book of the same title. See James Rosenau, *The Domestic Sources of Foreign Policy*, New York, Free Press, 1967. 'Peter Gourevitch drew attention to the converse in his 'The Second Image Reversed: The International Sources of Domestic Politics', *International Organisation*, 36:4 (1978), pp. 881–912. Hill, 'What is Left of the Domestic?', pp. 185–186, fn. 51.

34 Hill, *The Changing Politics of Foreign Policy*, p. 2. See, for example, Martin Hollis and Steve Smith, 'Two Stories about the Structure and Agency', *Review of International Studies*, 20:3 (July 1994); Alexander E. Wendt, 'The Agent-Structure Problem in International Relations Theory', *International Organisation*, 41:3 (Summer 1987); Roxanne Lynn Doty, 'Aporia: A Critical Exploration of the Agent-Structure Problematique in International Relations Theory', *European Journal of International Relations*, 3:3 (September 1997); Harry D. Gould, 'What Is at Stake in the Agent-Structure Debate?', in Vendulka Kubálková, Nicholas Onuf and Paul Kowert, eds, *International Relations in a Constructed World*, Armonk, New York, M.E. Sharpe, 1998.

35 See Richard Butweel *et al.*, eds, *Foreign Policy and Developing Nation*, Lexington, University of Kentucky Press, 1969; Christopher Clapham, ed., *Foreign Policy-Making in Developing States: A Comparative Approach*, Westmead, Saxon House, 1977; Bahgat Korany, *How Foreign Policy Decisions Are Made in the Third World: A Comparative Approach*, Boulder, CO: Westview, 1984; Peter Calvert, *The Foreign Policy of New States*, Brighton, Wheatsheaf Books, 1986.

36 Christopher J. Hill, 'Theories of Foreign Policy-Making for the Developing Countries', in Clapham, ed., *Foreign Policy-Making in Developing States*, p. 1.

37 K.J. Holsti, *International Politics: A Framework for Analysis*, New Jersey, Prentice Hall, 1988, p. 315.

38 Smith, 'Theories of Foreign Policy, p. 21.

39 Kenneth N. Waltz, *Man, the State and War: A Theoretical Analysis*, New York, Columbia University Press, 1959; Immanuel Wallerstein, 'The Rise and Future Demise of the World Capitalist System: Concepts for Comparative Analysis',

Comparative Studies in Society and History, 16:4 (September 1974); Immanuel Wallerstein, *Historical Capitalism*, London, Verso, 1993.

40   The best examples are: David Campbell, *Writing Security: United States Foreign Policy and the Politics of Identity*, Manchester, Manchester University Press, 1998; Henrik Larsen, *Foreign Policy and Discourse Analysis: France, Britain and Europe*, London, Routledge, 1997; Stephen Chan and Andrew J. Williams, eds, *Renegade States: The Evolution of Revolutionary Foreign Policy*, Manchester, Manchester University Press, 1994; Ilya Prizel, *National Identity and Foreign Policy: Nationalism and Leadership in Poland, Russia, and Ukraine*, Cambridge, Cambridge University Press, 1998.

41   Hudson, 'Foreign Policy Analysis', p.18; Peter J. Katzenstein, *Cultural Norms and National Security: Police and Military in Postwar Japan*, Ithaca: Cornell University Press, 1996; Shibley Telhami and Michael Barnett, eds, *Identity and Foreign Policy in the Middle East*, Ithaca: Cornell University Press, 2002, Brenda Shaffer, ed., *The Limits of Culture: Islam and Foreign Policy*, Cambridge, MA: MIT Press, 2006.

42   Wendt, 'The Agent-Structure Problem in International Relations Theory', pp.335–370; Alexander E. Wendt, *Social Theory of International Politics*, Cambridge: Cambridge University Press, 1999.

43   Stephen Saideman, 'Conclusion: Thinking Theoretically about Identity and Foreign Policy', in Telhami and Barnett, eds, *Identity and Foreign Policy in the Middle East*, p.177.

44   Friedrich Kratochwil, 'Constructing a New Orthodoxy: Wendt's "Social Theory of International Politics" and the Constructivist Challenge', *Millennium: Journal of International Studies*, 29:1 (2000), p.77.

45   Robert W. Cox, 'Social Forces, States and World Orders: Beyond International Relations Theory', *Millennium: Journal of International Studies*, 10:2 (1981), p.129.

46   Ibid.

47   Thomas R. Lindlof and Brian C. Taylor, *Qualitative Communication Research Methods*, 2nd edn, London, Sage, 2002, pp.51–52.

48   Cox, 'Social Forces, States and World Orders', p.129.

49   John Agnew and Stuart Corbridge, *Mastering Space: Hegemony, Territory and International Political Economy*, London, Routledge, 1995, p.48.

50   Robert C. Good, 'State-Building as Determinant of Foreign Policy in the New States', in L.W. Martin, ed., *Neutralism and Nonalignment: The New States in World Affairs*, New York, F.A. Prager, 1962, p.3.

51   Ibid., pp.4–10.

52   Joel S. Migdal, 'Internal Structure and External Behaviour: Explaining Foreign Policies of Third World States', *International Relations*, 14:5 (May 1974), p.520.

53   Ibid., p.523.

54   Hill, 'What is Left of the Domestic?', p.151.

55   Jung and Piccoli, *Turkey at the Crossroads*; Can Erimtan, *Ottomans Looking West?*, London, I.B. Taurus, 2008; Umit Cizre, ed., *Secular and Islamic Politics in Turkey*, London, Routledge, 2008, Resat Kasaba, *Turkey in the Modern World*, Cambridge, Cambridge University Press, 2008; Kemal Ciftci, *Tarih, Kimlik ve Elestirel Kuram Baglaminda Turk Dis Politikasi*, Ankara, Siyasal Kitabevi, 2010, pp.79–113; Emre Oktem, 'Turkey: Successor or Continuing State of the Ottoman Empire?', *Leiden Journal of International Law*, 24 (2011), p.562.

56   William Wallace, *The Transformation of Western Europe*, London, Pinter Publishers, 1990, p.29.

×××

57 Barrington Moore, Jr, *Social Origins of Dictatorship and Democracy: Lord and Peasant in the Making of the Modern World*, London, Penguin Books, 1987, p.159.
58 Wallace, *The Transformation of Western Europe*, pp.11–13.
59 Karl A. Wittfogel, *Oriental Despotism: A Comparative Study of Total Power*, New Haven, Yale University Press, 1967.
60 Moore, Jr, *Social Origins of Dictatorship and Democracy*, p.315.
61 Ibid., p.246.
62 Anthony Giddens, *The Consequences of Modernity*, Cambridge, Polity Press, 1990, pp.57–58.
63 Ibid., pp.11–12.
64 Ibid., p.57.
65 Bryan S. Turner, *Orientalism, Postmodernism and Globalism*, London, Routledge, 1994, p.10.
66 Moore, Jr, *Social Origins of Dictatorship and Democracy*, p.176.
67 Edward L. Morse, 'The Transformation of Foreign Policies: Modernisation, Interdependence and Externalisation', in Richard Little and Steve Smith, eds, *Perspectives on World Politics*, 2nd edn, London, Routledge, 1996, p.177.
68 Anthony Giddens' table provides a clear overall framework for the distinctions between pre-modern and modern cultures in broad connections between trust and risk, and between security and danger. See Giddens, *The Consequences of Modernity*, p.102, Table I. However, my concern is limited to the foreign policy-making of these states.
69 Morse, 'The Transformation of Foreign Policies', p.176.
70 Giddens, *The Consequences of Modernity*, p.57.
71 Ibid., p.62.
72 Larsen, *Foreign Policy and Discourse Analysis*, p.4; Steve Smith, 'Belief Systems and the Study of International Relations', in R. Little and Steve Smith, eds, *Belief Systems and International Relations*, Oxford: Basil Blackwell, 1988, p.12.
73 Migdal, 'Internal Structure and External Behaviour, p.520.
74 Robert L. Rothstein, 'Foreign Policy and Development Policy: From Nonalignment to International Class War', *International Affairs*, 52:4 (1976), p.599; A.I. Dawisha, 'The Principal Decision-Maker in Foreign Policy: The case of Nasser of Egypt', *International Relations*, 4:4 (November 1973), p.406; Ibrahim A. Karawan, 'Identity and Foreign Policy: The Case of Egypt', in Telhami and Barnett, eds, *Identity and Foreign Policy in the Middle East*, p.157.
75 H.J. Benda, 'Non-Western Intelligentsias as Political Elites', in J. Kautsky, ed., *Political Change in Underdeveloped Countries: Nationalism and Communism*, New York, R.E. Kieger, 1976, p.248; Howard Handelman, *The Challenge of Third World Development*, 7th edn, London: Pearson, 2013, pp.218–219.
76 David Singer, 'The Level-of-Analysis Problem in International Relations', in Klaus Knorr and Sidney Verba, eds, *The International System: Theoretical Essays*, Westport, Greenwood Press, 1961, p.89.
77 Ibid., p.91.
78 Wendt, 'The Agency Structure Problem', p.350.
79 Martin Hollis and Steve Smith, *Explaining and Understanding International Relations*, Oxford, Clarendon Press, 1991, p.88.
80 Gould, 'What Is at Stake in the Agent-Structure Debate', p.88.
81 Carlsnaes, 'The Agency-Structure Problem in Foreign Policy Analysis', p.263.
82 Hill, *The Changing Politics of Foreign Policy*, supra, p.5, note 3; see also, for the false

conflict between structuralism and unit level analysts, Barry Buzan, 'The Level of Analysis Problem in International Relations Reconsidered', in Ken Booth and Steve Smith, eds, *International Relations Theory Today*, Cambridge, Polity Press, 1995, pp. 212–214.

83 Hill, *The Changing Politics of Foreign Policy*, p. 6.
84 Ibid.
85 Joel S. Migdal, 'Vision and Practice: the Leader, the State and the Transformation of Society', *International Political Science Review*, 9:1 (1988), p. 40.
86 Larsen, *Foreign Policy and Discourse Analysis*, p. 21.
87 Rothstein, 'Foreign Policy and Development Policy', p. 599.
88 Larsen, *Foreign Policy and Discourse Analysis*, p. 10.
89 Ibid., p. 6.
90 Richard C. Snyder, H.W. Bruck and Burton Sapin, 'Decision-Making as an Approach to the Study of International Politics', in Richard C. Snyder, H. W. Bruck and Burton Sapin, eds, *Foreign Policy*, New York, Free Press of Glencoe, 1962, p. 110.
91 Ibid.
92 Cited in Walter Carlsnaes, *Ideology and Foreign Policy: Problems of Comparative Conceptualisation*, Oxford, Basil Blackwell, 1986, p. 47.
93 Ibid., p. 51.
94 Max Weber, *The Theory of Social and Economic Organisation*, New York, The Free Press, 1974, pp. 358–359.
95 Ibid., pp. 359–363.
96 Ibid., p. 362.
97 Benda, 'Non-Western Intelligentsias as Political Elites', p. 248.
98 Dankwart A. Rustow, *A World of Nations: Problems of Political Modernisation*, Washington, DC, 1967, pp. 163, 168; Robert Mantran, 'Mustafa Kemal Atatürk', in Roy, ed., *Turkey Today*, p. 119.
99 Bahgat Korany, 'Foreign Policy in the Third World: An Introduction', *International Political Science Review*, 5:1 (1984), p. 7.
100 Larsen, *Foreign Policy and Discourse Analysis*, p. 22.
101 Henry A. Kissinger, 'Domestic Structure and Foreign Policy', in *American Foreign Policy: Three Essays*, New York, W.W. Norton & Company, 1969, p. 11.
102 F.S. Northedge, 'The Nature of Foreign Policy', in F.S. Northedge, ed., *The Foreign Policies of the Powers*, London, Faber & Faber, 1974, p. 30.
103 Chris Brown, *Understanding International Relations*, London, Macmillan, 1997, p. 73.
104 Geoffrey Stern, *The Structure of International Society: An Introduction to the Study of International Relations*, London, Pinter, 1995, pp. 106–107.
105 Hill, *The Changing Politics of Foreign Policy*, supra note 3, p. 11.
106 Brown, *Understanding International Relations*, p. 69.
107 Northedge, 'The Nature of Foreign Policy', p. 11.
108 Morse, 'The Transformation of Foreign Policies, p. 171.
109 Rothstein, 'Foreign Policy and Development Policy', p. 598.
110 Hill, 'What is Left of the Domestic?', p. 153.
111 Ibid., p. 162.
112 Ibid.
113 Agnew and Corbridge, *Mastering Space*, p. 78.
114 Ibid., p. 51.
115 Hill, 'Theories of Foreign Policy-Making', p. 5.
116 However, as Hill reminds us, the domestic realm has fuzzy edges and may extend

to include diaspora. Hill, 'What is Left of the Domestic?', p. 162. In particular, in the context of Turkish nationalism, 'we' includes Turkish guest workers in Germany. In general, the 'other' is not always related to outside the state boundaries when nationalist feelings reach to the point of xenophobia.

117 William Wallace, 'Foreign Policy and National Identity in the UK', *International Affairs*, 67:1 (January 1991), pp. 65–66.

118 Ibid., p. 78.

2

The Turkish transition and alternative modernity

Having established the first pillar of an alternative approach to the foreign policies of transitional states in Chapter 1, this chapter explains why the study of modernity is chosen as the second pillar. The previous chapter argued that FPA as a 'bridging' sub-field of IR is helpful in bringing the arguments of historical sociology on modernity and state-building together within a new interdisciplinary approach to foreign policy of transitional states. To begin with, the concept of modernity is questioned in IR. Both what it means and how it relates to the study of international relations are problematised.[1] In order to establish a link between the studies of modernity and foreign policy within IR, a methodological attempt is made to investigate the relationship between the process of state-building and the construction of political identity during Turkey's transition to modernity.

First, modernisation theory is critically examined in order to demonstrate why the concept of modernity is the second pillar to base the new approach on. Having established what modernity means, the second section discusses the role of foreign policy in the transition to modernity. This section aims to show, on the one hand, the relationship between state-building and identity construction; and, on the other, how foreign policy contributes to the construction of a modern identity. The third section focuses on the implications of modernity for the Turkish transition. In particular, the Turkish integration into the capitalist international system and the intensification of its identity crisis at the margins of Europe is emphasised in order to analyse the internal and external causes of the Ottoman Empire's socio-political change. It is crucial to emphasise that to be 'on the margin' meant for Turkey not only its exclusion from Europe as 'the centre' but also identified its 'Otherness' in the European international system.[2] As explained in the previous chapter, one of the main concerns of this book is to understand the essence of socio-political changes in non-European societies in general, and in Turkey as a Muslim society in particular while engaging with Western modernity.

Understanding change in non-European societies

After the Second World War, especially with the process of de-colonisation, there was a great drive to grasp the dynamics of social, economic and political changes in non-European societies. Until the 1990s, three main paradigms – modernisation theory, dependency theory and world-system theory – dominated the discussions. There is a large amount of literature available on these theories, but they will be only briefly mentioned here.[3] Although it is beyond doubt that the debates between the two schools of modernisation and dependency are now *passé*, they were the most common point of departure for understanding the social and political transformations outside Europe. In the 1950s and the early 1960s, modernisation theory, represented by American sociologists, the most prominent of whom was Talcot Parsons, became part of the initial attempts to explain the evolution of the Third World by examining the socio-economic conditions conducive to modernisation.[4]

The reasons for beginning with modernisation theory are threefold. Turkey has been accepted as one of the most successful examples of modernisation theory;[5] there has been a recent resurgence of this theory since 9/11 in order to understand the socio-political changes in Muslim societies; and there is a parallel reasoning between modernisation theory and the idea of modernity.[6] In general, since Marx and Weber many orthodox political philosophers tend to assume tacitly that 'modern institutions and technical rationality' are essentially incompatible with other cultures since they arose in the West first.[7] Hence, Islam as a belief system is commonly identified as irrational and traditional, and, therefore, incompatible with European modernity.[8] In order to explain how Turkey's unique socio-historical experience challenges these assumptions about Islam's incompatibility with modernity and why the modernisation theory fails to explain the complex interplay between internal and external dynamics during transition to modernity, I turn to historical sociology.[9]

There are three main theoretical concerns of historical sociology that are explicitly related to the interdisciplinary approach of this book: first as highlighted in Chapter 1, it concerns 'the analysis of social change' over a broad historical context and it deals 'with social structures' rather than providing the narrative of events and emphasising the role of individuals as agents.[10] Second, by 'bringing the state back in', historical sociology contributed towards the possibility of a wider agenda for an interdisciplinary approach.[11] The major contribution of historical sociologists has been the emphasis on locating the analysis of the state within an international system.[12] Third, as Fred Halliday argues, the approach of historical sociology to the state created a 'second agenda' for IR.[13] On the one hand, he emphasises the difference between the traditional realist IR views of the state as 'the social-territorial totality' and those of historical sociology as 'a specific set of coercive and administrative institutions'. On the other hand, he suggests that the historical sociology approach provides 'an alternative way' in which its key themes are relevant to main discussions of IR.[14]

The most significant theme for IR occupying historical sociology literature is that the state as an actor or an institution operates in two realms, the domestic and the international.[15] This is where FPA and historical sociology overlap, since the separation of the domestic and foreign realms of the state have been a central occupation of FPA. As discussed in Chapter 1, a new trend in FPA has also developed by bringing foreign policy back into IR in line with post-positivist turn. Consequently, the impacts of the socio-political changes of the Ottoman Empire on Turkish foreign policy can only be examined by bringing historical sociology and FPA together within a broad historical context. The next section will critically explore modernisation theory in order to discuss why it is necessary to search for an alternative modernity from the perspective of historical sociology in analysing Ottoman socio-political changes.

The critique of modernisation theory

The notions of 'modern', 'modernisation', and 'modernity' have been the key terms in characterising social change of non-European societies since the 1960s. The concept of 'modernity' was used to describe the common characteristics of developed countries that are most advanced in technological, political, economic and social spheres. The definition of 'modernisation' referred to the process by which states – European or non-European – acquired these characteristics.[16] This process has been described, not only as 'modernisation', but also as 'Europeanisation' and 'Westernisation'. In specific terms, 'modernisation' can be defined 'as the process by which historically evolved institutions are adapted to the rapidly changing functions that reflect the unprecedented increase in man's knowledge, permitting control over his environment, that accompanied the scientific revolution'.[17] Modernisation theorists emphasise the importance of industrialisation, urbanisation, education, wealth and social mobilisation as complex and diversified structures.[18] However, modernisation theory failed to identify what these complex structures are and, more importantly, how non-European societies responded to the challenges of rapid changes through the 'prism' of their own cultures and the historical 'background'.[19] In the case of Turkey, the challenge has been how its historical background in religious practices and traditions can be channelled into modern conditions.

There are three major tenets of modernisation theory. First, in constructing their understanding of social change, modernisation theorists drew on the dichotomy between tradition and the modernity of classical sociologists like Durkheim and Weber.[20] In general, as mentioned above, modernisation referred to the process of transition from traditional to modern principles of social and political organisations, and this process was expected to expand to the rest of the world, to Asia, Africa and Latin America.[21] Second, modernisation as the process of change towards modern socio-political formations has been identified with the development of industrialisation in the West. However, it was no longer seen as 'something unique' to the West, as Weber thought, but as 'the blueprint for development' throughout the world.[22] Third, while the replacement of 'tradition' by modernity was taken for granted, a lack of development was found in the traditional internal factors of non-European societies.[23]

In a broad sense, modernisation theory might be described as 'nationalist'.[24] This argument became the point of departure for dependency theory, which claimed that the process of underdevelopment must be placed within a globally defined historical context. According to Samir Amin, both internal conditions and external factors determined the new specificity of the Third World when countries attempted to construct a bourgeois national state at every stage of world-capitalist expansion.[25] Therefore, the key element lies not only in the internal characteristics of non-European societies such as religion and/or culture but also in the structure of the Western international system.[26]

The following three main criticisms of modernisation theory will help us to understand why the ideas of 'multiple modernities' and 'alternative modernities' take the analysis further than the point where modernisation theory failed.[27]

First, the difficulties and issues of modernisation proved that 'modernity' and 'Westernisation' were not necessarily identical.[28] Furthermore, the dichotomy in modernisation theory between 'tradition' and 'modernity' leads to an ahistorical analysis, which ignores the complexity of social formations. More importantly, modernisation theories do not explain how local traditions respond and/or adapt to the common structural pressures of modernity.[29] The Ottoman engagement with European modernity must be understood within an historical structure, as a 'dialogical relation' between the forces of Islamic tradition and the pressures of European modernity, rather than seeing them as two opposed forces. It is only through this interaction that Turkey has synthesised the characteristics of Islamic and Western civilisations and produced its hybrid identity as Muslim and secular.[30]

Second, the enthusiasts of modernisation theory preferred to focus on the social changes and political order of transitional societies.[31] They, therefore, entirely ignored the impacts of the international system on the transition process. The question lies not just in the process itself but also rather in its complex of political, economic and international dimensions, which cannot be reduced to a mono-causal explanation, such as domestic/national structure. Yet, as will be argued later, historically the Ottoman Empire's relations with European states cannot be separated from its attempts at modernisation, and vice versa.

Third, the replacement of tradition by modernity remains deeply problematic. The advent of modernity does not necessarily mean the abandonment of traditional patterns of society in general and Islamic practices in particular. Not only in Turkey as a Muslim society but in modern industrial societies in the West traditional values still persist and actually play an important role in keeping these values going.[32] This is probably because the idea of tradition is itself 'a creation of modernity'. As Giddens highlights, it does not 'mean that one should not use it in relation to pre-modern or non-Western societies, but it does imply that we should approach the discussion of tradition with some care'.[33]

In short, the criticisms of modernisation theory are well taken, but this does not mean the concepts of modernity, or equivalent terms, are empty words.[34] The concept of modernity is more complicated than has been addressed by modernisation theory. Thus, the task of the next section is to illustrate how the idea of 'multiple modernities' has started a new debate to understand the socio-economic and political changes of non-Western societies and why the notion of 'alternative modernities' offers a better explanation of the essence of Turkey's engagement with European modernity.

I carefully refrain from interpreting this attempt as the creation of just another meta-theory. On the one hand, I am aware that '[t]he search for a single paradigm, for a "normality" defined in Kuhnian terms, has produced a situation of, for many, unsatisfactory pluralism' in the past.[35] On the other hand, intellectuals and politicians in both European and non-European countries are aware that 'no single text or paradigm is likely to suffice' to understand the complexity of the modern world.[36] As Ashcroft argues:

> Alternative, or non-Western modernities emerge either by the development of hybridized cultural forms through the appropriation of those of Western modernity or by the introduction of innovative, and thus truly alternative forms of modernity. Yet neither of these forms has emerged out of thin air. They emerge out of a *relation* to other modernities and the processes of appropriation, adaptation, and transformation have been their characteristic features.[37]

Hence, the main aim of the next section is to highlight some of the pluralistic characteristics of modernity and how Turkey produced its own historical synthesis from a non-Western, Islamic perspective.

Searching for a new paradigm: alternative modernities

If one accepts that a contemporary international system was created in Europe with its own peculiar political units one can hardly disagree with the expansion of a Eurocentric state system to the rest of the world. In a general sense, post-feudal European institutions and modes of behaviour have become world-historical in their impacts in the twentieth century and beyond.[38] More specifically, the notion of multiple modernities rightly emphasises the inclusionary dynamic of 'modernity' that accepts borrowing, blending and cross-fertilisation among different civilisations.[39] Therefore, it convincingly refutes the logic of exclusionary divergence and binary oppositions between traditional and modern, or the clash of civilisations between Islam and the West.[40] Moreover, by accepting 'the multiplicity of the model of modernity' it acknowledges the existence of different socio-historical and political experiences.

Modernity is an essentially contested concept which has cultural, political and economic aspects. 'The project of modernity formulated in the eighteenth century by the philosophers of the Enlightenment consisted in their efforts to develop objective science, universal morality and law, and autonomous art according to their inner logic.'[41] In its simplest terms, modernity is defined here as 'gaining rational control of the physical and social environment, building a liberal democratic state, participating in world culture, and joining the scientific revolution'.[42] There is a general consensus that Kantian 'universal reason' and Weberian 'instrumental rationality' have identified the conditions of modernity.[43] According to Habermas, 'Max Weber characterised cultural modernity as the separation of the substantive reason expressed in religion and metaphysics into three autonomous spheres. They are: science, morality and art.'[44] Based on these assumptions, one can argue that, despite the existence of deeper differences in cultural terms among civilisations, 'an alternative modernity' is possible if European modernity is not presented as a blueprint for non-European societies.[45]

Göran Therborn defines modernity culturally 'as an *epoch turned to the future*, conceived as likely to be different from and possibly better than the present and the past'.[46] There is a difference between tradition and modernity in terms of a prevailing concept of time: while pre-modernity looks back to the experiences of the past, modernity 'looks at the future, hopes for it, plans for it, constructs it, builds it'.[47] In this understanding of modernity, human action seems to be related to the organisation of space and time in the Enlightenment vision of universal progress and change. Both individuals and societies not only situate themselves spatially but also possess modes of time-reckoning in a sense of past, present and future.[48] 'Assuming that modernity is best understood as an attitude of questioning the present', one can make sense of alternative modernities, and the dilemmas of 'modernity' universally from a transcultural and transnational perspective.[49]

> What is meant by the notion of an alternative modernity, and is it really plausible? What I will call the 'content approach' to alternative modernity emphasises such ethnic and ideological differences as the kinds of food people eat, the role of family or religion, the legal forms of property and administration, and so on. These are weak bases for an alternative because modernisation, as we should know since Marx and Weber, consists precisely in erasing or incorporating such ethnic and ideological contents in a convergent model of civilisation. The universalist view, which uncritically confounds Westernisation and modernisation, is still persuasive compared to this.[50]

When we apply a similar 'content approach' of alternative modernity to international politics, the most prominent form of modernity over space and time translates itself as the *modern nation-state*. In the modern international system, despite the challenges of globalisation, the political structure of the nation-state is still persuasive to preserve spatial integrity through territoriality, sovereignty and national identity at local levels.

However, the main features of modernity are also closely associated with the development of *capitalism* and its 'structural features'.[51] It is beyond any doubt that the three aspects of modernity – economic, political and cultural – are closely related to each other.[52] More crucially, it seems that the problematic nature of political modernity appearing in Muslim countries at the periphery is generally related to their cultural characteristics as well as their economic backwardness without questioning the central role of the international system itself.[53] In the case of Turkey, the nation-state engineers under the leadership of Mustafa Kemal Atatürk understood 'modernity' in clearly European modern terms as the emergence of scientific, rational progress and a liberal market economy in opposition to the religious-bound traditions and practices of the Ottoman Empire. In order to understand the link between capitalist progress and political modernity in a

Muslim society, the implications of modernity for the Turkish socio-historical experience as an alternative path must be related to its integration into the capitalist international system from a broad historical context, as highlighted earlier.

In international relations, there are four implications of political modernity: the political form of modernity is the 'nation-state', which has expanded from the West to the rest of the world.[54] Modernity provides an understanding of social transformations within a structural framework; it places the non-European societies in world history by 'pointing to different societal paths to modernity', and it emphasises the importance of collective identity construction in the modern world.[55]

The first implication is that the nation-state becomes the most prominent social form of modernity. From a sociological point of view, a crucial feature of a *modern state* is that its resources of power are reducible neither to its internal military power nor its parameters of population and territory. The power resources of the modern state depend significantly on its capacity to develop the potentials of the population and of the territory, through scientific revolution, technological advance, education, recruitment, infrastructural construction, etc.[56] It is not an historical coincidence that for most Third World countries, in particular, the main agent of this development has been the state.[57] Consequently, a necessary focus on multiple modernities brings to light the place of state in the structural transformation of societies, European and non-European alike.

Second, the notions of 'multiple modernities' and 'alternative modernities' add new dimensions in that structural transformation is especially important for non-European societies in which the validity of Western modernity has been questioned.[58] Suffice it to say that, on the one hand, the creation of a new type of structure involves 'the destruction of the old structure', and, on the other hand, that 'breaking with the past' is not always a very manageable task in practice.[59] Maybe that is why some societies – in particular Muslim ones – outside Europe are still facing distinctive problems with, and unprecedented consequences of, modernity. However, the problem lies not in the nature of modernity but in its uneven character, given the fact that modernity brings different contradictions and tensions to different parts of the world while still becoming a global phenomenon. The problems Asian, African and East European societies face today can be related to this contradictory character and dilemmas of modernity. As Gaonkar argues:

> the attitude of questioning the present is both pervasive and embattled: It is pervasive because modernity has gone global and it is embattled because it faces seemingly irresolvable dilemmas. In fact, the very idea of alternative modernities has its origin in the persistent and sometimes violent questioning of the present precisely because the present announces itself as the modern at every national and cultural site today.[60]

In relation to the third implication, the uneven development of non-European societies can be explained by specifying the different paths to modernity. According to Therborn, there are four institutionally different paths to modernity:[61]

(1) *The pioneering European route*: In the case of Europe, the idea of modernity developed against indigenous traditions. While modernity generated the European pattern of internal revolutions, 'doctrinal-isms, ranging from legitimism and absolutism to socialism and communism, via nationalism, ultramontanism and liberalism', brought major disasters such as two world wars, Fascism, the Holocaust, Stalinism.[62]

(2) *The new worlds*: represented primarily, but not exclusively, by the Americas, South as well as North. In this group, while modernity was 'created by early modern conquest and mass migration, the theoretical and practical struggle for modernity was largely external, against colonial Europe and by the colonised aliens against the colonists'.[63]

(3) *The colonial zone*: stretching from North-Western Africa to Papua New Guinea and the South Pacific. Modernity was introduced in the form of an alien conquest and destruction. After the domestic resistance to modernity was crushed, colonial modernity learned 'the appropriate ideas of the colonisers – popular sovereignty, national self-determination, socio-economic development' and turned against the colonisers.[64] Contradictions of modernity in the Colonial Zone emerged in the form of civil wars, social fragmentation and the national question.

(4) *Emulative modernisation*: in this route, modernity was selectively imported by a group of the ruling élite. Here we are talking about the Japan of the Meiji Restoration, the Ottoman Empire with its Turkish and Arab successors, and China. 'The designation refers to polities seriously threatened but never fully subjugated by alien imperialism; polities which managed to survive into the modern world by adopting modern state institutions from abroad and grafting them on to indigenous rule and indigenous society.'[65]

In conclusion, there is no disagreement that while modernity was organically developed in Europe, it was externally derived in the rest of the world. More importantly, imitating Europe was not only the voluntary act on the part of the late-comers but also the consequence of the ineluctable expansion of capitalist modernity.[66] If there are widespread feelings that we are either at some sort of a turning point or at the end of modernity, these 'have less to do with the ending of an era than with the fact that modernity today is global and multiple and no longer has a governing centre and master-narratives to accompany it'.[67] There are new challengers of master-narratives.

The fourth implication of political modernity is the relationship between modernity and identity. One of the main characteristics of modernity is the construction of individual and collective identity. When modernity replaces the protective framework of small communities with impersonal organisations, this process also affects the sense of 'self' and 'society'.[68] In this context, what is important about modernity is that the emerging new social forms, of which the most prominent is the state, mediate claims of identity by replacing pre-modern institutions. Accordingly, the relationship between modernity and identity is prevalent in a discourse of the 'state' itself.[69] The erosion of traditional social relations leads to a crisis of identity at individual and collective levels. In solving this crisis, the new identity at any level can be constructed in relation to an 'other'. Since our concern is limited to the state level, a basic assumption here is that the identity and interests of states (and other actors) are formed in interaction with one another.[70] Hence, I argue that foreign policy plays a crucial role during this interaction. The next section will explore the role of foreign policy in the construction of political identity at national and international levels.

The role of foreign policy in the construction of political identity

Under the conditions of the transition to modernity, the construction of a new political identity cannot be achieved without the channel of foreign relations. The so-called traditional societies did not come into existence from a *tabula rasa*, but had a specific form of identity beyond that of the 'nation' and 'modern state'. This sense of identity might be based on family, clan, religious ties, in different stages of their history. In contemporary international relations, these identities are expected to either disappear or be replaced by modern identities of sovereign nation-states in order to become part of the current system. Put succinctly, modern political identities are determined by the socio-historical structures of the existing system that the actors inhabit. In this case, the main task is to understand the relationship between identity formation and modernity as an integral part of the contemporary international system. Surprisingly, the studies of IR and FPA have neglected until recently not only what William Bloom refers to as 'identification theory' but also the linking of national identity to foreign policy.[71] Thus, I explore the role of foreign policy-making in the creation of political identity at three levels: first, the correlation between modernity, territoriality and state identity; second, the explicit link between modernity and national identity construction; and, third, foreign policy's contribution to the creation of modern identity.

Modernity, territoriality and state identity

It has been argued that while Western modernity has become a universal phenomenon with its alternative types for different societies, the modern state is accepted as its key political feature worldwide. As Gaonkar argues, '[m]odernity has travelled from the West to the rest of the world not only in terms of cultural forms, social practices and institutional arrangements but also as a form of discourse that interrogates the present'.[72] At the end of the twentieth century, we witnessed a contradictory metamorphosis of the modern state. While it is 'withering away' in accordance with globalisation, for some societies it is becoming more urgent than ever. Ulrich Beck reduces it to a formula: 'withering away plus inventing equals metamorphosis of the state. That is how one can sketch and fill out the image of a state that, like a snake, is shedding the skin of its classical tasks and developing a new global "skin of tasks".'[73] However, the traditional state's 'withering away' should not be accepted as being synonymous with its failure.[74] In the 1990s, the disintegration of the Soviet Union, Yugoslavia and Czechoslovakia indicated that Europe, as the historical origin of the modern nation-state and nationalism, once again witnessed the rebirth of the nation-state rather than its demise. Similarly, the Arab Spring of 2011 has proved the importance of stable and sustainable nation-states in the modern Middle East. Hence, it is necessary to explain clearly what we mean by the state.

As John Hoffman says, despite its complexities, the state can be defined.[75] But the problem is, how? There have been many definitions of the state 'since Machiavelli used the word in its modern sense'.[76] It is not only a mere institution or actor, or an organisation of class domination: the state is an historically modern phenomenon since there have been times in human history when 'the state' as we know today it did not exist.[77] In Christopher Piersen's analysis of the modern state, there are a certain number of characteristics which can be identified with the epoch of modernity: industrialisation, demographic change, the commercialisation and subsequent commodification of economic relationships, the rise of capitalism, the growing social division of labour, the rise of the scientific mode of thought and the transformation of modes of communication, urbanisation, and democratisation. Although some might argue that this list does not represent the most important features of modernity, it still indicates a wide range of changes with the emergence of a modern state and social order.[78]

Within the literature of historical sociology, Charles Tilly argues that there have been three main stages of state-making:

(1) formation and consolidation of the first great national states in commercial and military competition with each other, accompanied by their economic penetration of the remainder of Europe and of important parts of the world outside of Europe: roughly 1500 to 1700;
(2) regrouping of the remainder of Europe into a system of states, accompanied by the extension of European political control into most of the non-European world, save those portions already dominated by substantial political organisation (e.g., China and Japan): roughly 1650 to 1850;
(3) extension of the state system to the rest of the world, both through the acquisition of formal independence by colonies and clients, and through the incorporation of existing powers like China and Japan into the system: roughly 1800 to 1950.[79]

This is possibly why Tilly assumes that if the above scheme is correct, 'a state which has adopted Western forms or organisation will have an easier time in the international system; after all, the system grew up in conjunction with those forms'.[80] The existence of states as independent political units is the starting point of international relations. The realist paradigm of IR also provides a detailed definition of the state:

> The state is a *territorially-based political unit* characterised by central decision-making and enforcement machinery (a government and an administration); the state is legally 'sovereign' in the sense that it recognises neither an external superior, nor an internal equal; and the state exists in a world composed of other, similarly characterised, territorial, sovereign political units.[81]

There are four main characteristics of the modern state: it possesses a *government*; it asserts internal and external *sovereignty*; it claims its authority within a clearly defined *territory*; and it represents a particular group of *people*.[82] In particular, the creation of new states was a result of reconciliation between the principle of sovereignty and that of national self-determination.[83] On the one hand, sovereignty means not only that the state is the supreme power over all other authorities within its territory and population but also that it is independent of external authorities.[84] On the other hand, the doctrine of self-determination assumes that a group of people must discover its-'self' according to nationality, and each 'nation' has a right to constitute a separate state. Consequently, under the impact of nationalism, the idea of self-determination as a 'product of specifically *historical* consciousness' was inevitably codified into the principle of sovereignty.[85]

Among these characteristics, the differentiation between state and nation is crucial in understanding the state-led developments in non-European societies in general and Muslim societies of the Middle East and North Africa in particular. The concept of nation-state, or more precisely the concept of 'state-nation', becomes the main reference point of analysing non-European societies.[86] In general, as has been pointed out by many scholars, the usage of 'international' 'confused the issue by denoting as between nations what are usually relations between states'.[87] The common historical trend of the modern era has been the unification of two conceptually different processes of state-building and nation-building. While nationhood determines the sense of individual and collective identity, statehood conforms this identity with its demarcated sovereignty in the inter-state system through foreign relations. In this context, statehood has two important functions for transitional states.

The first function is the homogenisation of a nation within a demarcated territory. Every nation makes the same argument about a particular territory as a cradle of its existence and homeland, and territory normally consists of geographically determined boundaries. But the question relates to how these boundaries are fixed because 'the state does not *have* a territory, it *is* a territory' in the modern world.[88] In this context, what is important is the way in which nationhood and statehood are defined territorially.

The second function of a state as 'a territorial political unit' is the conformation of this political identity in the international arena.[89] In this chapter, 'state-making is seen as the political dimension of modernisation'.[90] The main characteristics of state-building within a demarcated territory are nation-building, secularisation, modernisation and socio-economic development. Although all of these factors seem to be inextricably linked, the focus here has been limited to the construction of political identity and the demarcation of territorial borders since the 'state' is itself an identity in the political sphere of international relations.

In conclusion, the territoriality and the sovereignty of a state imply that the state as a political identity exists in two environments: the internal environment, which is composed of all the other institutions of the territorial state, and the external environment, which is composed of all other states and the interactions between them. '*The very term "international" only has full meaning with the emer-*

gence of nation-states which, because of their strictly demarcated character, give a very particular shape to "internal" versus "external" relations.'[91] According to mainstream IR theories, the state constantly engages in 'domestic' and 'foreign policy'.[92] As explained in Chapter 1, the separation between domestic and foreign policies blurs under the conditions of transitional process. Internal and external become two poles of the same continuum rather than two polar opposites. The next section aims to show how this interaction between the two spheres of policy takes place during the construction of national identity as an integral part of modernity.

Modernity and national identity construction

The concept of 'national interest' has been a common departure point in analysing foreign policy. However, the definition of national interests in domestic and foreign affairs can make better sense in relation to what 'national identity' means.[93] '*National Identity* describes that condition in which a mass of people have made the same identification with national symbols – have internalised the symbols of the nation – so that they may act as one psychological group when there is a threat to, or the possibility of enhancement of, these symbols of national identity' (emphasis in the original).[94] Hence, construction of national identity cannot be explained by referring only to domestic politics.

As proposed in Chapter 1, foreign policy is partly a reflection of the search for national identity. In particular, for transitional states, it is important to identify 'who they are' during the erosion of traditional identities. During this search, foreign policy becomes an essential element in defining the new identity within the boundaries of state and relating to the others outside these boundaries. Before establishing this link between national identity and foreign policy, it is necessary to examine the process of identity construction which will help us to understand the correlation between 'us' and 'them', 'inside' and 'outside', 'domestic' and 'foreign'.

This chapter emphasises that the idea of modernity not only represents an era of rapid socio-political, economic and technological changes, but also represents a modern identity as part of new consciousness of temporality.[95] Among other complex aspects, it becomes clear that modernity means a new, 'individual-cum-collective' identity, both in the direction of individuality and in that of chosen collective, of nation and state. 'One important expression of this modern individualism/collectivism is the demand for political rights, for citizenship.'[96] Historically, as in the case of Turkey, to be a citizen instead of a subject of an imperial state requires a new political form of the state, namely a nation-state, since nationality and citizenship complement each other in the modern international system. Hence, the emphasis is given to the collective level – national identity – while investigating the relationship between modernity and political identity construction.

According to Therborn, '[i]dentity is post-classical Latin and means sameness. As such it is operative only dialectically, i.e. in connection with its opposite, otherness'.[97] There are three crucial stages in identity construction: differentiation,

settlement of self-image and the recognition of other.[98] The first, differentiation, refers to the separation of the potential 'me' or 'us' from the environment.
Experience of an 'other' and discoveries of a 'self' are the two related aspects of
this process.[99] Second, identity should not be seen as the negation of 'other' but
as something positive – as an identification with someone after an awareness of
separateness. For collective identities, especially, this self-reference may be based
on a common origin, a common task or on certain values. The last, but most
crucial, stage is recognition. Self-identity depends not only on separating from
the 'other' but also on being recognised by the 'other'. For Therborn, these stages
are not in chronological order. Recognition by the 'others' might come before
differentiation.[100]

In this context, the distinction between 'inside' and 'outside' emphasises the
construction 'we' and 'they': 'all too often, "we" turn out to be those who have
"progressed", "developed" or "modernised", to be distinguished from "they who
have not"'.[101] Thus, identity construction is a consequence of a new procedure
by containing and negating the 'other'. Moreover, the construction of identity is
achieved through the drawing of territorial boundaries that serve to separate an
'inside' from an 'outside', a 'self' from an 'other', a 'domestic' from a 'foreign'.[102]
These three stages of the identification process are intrinsically crucial for political integration of a nation within a state. The achievement of political integration
implies a successful 'nation-building' that relates to the process within which the
inhabitants of a territorial unity are recognised as *loyal* citizens of the state.[103] In
this understanding, although nation-building is related to the creation of a state
as a new political entity and to a sense of national identity, it does not imply that
the nation precedes the state but the other way around. As discussed in the previous chapter, the construction of a nation is possible within an established state.
Specifically, 'national identity, by definition, reflects a nation's relationship to
"the other", that national identity is an outgrowth of contact between at least two
distinct groups.'[104] In the context of international relations, the contacts between
distinct groups are mainly the relations between states. After explaining the two
layers of the formation of new territorial identity – state identity – and collective
political identity – national identity – the final stage of identity construction is
related to foreign policy. Hence, the next section examines the role of foreign
policy as the third layer of identity construction during transitional periods.

Foreign policy's contribution to the construction of modern identity

In the process of the collective identity formation of transitional states, neither the
construction of self-image nor the differentiation between 'inside' and 'outside'
can be achieved without the channel of foreign policy. 'Foreign policy represents
the ways in which a domestic unit deals with other such units whose perceptions
and interests differ, as they will even where underlying values are shared.'[105] Most
importantly, recognition as the essential stage of new identity formation will not
be achieved without the help of foreign policy.

As explained earlier, if foreign policy is partly a reflection of the search for
identity, it clearly serves two functions: it constructs and secures identity on

the 'inside' and locates it on the 'outside'. David Campbell states that this has to be achieved by 'creating the myths of identity through foreign adventures' and demarcating the boundaries of states in the international system.[106] In this understanding, foreign policy needs 'to be retheorised as a boundary-producing practice central to the production and reproduction of the identity in whose name it operates'.[107]

It can be suggested that the understanding of foreign policy must be reconsidered in conjunction with the process of identity construction within modernity. This mode of thought might be valid for all states; however, it is more noticeable in the case of transitional states when they are trying to locate their new political entities in the international system. 'A state cannot exist and act as such unless it is recognised by others.'[108] The recognition of a state by other members of international society cannot be achieved without the channel of foreign policy.

As argued earlier, the importance of 'statehood' for transitional states is twofold: it homogenises a nation within a delimited territory; and, the new political identity must be recognised by other members of international society. That is how foreign policy becomes crucial for any transitional state to declare its statehood on an international level after securing its national identity in domestic politics. As Ilya Prizel argues, 'the interaction between national identity and foreign policy is a key element in both established and nascent polities, but this interaction is particularly important in newly emerging or re-emerging states since nationalism and national identity are often the main, if not the sole, force binding these societies together'.[109] Therefore, foreign policy as a way of differentiating between 'inside' and 'outside' becomes an important element of identity construction in the modern international system.

In conclusion, the correlation between foreign policy and political identity construction can be seen at two levels. First, the differentiation between 'inside' and 'outside' through the channel of foreign policy is important during the nation-building process. The foreign policy of a transitional state is heavily influenced by the construction of national identity which is based on the differentiation between 'us' and 'them'. Thus, it is clear not only that national identity, by definition, reflects a nation's relationship to the 'other' but also that foreign policy becomes an essential element in defining and relating to this other. Second, the recognition of a new political identity by other members becomes crucial in placing the new identity in an existing system. The act of recognition through the different channels of foreign policy affirms the equality of states based on the principle of sovereignty. A new political identity takes its place *on a par* with other states in the society of states when it is recognised as sovereign.[110]

The construction and recognition of new political identity is especially crucial in the Turkish context. As an Islamic entity, during the Ottoman Empire people associated themselves with each other according to their religion in the *millet* System – i.e. Muslim subjects and non-Muslim subjects (Christians and Jews) of the empire. The replacement of the '*umma*' identity by a secular 'national' identity was seen as a consequence of the transformation to modernity. First, the majority of Muslim Anatolian people discovered their Turkishness. Second, due to the need to construct a new collective identity, they would have gone through a process of differentiating themselves from the others, i.e. the Greeks and the Armenians, and by claiming national self-determination over Turkish territory. During this process, Turkish–Bolshevik co-operation would become important, not only for demarcating Turkish territory but also for conforming its new identity on the international level.

Before dwelling on these aspects of Turkish foreign policy it is worth examining what modernity meant in the Turkish context. The Turkish integration into the capitalist international system will be emphasised in order to analyse the implications of alternative modernity for the Turkish transition within a broader historical structure. The identity crisis of the Ottoman Empire is then examined, so as to understand the relation between modernity and identity construction.

The implications of alternative modernities for the Turkish state transformation

When it comes to understanding the political changes of the Ottoman Empire, the modernisation theorists described it mainly as an imitation, or externally introduced by the Western educated elites. On the contrary, world-system theory emphasised the importance of the international economic system while ignoring the internal dynamics of Ottoman changes.[111] In contrast, my aim is to identify both the internal and external dynamics of these complex changes and emphasise their socio-historical and economic dimensions.[112] In particular, the Ottoman identity crisis will be analysed through its integration into the capitalist international system. Historically, the Ottoman Empire had to accept the requirements of the international system when it was admitted as a legitimate member of the European Concert to participate in the advantages of European public law with the Treaty of Paris of 1856.[113] However, this legal equality was only on a theoretical level. The empire was never accepted as a member of the 'Christian club', despite the fact that it had been an important European power since the fourteenth century. It was routinely regarded in the West as the 'sick man of Europe' after Tsar Nicholas so described the declining empire's condition in 1853.[114] After 1856, despite Ottoman statesmen's claims, the principle of Ottoman membership in the Concert did not change the attitude of the European states towards the empire of failing to treat it as an equal.[115] Therefore, it is worth analysing further the status of the empire in the practice of international relations.

For the Ottoman Empire, the legitimisation of its membership in the European system had unprecedented consequences: *the empire implicitly accepted the validity of European modernity and tried to overcome its imposed otherness by participation in this different system.*[116] At this point, on the theoretical level, Sudipta Kaviraj's emphasis on the dialectical relationship between modernity and the existing structures becomes the crux of the argument. '[M]odernity does not build institutions in an empty space. It has to rework the logic of existing structures, which have their own, sometimes surprisingly resilient, justificatory structures.'[117] In this account, the construction of the Turkish nation-state was a clear result of the perpetual historical metamorphosis of the Islamic empire that had been going on since the nineteenth century. The most distinctive sign of this historical movement was the emergence of Turkish nationalism at the beginning of the twentieth century, as will be explained in the next chapter. Under the impact of nationalism, the construction of a modern nation-state as an integral part of the adaptation to modernity became the determining structure of Turkey's unique socio-political experience. At this point, it becomes necessary to define what this determining structure means in order to grasp the essence of the Turkish transition.

The concern to define social structure in relation to human action has been the main preoccupation of social theory.[118] In the literature of IR and in particular that of the 'English School', a social structure in international society has been accepted primarily as 'the structure among states' or 'the states system'.[119] Chapter 1 pointed out that among the recent concerns of both traditional IR and FPA are the issues of the 'agency-structure' debate. Realist theory was always interested in the role of structure in the sense of constraining what actors such as states, social movements, or individuals can do.[120] But Giddens' structuration theory then explicitly focused on 'the mutual dependence of structure and agency'.[121] However, as in Rosenberg's attempt to formulate the relationship between social structure and geopolitical systems, the concern with structure here is not only concerned with 'a theoretical resolution of the tension between the concepts of agency and structure, it concentrates instead on specifying the actual social relationships themselves which comprise the fabric of any society, and on tracing the particular institutional forms and distribution of resources which are reproduced by those relationships'.[122]

In Giddens' terminology, 'structure' is also linked with the notion of transformation and a structural analysis of social relationships, which 'is considered to penetrate below the level of surface appearances'.[123] In addition, structure denotes long-term or abrupt changes that the human will cannot prevent or resist. 'Structure' becomes not only a matter of constraint but a source of both change and resistance to change.[124]

The reasons for applying this understanding of structure to the Turkish transition are twofold: (a) Turkish politics, both domestic and foreign, cannot be analysed independently from society's social changes; (b) the structural analysis of Ottoman social relations shows how the transition took place in the Turkish path to European modernity.

In the context of Ottoman social relations, therefore, structure denotes the historical relations between the empire and the European international system which caused socio-political changes in the empire in accordance with the dominant form of the existing international system. Clearly, these theoretical explanations do not go beyond an abstract level unless we try to elaborate them in history. Given the fact that this is a difficult and complex task, I shall restrict my concern to two primary aspects of the structure:

First, in relation to the 'structure and agency' debate in FPA, the emphasis must be on the interrelation between structure and actors. On the one hand, an actor

(decision-maker) is a member of a social system (society) which itself is determined by the 'structure'. On the other hand, 'human actions had to be seen in the
context of events and processes that were beyond their control'.[125]

Second, the connection between the idea of a modern nation-state and modernity has been accepted as the determining structure of Ottoman socio-political
change. Furthermore, I argue that there were two 'structural forces' in this
transition as a consequence of historical relations between the empire and the
European system. The next section will argue that the first structural force was
the integration of the empire into the capitalist international system. The second
structural force was the move to solve the Ottoman Empire's identity crisis by
changing its Islamic character to the secular character of the European system.

Turkish integration into the capitalist international system

Historically, when the empire's adhesion to the European system was approved
with the Treaty of Paris in 1856, the *Islahat Fermanı* (Reform Decree) was issued
in order to introduce domestic reforms in the same year. It would be naive to
interpret this as a coincidence. Rather, it was a result of incorporation into the
existing international system which imposed domestic adjustments on the empire
within which the transition had started. It seems that the socio-political change
progressed from outside to inside during the transformation of the Ottoman
Empire into a nation-state. First, the emergence of the nation-state, specifically in
Europe, 'was integrally bound up with the expansion of capitalism'.[126] When the
form of the European 'nation-state' expanded to the rest of the world, it was inextricably linked to the spread of capitalism. Second, the transition of the Ottoman
Empire was not immune from this general trend. I argue, therefore, that the
transformation of the Ottoman Empire into a modern nation-state exemplifies
the spread of capitalist European modernity to a non-European society within a
broad historical structure and long process.

According to Haldun Gülalp, in a very broad sense the history of Ottoman
modernisation can be divided into three conceptual stages which are not necessarily 'historically watertight categories':[127]

1. The first stage was the reorganisation of the military structure between 1789
and 1839: It resulted from inter-state military pressures. The modernisation of
the Ottoman state had started when the empire perceived the European powers'
military superiority, and the first precaution was to reorganise its own military
structure. 'This took place in the initial period of the rationalisation of the army
and bureaucracy under Selim III (1789–1807) and Mahmud II (1808–1839).'[128]
This stage coincides perfectly with the explanation of modernisation theorists
about the imitation of the West. But the imitation was only on an administrative
level, through the modernisation of its military structure. Most importantly, the
relations between the empire and the European states were not based on economic issues. The Ottoman economy was a largely rural economy with its pre-
capitalist features, such as the lack of bourgeoisie, private property and national
capitalist accumulation. As long as the transportation and export of manufactur-

ing goods, e.g. silk and grains were under the control of central government, mercantile accumulation did not threaten the imperial economic system.[129] At this stage, there was no need for the empire's economic integration with European capitalism.

2. The second stage was the *Tanzimat* period starting with the *Gülhane Hatt-ı Hümayunu* (Imperial Decree of the Rose Chamber) of 1839; this was a critical stage in the economic integration of the empire into the world capitalist system.

> Corresponding to this process was the capitalist transformation of the state. The Ottoman state began to acquire *legal–rational* features for the first time in this period. The proclamation of the *Tanzimat* in 1839 was preceded by the signing of the Free Trade Treaty with Britain in 1838. In this period of Ottoman history, new classes emerged and new class alliances developed. The class basis of the transformed state was an alliance between the European industrial bourgeoisie and the local commercial bourgeoisie with section of the traditional ruling class.[130]

The *Tanzimat* era signalled the beginning of the transition of the Ottoman Empire to a modern state. The sultan's power, which he traditionally exercised in the name of Islamic law, was challenged for the first time by the *Tanzimat* reforms. The sultan now had to share his power with a new Westernised state apparatus.[131] 'The *Tanzimat* Charter proclaimed a new order by instituting private property and declaring the equality of all subjects of the empire before the law without regard to ethnicity or religion. This signified the beginnings of the emergence of a civil society based on market relations and its separation from the state.'[132] However, until the end of the nineteenth century, the Young Ottoman elites were interested less in promoting economic activities than in the modernisation of administration and education.

3. The final stage started with the revolution of 1908 which brought the Young Turks to power until 1918: 'Until the arrival of the Committee of Union and Progress (CUP) in 1908, the successive waves of modernisation could not achieve a permanent balance in favour of a modern state mechanism conducive for the sustained development of capitalism.'[133] The most significant efforts of the Young Turks 'concerned the socio-economic sphere. They were keenly aware of the absolute necessity to promote a national economy'.[134] The Young Turk period ended in 1918 with the defeat of the Ottoman Empire in the First World War. During this final stage, the differences between the persistent pre-capitalist features of the state and its increasingly capitalistic nature would be resolved by the Turkish nationalists. The Ottoman Empire's social structure was different prior to its 'capitalist incorporation'.[135] Pre-capitalist power structures were legitimised by divine law – *Şeriat* in modern Turkish and *Sharia* in Arabic – and the identity was defined by religion – *umma*. Thus, secularisation was a necessity which signified two interrelated processes: the homogenisation of the people, ruled by the same centralised state, and the transformation from an 'umma' identity to a 'secular' identity. The result was the construction of the Turkish national identity within

the boundaries of the modern Turkish state by the Kemalist project.[136] The above-outlined three stages, in fact, show that Ottoman socio-political changes must be investigated in conjunction with the empire's adaptation to European capitalism. However, as Ashcroft argues, the processes of appropriation, adaptation and transformation have been main characteristic features of 'alternative moderni-ties', which 'emerge out of a *relation* to other modernities'.[137]

In the final analysis, the transformation of the empire was a dialectical result of competing prescriptions on how to modernise the state based on the model of Western modernity. It is ironic that the initial reason for modernising the empire, that is to withstand the West militarily, brought its pre-modern features towards an unexpected end when the empire started to integrate into the European capi-talist system. Simon Bromley suggests the necessity for a new analysis, based on three pillars, to understand the process of Ottoman decline, European expansion and state building and the legacy left for the Arab successor states of the Ottoman Empire in the Middle East and North Africa. First, the nature of Ottoman disin-tegration and European penetration should be examined; second, the character of European and especially British interests in the region should be reconsid-ered; and, third, this investigations would then allow us to rethink the 'Eastern Question' itself.[138] Bromley argues that 'it was unlikely that any localised conflict would bring about a complete collapse of Ottoman rule. Rather it was to take the general crisis of European imperialism to restructure the state system in the Middle East.'[139] If we take this analysis one step further, these external factors also had some unprecedented consequences and impacts on the internal dynamics of the empire, which together contributed towards the destruction of the Ottomans.

Although it is generally accepted that concepts of nation and nation-state became known towards the end of the eighteenth century in the Ottoman Empire, 'it is apparent from reading such key documents as the [*Gülhane Hatt-ı Hümayunu*] of 1839 … that the sultan and his government were indeed striving to initiate what amounts to a nationalising project'.[140] While the main concern was how to save the empire, the ideas of the French Revolution – equality, liberty and brotherhood – started a snowball effect that planted the seeds of its own destruction.[141] In specific terms, these new concepts undermined the empire, so that when the First World War brought the empire to an end, it was vulnerable to the combined force of internal and external pressures. Interestingly enough, they also created some of the building blocks for the construction of a new Turkish political identity and a modern nation-state at the beginning of the twentieth century, which has a residual effect upon its current relations with the EU.

Intensifying Turkey's identity crisis at the margins of Europe

As argued earlier, the Turkish nationalists inherited an 'identity crisis' from the Ottoman Empire. The major non-European societies, i.e. China, Japan and the Ottoman Empire, were not accepted as equal members of the European interna-tional system until the mid-nineteenth century. They were, mainly, the 'other' for Europeans. As Therborn argues, '[l]ike nationally or ethnic identity, Europeanism is a historically constructed, historically variable, historically moulded chosen collective identity'.[142] In this context, one can submit that European identity, like any other collective identity, developed itself in relation to the existence of the 'other'. Accordingly, the Ottoman Empire was one of the 'others' until the nineteenth century, when internal and external change threw its position and sense of self into crisis.

The previous section explained that the Turkish transformation was an outcome of an historical process with both internal and external dimensions. It was 'a prolonged process of resistance-and-accommodation to capitalism' and adaptation to Western modernity.[143] 'The entire process took almost a century, starting with the *Tanzimat* of 1839 and culminating in the foundation of the Turkish Republic in 1923.'[144] During this long process, the Turkish nationalists tried to find a solution to the 'identity crisis' by transforming the state structure into the dominant form of the international system, that of a modern nation-state.

A very brief summary of Anthony Giddens' classification of nation-states will be helpful for understanding the essence of Turkey's identity crisis. He lists four different types of nation-states: classical, colonised, post-colonial and modernising.[145] Classical nation-states refer mainly to the European states originating in the eighteenth and nineteenth centuries. What is specifically important for this study is that he considers Turkey to be in this group. Giddens argues that '[n]ot all nation-states that can be placed in the classical type were established in the eighteenth and nineteenth centuries. Those set up in Europe and around the margins of Europe following the world wars (including ex-imperial states like Austria or Turkey) belong in this category.'[146]

I think that the main reason for considering Turkey among the classical nation-states is its geographical closeness to Europe – 'around the margins of Europe', as Giddens describes it. This is also a crucial point in understanding its 'identity crisis'. With the Treaty of Paris in 1856, the Ottoman Empire had been accepted into the European system without being part of it, and the new Turkish Republic inherited this historically ambiguous status.

One can argue that history and geopolitics may play an important role in the political identities of some countries. Turkey and Russia alike have inherited the historical legacies that restrain their modern policy orientations. 'For example, the recently revived dispute in Russia between the Slavophiles and the Westernisers as well as the current contention in Turkey between the Islamists and the secularisers reflect the geopolitical dilemmas of states with mixed European and Asian roots.'[147] Turkey's geo-culturally determined 'Euro-Asian' identity implies its 'hybridity' in-between cultures and modernities. Despite the continuity of the current Turkish government's pro-Western foreign policy orientations, Turkish society oscillates between secular and Islamic ideas in domestic affairs. Hence, these tensions not only highlight the main characteristic of the Turkish model as 'hybridised' but also question how Turkey's alternative modernity will appropriate and transform 'global cultural forms to local needs, beliefs and conditions'.[148]

Historically, one of the necessary consequences of the Turkish adaptation to modernity was incorporation into the capitalist international system with its own political identity, nation-state. Suffice it to say that modern Turkey still has to face the dilemmas of this transformation and adaptation as a litmus test in the twenty-first century. In fact, European modernity itself should be neither credited with nor cursed for the existence of other culturally situated alternative modernities in the non-European world. In the twentieth century, the Turkish transformation to a secular nation-state from an Islamic empire provided an alternative way of constructing modern identity in a Muslim society on both the individual and collective levels. It is the task of the rest of the book to examine the role of Turkish foreign policy in constructing a new political identity in the international system and to show why developments in the South Caucasus were important during this process.

Concluding remarks

This chapter explained why the concept of modernity is chosen as the second pillar of a new theoretical framework. One of the key findings is that the Ottoman transformation to a modern nation-state was an unintended consequence of a long historical process produced by its simultaneous resistance and accommodation to the expansion of capitalism and European modernity since the beginning of the nineteenth century. Having said that, two of modernity's 'structural forces' have been particularly identified: Ottoman incorporation into the capitalist international system and the Turkish identity crisis at the margins of Europe. The historical evolution of Ottoman participation in the modern international system is emphasised for two reasons: the legacy of 'identity crisis' of the empire in the European system, and how foreign policy played an important role in solving this crisis during the construction of a new political identity.

It has been proposed that there are two important implications of multiple and alternative modernities for the Turkish transition: the nation-state is the most prominent political form of modernity, and there is a direct relation between modernity and identity construction during the transition process. This is where the state theories of historical sociology and FPA come together: the emergence of the modern nation-state has to be placed within a wider historical structure, and during this emergence foreign policy plays a crucial role in locating a new political identity in the international system. It was also argued that the role of foreign policy in the construction of political identity shows how the distinction between foreign and domestic policies blurs under the conditions of transition to modernity. The next chapter will explain why the study of nationalism has become the third pillar on which a new interdisciplinary approach is based. In particular, modernity, nationalism and foreign policy are connected to each other during the transition process: one of the main goals of transitional states is nation-state building, which is an integral part of the ideology of nationalism.

Notes

1 Richard Devetak, 'The Project of Modernity and International Relations Theory', *Millennium: Journal of International Studies*, 24:1 (Spring 1995), p. 27; James Mayall,

'Nationalism in the Study of International Relations', A.J.R. Groom and Margot Light, eds, in *Contemporary International Relations: A Guide to Theory*, London, Pinter, 1994, p. 182.

2 Rob Shields, *Places on the Margin: Alternative Geographies of Modernity*, London, Routledge, 1991, p. 276.

3 In the late 1960s, as a result of the Marxist revival of development–underdevelopment approaches, dependency theory, represented in the work of Andre Gunter Frank, criticised modernisation theory and formulated an alternative view. The central concern of this school was to place the economic development and general modernisation of peripheral countries into the context of their relations with the developed capitalist countries. Thomas R. Shannon, *An Introduction to the World-System Perspective*, Boulder, CO, Westview Press, 1996, p. 15; See also, David Harrison, *The Sociology of Modernisation and Development*, London, Routledge, 1993. In the 1970s, world-system theory, articulated by Immanuel Wallerstein, emerged as a response to dependency theorists' overemphasis of external rather than internal factors in explaining the problems of the periphery. The nature of the exploitation of the periphery was located in relationship of the core to the periphery. Shannon, *An Introduction to the World-System Perspective*, p. 19. World-system theorists provided a detailed historical analysis of the study of social change, which became an alternative to modernisation theory. World-system theory also overcame dependency theory's flawed conclusion that the integration of peripheral societies into the world-economy will always remain at the level of 'dependent development'. During this perpetual search to understand the Third World's evolution, 'historical sociology' became the dominant discipline concerned with the analysis of the dynamics of large-scale social change. Ibid., p. 210.

4 Andrew Webster, *Introduction to the Sociology of Development*, London, Macmillan, 1993, p. 49.

5 Jung, Dietrich and Wolfango Piccoli, *Turkey at the Crossroads: Ottoman Legacies and a Greater Middle East*, London: Zed Books, 2001; Tim Jacoby, *Social Power and the Turkish State*, London, Routledge, 2004, p. 60.

6 See, Sibel Bozdoğan and Reşat Kasaba, eds, *Türkiye'de Modernleşme ve Ulusal Kimlik*, İstanbul, Tarih Vakfı Yurt Yayınları, 1998; Ersin Kalaycıoğlu and Ali Y. Sarıbay, *Türkiye'de Politik Değişim ve Modernleşme*, İstanbul, Alfa, 2000; Fuat Keyman, *Remaking Turkey: Globalization, Alternative Modernities, and Democracies*, Lexington Books, 2007.

7 Andrew Feenberg, *Alternative Modernity: The Technical Turn in Philosophy and Social Theory*, California, University of California Press, 1995, p. 214.

8 Ayla Göl, 'Editor's Introduction: Views from the "Others" of the War on Terror', *Critical Studies on Terrorism*, 3:1 (2010), pp. 1–5.

9 Jacoby, *Social Power and the Turkish State*, p. 5.

10 Stephen Hobden, *International Relations and Historical Sociology: Breaking Down Boundaries*, London, Routledge, 1998, p. 3.

11 Theda Skocpol, 'Bringing the State Back In: Strategies of Analysis in Current Research', in Peter B. Evans, Diethrich Rueschemeyer and Theda Skocpol, eds, *Bringing the State Back In*, Cambridge, Cambridge University Press, 1985, pp. 3–4.

12 Hobden, *International Relations and Historical Sociology*, p. 2.

13 Fred Halliday, 'State and Society in International Relations: A Second Agenda', *Millennium: Journal of International Studies*, 16:2 (Summer 1987), p. 215.

14 Ibid., p. 218.

15 Ibid., p.221; Fred Halliday, *Rethinking International Relations*, London, Macmillan, 1994, p.84; Fred Halliday, *The Middle East in International Relations: Power, Politics and Ideology*, Cambridge, Cambridge University Press, 2005, p.41.
16 C. Black, 'Dynamic of Modernisation', in Robert Nisbet, ed., *Social Change*, Oxford, 1972, p.242.
17 Ibid., p.243.
18 Samuel P. Huntington, *The Clash of Civilisations and the Remaking of the World Order*, London, Touchstone Books, 1997, p.68.
19 Nora Fisher Onar and Meltem Mutfuler-Bac, 'The Adultery and Headscarf Debates in Turkey: Fusing "EU-niversal" and "Alternative" Modernities?', *Women Studies International Forum*, 34 (2011), p.380.
20 Webster, *Introduction to the Sociology of Development*, p.49.
21 Colin Leys, 'Samuel Huntington and the End of Classical Modernisation Theory', in Hamza Alavi and Thedor Shanin, *Introduction to the Sociology of 'Developing Societies'*, New York, Monthly Review Press, 1982, p.333.
22 Webster, *Introduction to the Sociology of Development*, p.53.
23 Shannon, *An Introduction to the World-System Perspective*, p.7.
24 Christopher Clapham, *Third World Politics: An Introduction*, London, Routledge, 1988, p.6.
25 Samir Amin, 'The Social Movements in the Periphery: An End to National Liberation?', in S. Amin, G. Arrighi, Andre Gunder Frank and Immanuel Wallerstein, *Transforming the Revolution: Social Movements and the World-System*, New York, Monthly Review Press, 1990, p.102.
26 Tony Smith, 'The Underdevelopment of Development Literature: The Case of Dependency Theory', in Atul Kohli, ed., *The State and Development in the Third World*, Princeton, NJ: Princeton University Press, 1986, p.26.
27 Onar and Mutfuler-Bac, 'The Adultery and Headscarf Debates in Turkey'.
28 Bill Ashcroft, 'Alternative Modernities: Globalization and the Post-colonial', *A Review of International English Literature*, 40:1 (2009), p.82.
29 Onar and Meltem Mutfuler-Bac, 'The Adultery and Headscarf Debates in Turkey', p.380.
30 Nilufer Göle, 'Islam in Public: New Visibilities and New Imaginaries', *Public Culture*, 14:1 (2002), p.174; Ayla Göl, 'The Identity of Turkey: Muslim and Secular', *Third World Quarterly*, 30:4 (2009), p.795.
31 The best examples are: Dankwart A. Rustow, *A World of Nations: Problems of Political Modernisation*, Washington, DC, 1967; S. P. Huntington, *Political Order in Changing Societies*, Yale University, 1968.
32 Webster, *Introduction to the Sociology of Development*, p.57.
33 Anthony Giddens, *Runaway World: How Globalisation is Reshaping Our Lives*, London, Profile Books, 1999, p.39.
34 Anthony Giddens, *The Nation-State and Violence*, Cambridge: Polity Press, 1985, p.169.
35 Halliday, 'State and Society', p.215.
36 Sudipta Kaviraj, 'On State, Society and Discourse in India', in James Manor, ed., *Rethinking Third World Politics*, London, Longman, 1991, p.9.
37 Ashcroft, 'Alternative Modernities', p.83.
38 Philip Cassell, ed., *The Giddens Reader*, London, Macmillan, 1993, p.288.
39 The idea of 'modernity', as a mode of social life or organisation, emerged in Western Europe after the English Industrial Revolution and the French Revolution

and became dominant world-wide. Anthony Giddens, *The Consequences of Modernity*, Cambridge, Polity, 1990, p. 1; Nicos Mouzelis, 'Modernity, Late Development and Civil Society', in John A. Hall, ed., *Civil Society: Theory, History, Comparison*, Cambridge, Polity, 1995, p. 224. However, this diffusion does not imply that the concept of modernity is simple to define. Classical sociologists have attempted to analyse 'a single overriding dynamic transformation in interpreting the nature of modernity': for Marx, 'the emergent social order of modernity is *capitalistic* in both its economic and its other institutions'; for Durkheim, the nature of modern institutions was bound 'primarily to the impact of *industrialism*'; for Weber, considering the impact of capitalism rather than industrialism, '[r]ationalisation as expressed in technology and in the organisation of human activities, in the shape of bureaucracy is the keynote'. Giddens, *The Consequences of Modernity*, pp. 11–12.

40 Nilufer Göle, 'Snaphots of Islamic Modernities', *Deadalus*, 129:1 (2000), p. 91.
41 Jürgen Habermas, 'Modernity – An Incomplete Project', in Thomas Docherty, ed., *Postmodernism: A Reader*, New York, Harvester, 1993, p. 103.
42 Timothy W. Luke, *Social Theory and Modernity: Critique, Dissent and Revolution*, London, Sage Publications, 1990, p. 212.
43 R.B.J. Walker, *Inside/Outside: International Relations as Political Theory*, Cambridge University Press, 1993, p. 71.
44 Habermas, 'Modernity', p. 103.
45 Feenberg, 'Alternative Modernity', p. 214.
46 Göran Therborn, *European Modernity and Beyond: The Trajectory of European societies 1945–2000*, London, Sage Publications, 1995, p. 4.
47 Ibid.
48 Anthony Giddens, *Modernity and Self-Identity: Self and Society in the Late Modern Age*, Cambridge, Polity Press, 1993, p. 16.
49 Dilip P. Gaonkar, 'On Alternative Modernities', *Public Culture*, 11:1 (1999), p. 13.
50 Feenberg, 'Alternative Modernity', pp. 213–214.
51 Martin Riesebrodt, 'From Pathriarchalism to Capitalism: The Theoretical Context of Max Weber's Agrarian Studies (1892–3)', in Keith Tribe, ed., *Reading Weber*, London, Routledge, 1989, pp. 138–141; Ellen M. Wood, 'Modernity, Postmodernity, or Capitalism?', *Monthly Review*, 48:3 (July–August 1996), p. 27; Anthony Giddens, *Capitalism and Modern Social Theory: An Analysis of the Writings of Marx, Durkheim and Max Weber*, Cambridge, Cambridge University Press, 1994, p. 179. See also, R. Collins, 'Weber's Last Theory of Capitalism: A Systematisation', *American Sociological Review*, 45:6 (1980), pp. 925–942.
52 Giddens, *The Nation-State and Violence*, pp. 5, 169.
53 Ali Kazancigil, 'Paradigms of Modern State Formation in the Periphery', in Ali Kazancigil, ed., *The State in Global Perspective*, Paris, Gower, 1986, p. 127; Geoffrey Hawthorn, '"Waiting for A text?": Comparing Third World Politics', in James Manor, ed., *Rethinking Third World Politics*, London, Longman, 1991, p. 28.
54 Gaonkar, 'On Alternative Modernities', p. 13.
55 Gerard Delanty, 'Modernity and the escape from Eurocentrism', in G. Delanty, ed., *The Handbook of European Social Theory*, Abingdon: Routledge, 2006, p. 272.
56 Göran Therborn, 'The Right to Vote and the Four World Routes to/through Modernity', in Rolf Torstendahl, ed., *State Theory and State History*, London, Sage, 1992, p. 63.
57 Atul Kohli and Vivienne Shue, 'State Power and Social Forces: on Political Contention

and Accommodation in the Third World', in Joel S. Migdal, Atul Kohli and Vivienne Shue, eds, *State Power and Social Forces*, Cambridge University Press, 1994, p. 300.

58 Ashcroft, 'Alternative Modernities', pp. 82–83.

59 Black, 'Dynamic of Modernisation', p. 263.

60 Gaonkar, 'On Alternative Modernities', p. 13.

61 Therborn, 'The Right to Vote', p. 64.

62 Therborn, *European Modernity and Beyond*, p. 5; Therborn, 'The Right to Vote', p. 64.

63 Göran Therborn, 'Dialectics of Modernity: On Critical Theory and the legacy of Twentieth-Century Marxism', *New Left Review*, 215 (January/February 1996), p. 77.

64 Therborn, *European Modernity and Beyond*, p. 6.

65 Therborn, 'The Right to Vote', p. 65.

66 It must be pointed out at this juncture of the analysis that there are also other inter-pretations of the transformation of non-European societies. For instance, Tosun Arıcanlı and Mara Thomas argue that '[t]he historical trajectory of Western Europe can neither define the course of a non-European historical transformation nor is it suitable for constructing a comparative model encompassing both the European experience and the rest of the world'. Tosun Arıcanlı and Mara Thomas, 'Sidestepping Capitalism: On the Ottoman Road to Elsewhere', *Journal of Historical Sociology*, 7:1 (March 1994), p. 25.

67 Gaonkar, 'On Alternative Modernities', p. 13.

68 Giddens, *Modernity and Self-Identity*, p. 33.

69 David Campbell, *Writing Security: United States Foreign Policy and the Politics of Identity*, Manchester, Manchester University Press, 1998, p. 43.

70 John Agnew and Stuart Corbridge, *Mastering Space: Hegemony, Territory and International Political Economy*, London, Routledge, 1995, p. 16.

71 William Bloom, *Personal Identity, National Identity and International Relations*, Cambridge, Cambridge University Press, 1990, p. 23; S. Telhami and M. Barnett, eds, *Identity and Foreign Policy in the Middle East*, Ithaca, Cornell University Press, 2002.

72 Gaonkar, 'On Alternative Modernities', p. 13.

73 Ulrich Beck, Anthony Giddens and Scott Lash, *Reflexive Modernisation: Politics, Tradition and Aesthetics in the Modern Social Order*, Cambridge, Polity Press, 1994, p. 38.

74 Ibid., p. 39.

75 J. Hoffman, *Beyond the State: An Introductory Critique*, Cambridge, 1995, p. 19.

76 Ali Kazancigil, ed., *The State in Global Perspective*, Paris, Unesco, 1986, p. xii.

77 Stuart Hall, 'The State in Question', in Gregor McLennan, David Held and Stuart Hall, eds, *The Idea of the Modern State*, Milton Keynes, Open University Press, 1990, p. 1.

78 Christopher Pierson, *The Modern State*, London, Routledge, 1996, pp. 36–37.

79 Charles Tilly, 'Western State Making and Theories of Political Transformation', in Charles Tilly, ed., *The Formation of National States in Western Europe*, Princeton, NJ, Princeton University Press, 1975, p. 637.

80 Ibid., p. 638.

81 Chris Brown, *Understanding International Relations*, London, Macmillan, 1997, pp. 67–68.

82 Hedley Bull, *The Anarchical Society: A Study of Order in World Politics*, London, Macmillan, 1977, p. 8.

83 James Mayall, *Nationalism and International Society*, Cambridge, Cambridge University Press, 1990, p. 35.

84 Bull, *The Anarchical Society*, p. 8.
   For a well-argued examination of the ambiguity of the concept of sovereignty see Öyvind Österud, 'The Narrow Gate: Entry to the Club of Sovereign State', *Review of International Studies*, 23:2 (April 1997), pp. 167–184.
85 Mayall, *Nationalism and International Society*, pp. 38–41.
86 Anthony Giddens uses the concept of 'state-nation' to describe the post-colonial states which 'are based upon state apparatuses originally established by the colonising societies'. Giddens, *The Nation-State and Violence*, p. 272.
87 Halliday, 'State and Society', p. 219; Geoffrey Stern, *The Structure of International Society: An Introduction to the Study of International Relations*, London, Continuum, 1995, p. 96.
88 Gianfranco Poggi, *The State: Its Nature, Development and Prospects*, Cambridge, Polity Press, 1990, p. 22.
89 Brown, *Understanding International Relations*, p. 68.
90 Poggi, *The State*, p. 86.
91 Giddens, *The Nation-State and Violence*, p. 170.
92 Brown, *Understanding International Relations*, p. 73.
93 Ilya Prizel, *National Identity and Foreign Policy: Nationalism and Leadership in Poland, Russia, and Ukraine*, Cambridge, Cambridge University Press, 1998, p. 14; See, Shibley Telhami and Michael Barnett, 'Introduction: Identity and Foreign Policy in the Middle East', in Shibley Telhami and Michael Barnett, eds, *Identity and Foreign Policy in the Middle East*, Ithaca: Cornell University Press, 2002, p. 6.
94 Bloom, *Personal Identity*, p. 52.
95 Walker, *Inside/Outside*, p. 9.
96 Therborn, 'The Right to Vote', p. 63.
97 Therborn, *European Modernity and Beyond*, p. 229.
98 Ibid.
99 Prizel, *National Identity and Foreign Policy*, p. 17.
100 Therborn, *European Modernity and Beyond*, pp. 229–231.
101 Walker, *Inside/Outside*, p. 27.
102 Campbell, *Writing Security*, p. 9.
103 Bloom, *Personal Identity*, p. 55.
104 Prizel, *National Identity and Foreign Policy*, p. 8.
105 Christopher Hill, 'What is Left of the Domestic? A Reverse Angle View of Foreign Policy', in Michi Ebata and Beverly Neufeld, eds, *Confronting the Political in International Relations*, London, Macmillan, 2000, p. 164.
106 David Campbell, 'Global Inscription: How Foreign Policy Constitutes the United States', *Alternatives*, 15:3 (Summer 1990), p. 266.
107 Ibid.
108 Agnew and Corbridge, *Mastering Space*, p. 16.
109 Prizel, *National Identity and Foreign Policy*, p. 2.
110 Mayall, *Nationalism and International Society*, p. 19.
111 Fatma Müge Göcek, *Rise of the Bourgeoisie, Demise of Empire: Ottoman Westernisation and Social Change*, New York, Oxford University Press, 1996, p. 18.
112 The economic dimension of the Ottoman transition has been studied through its mode of production, lack of bourgeoisie, peripheral relations. See, for instance, Şevket Pamuk, *The Ottoman Empire and European Capitalism, 1820–1913: Trade, Investment and Production*, Cambridge, Cambridge University Press, 1987; Halil İnalcık and Donald Quataert, eds, *An Economic and Social History of the Ottoman*

Empire, Vol. 1. 1300–1660 and *Vol. 2. 1600–1914*, Cambridge, Cambridge University Press, 1997.

113 The signature of the Treaty of Paris between Britain, Austria, France, Prussia, Russia, Sardinia and the Ottoman Empire on 30 March 1856 indicated that 'the Sublime Porte should be "admitted, to participate in the advantages of the public law and system (*concert*) of Europe"'. A.L. Macfie, *The Eastern Question: 1774–1923*, London, Longman, 1994, p. 100; Doc. 16, Article VII of the Treaty of Paris.

114 Simon Bromley, *Rethinking Middle East Politics: State Formation and Development*, Cambridge, Polity Press, 1994, p. 46.

115 Roderic H. Davison, 'The Westernisation of Ottoman Diplomacy in the Nineteenth Century', in Edward Ingram, ed., *National and International Politics in the Middle East: Essays in Honour of Elie Kedourie*, Franc Cass, 1986, p. 57.

116 Çağlar Keyder, 'The Dilemma of Cultural Identity on the Margin of Europe', *Review*, 16:1 (Winter 1993), p. 19.

117 Kaviraj, 'On State, Society and Discourse in India', p. 7.

118 Justin Rosenberg, *The Empire of Civil Society: A Critique of the Realist Theory of International Relations*, London, Verso, 1994, p. 47; Fred Halliday, *Revolution and World Politics: The Rise and Fall of Sixth Great Powers*, London, Macmillan, 1999, p. 9.

119 Evan Luard, *International Society*, London, Macmillan, 1990, p. 72; Bull, *The Anarchical Society*, p. 257.

120 Halliday, *Revolution and World Politics*, p. 9.

121 Anthony Giddens, *Central Problems in Social Theory: Action, Structure and Contradiction in Social Analysis*, London, Macmillan, p. 69.

122 Rosenberg, *The Empire of Civil Society*, p. 47.

123 Giddens, *Central Problems*, p. 60.

124 Halliday, *Revolution and World Politics*, p. 9.

125 Ibid., p. 10.

126 Anthony Giddens, *A Contemporary Critique of Historical Materialism*, London, Macmillan, 1981, p. 12.

127 Haldun Gülalp, 'Capitalism and the Modern Nation-State: Rethinking the Creation of the Turkish Republic', *Journal of Historical Sociology*, 7:2 (June 1994), p. 166.

128 Ibid.

129 Çağlar Keyder, 'The Dissolution of the Asiatic Mode of Production', *Economy and Society*, 5:2 (May 1976), p. 179.

130 Gülalp, 'Capitalism and the Modern Nation-State', p. 167.

131 Ali Kazancigil, 'The Deviant Case in Comparative Analysis – High Stateness in a Muslim Society: The Case of Turkey', in Mattei Doğan and Ali Kazancigil, eds, *Comparing Nations: Concepts, Strategies, Substance*, Oxford, Blackwell, 1994, pp. 223–224.

132 Gülalp, 'Capitalism and the Modern Nation-State', p. 168.

133 Çağlar Keyder, 'The Political Economy of Turkish Democracy', *New Left Review*, 115 (May–June 1979), p. 5.

134 Kazancigil, 'The Deviant Case in Comparative Analysis', p. 225.

135 Çağlar Keyder, *Sate and Class in Turkey: A Study in Capitalist Development*, London, Verso, 1987, p. 7.

136 Gülalp, 'Capitalism and the Modern Nation-State', p. 167.

137 Ashcroft, 'Alternative Modernities', p. 83.

138 Bromley, *Rethinking Middle East Politics*, pp. 47–48.

139 Ibid., p. 70.

140 Dror Ze'evi, '*Kul* and Getting Cooler: The Dissolution of Elite Collective Identity and the Formation of Official Nationalism in the Ottoman Empire', *Mediterranean Historical Review*, 11:2 (December 1996), p. 179.
141 Ibid., pp. 194–195.
142 Therborn, *European Modernity and Beyond*, p. 242.
143 Gülalp, 'Capitalism and the Modern Nation-State', p. 166.
144 Ibid., p. 156.
145 Giddens, *The Nation-State and Violence*, p. 269.
146 Ibid., p. 270.
147 Stern, *The Structure of International Society*, p. 86.
148 Ashcroft, 'Alternative Modernities', p. 83.

3

Modernity, nationalism and Islamic identity

Having suggested a new approach to understanding the foreign policies of transitional states by using FPA and historical sociology, this chapter shows why the study of nationalism is the third pillar that completes the new theoretical framework. Chapter 1 argued that the foreign policies of transitional states reflect their preoccupation with domestic politics – which indicates nation-state building as an integral part of modernity. Chapter 2 then explained what the transition to modernity meant in Turkish politics and this chapter now examines the relationship between nationalism and modernity in order to understand the emergence of Turkish nationalism.

This chapter will, first, argue why the emergence of Turkish nationalism can be better explained by the modernist approach, which explicitly recognises the correlation between modernity and nationalism. Afterwards, the second part of the chapter aims to understand the emergence of Turkish nationalism and its impacts on Turkish foreign policy towards the East. The emphasis here is placed on Ottoman modernisation since the beginning of the nineteenth century and how this influenced the emergence of Turkish nationalism in the twentieth century. Based on critical theory as highlighted in Chapter 1, neither the rise of nationalism is taken for granted nor the concept of nation as a given. Furthermore, the five dimensions of the foreign policies of transitional states were also illustrated in Chapter 1. Accordingly, this chapter particularly attempts to locate the rise of Turkish nationalism as part of Turkey's transition to modernity within a broader historical context. Hence, this chapter aims to contextualise the theoretical argument, with reference to historical continuity and change as the first dimension of foreign policy in state transformation.

Modernity and nationalism

Nationalism has been one of the most influential forces of international politics in contemporary history.[1] Before explaining how and why nationalism became part of social and political changes in the history of the Ottoman Empire, as a non-European Islamic empire it is necessary to understand the link between

modernity and nationalism. As John Breuilly argues, nationalism can be interpreted as one aspect of an 'unintended modernity'.[2] As explained in Chapter 2,
the transition to modernity assumes, drawing on the mainstream sociological
theorists, 'the existence of three stages of the modernisation process: tradition,
transition, modernity'.[3] In this understanding, nationalism as one of the main
forms of organising social relations among people is seen as an outcome of the
'transitional phase'.[4] During this phase, nationalism has the potential to act like a
'prism' through 'which are preserved, albeit in changed forms, some of the continuities with the past and the transformations of modernity'.[5] In this case, there is
an explicit link between nationalism and modernity since both were at the centre
of major changes around 1800 in Europe. Historically, they seem to be apt to
explain each other in the European context. For Otto Dann, 'the term modernity,
used to denote the historical epoch we live in, is the broader context and thus it
figures as the *explanas*, while nationalism is the *explanandum*'.[6]

On the other hand, Liah Greenfeld's influential book, *Nationalism: Five Roads
to Modernity*, challenges the current sociological literature on modernity and
nationalism by seeing modernity as defined by nationalism rather than by defining nationalism through its modernity.[7] Greenfeld argues that the national idea
first arose in England in the early sixteenth century before modernisation and that
'the emergence of nationalism in France, Russia, Germany, and the United States
all predated industrialisation'.[8] It is the former approach that will be applied to
the case of Ottoman Empire since the latter fails to answer why any particular
national identity is important to people in the contemporary world.[9] As critically
explored in the previous chapter, the process of modernisation is not interpreted
as industrialisation and the concept of modernity is not seen as a single wave.[10]

Otto Dann identifies five different phases of political modernity: state-building
as a new form of government, the process of nation-construction, the expansion
of political participation through democratisation, the demand for social justice
through the redistribution of the resources of state and society and the growth of
internationalism of the political world.[11] Among these phases, state-building and
nation-construction become the most problematic phases of political modernity
in Turkey's transformation from an Islamic empire to a nation-state. However,
two essentially contested concepts, 'nation' and 'state', which are two different phenomena, will help us in understanding not only nationalism but also its
relation to modernity.[12]

To begin with, the main studies of nationalism agree that as a doctrine it translates into international politics as a neatly organised world of nation-states.[13] As
already clarified, the nation-state is the most recognised political unit and prominent form of modernity despite the fact that, as has often been argued, 'there are
actually very few genuine "nation-states" today'.[14] It would be more appropriate
to describe the main actors of international politics as 'state-nations'. Moreover,
epistemologically, the name of international politics is a misnomer since the main
theoretical concerns of IR are related to states not nations.

In general, the definition of state might seem to scholars easier to grasp than
the definition of nation. As highlighted in the previous chapter, there is general

agreement on the definition of state as a 'territorially based' political organisation; but nation remains to be one of the most 'puzzling and tendentious items in the political lexicon'.[15] However, Arthur Waldron emphasises that '"nation" captures something that "state" misses: a feeling, a passion, a legitimising power that the word "nationalism" possesses to an unequalled degree'.[16] Hence, nationalism as a sociological phenomenon and ideology is not just a clear-cut concept like state and nation. Paradoxically, while the definitions of nationalism, nation and state are closely interlinked with each other, they are regarded as different phenomena. How can one solve this puzzle?

I suggest starting with the understanding of nation for two reasons: nation captures what state misses on societal level, as people; and the construction of state identity cannot be detached from its national context. Consequently, nationalism is defined 'as any political movement which seeks to take or exercise state power and justifies this in national terms'.[17] The 'core doctrine' of these nationalist terms consist of three assertions: national identity, national unity and national autonomy.[18]

1. There is a nation – usually, but not invariably, identified as a multi-class society occupying a particular territory – which can be recognised by certain collective characteristics which give it a peculiar identity.
2. The nation has an overriding claim to collective loyalty from those who belong to it.
3. The nation has a right to autonomy, usually but not invariably taking the form of a sovereign state for the national territory.[19]

Although all scholars of nationalism – that is, the primordial and perennial, and the ethno-symbolist accounts – have not accepted the modernity of the nation, there is a general agreement among all theories of nationalism that nationalism is a global political movement and a peculiarly modern phenomenon.[20]

Modernity of nationalism and the Turkish transformation

The modernist approach stems from the intellectual traditions that go back to the classical social theorists, Emile Durkheim, Max Weber and Karl Marx.[21] The modern theories of nationalism reflect different kinds of causal explanations, in one way or another, based on the concept of capitalism (Anderson), industrialism (Gellner), or rationalism (Breuilly).[22] However, they all conceive of nationalism as the most important 'political ideology of the modern era' and a by-product of modernity.[23] In particular, Hobsbawm and Anderson regard nationalism as the product of fiction and invented traditions.[24]

The political units of human history – small tribal units or village units, city states, dynastic empires, religious communities – seldom and accidentally coincide with those of 'nations'. The main paradox is that nations can be defined only in terms of the 'age of nationalism' rather than the other way round. To put it more precisely: 'Nationalism is not the awakening of nations to self-consciousness: it invents nations where they do not exist.'[25] Consequently, for the modernists, nationalism is an unnatural modern phenomenon and not taken for granted in human history.

The modernists argue that there are three causes behind the rise of nationalism: the psychological losses of identity, which have appeared through the erosion of tradition; the needs of modernisation; and the development of communication, culture and modern forms of class conflict. Thus, the site of investigation encompasses the economic, political and ideological levels of the social formation of each national ideology.[26] Also, attachment to the principle of the social forms, i.e. nation(states), does not necessitate the understanding of nationalism in all cases. But it has been suggested that there is no single, universal theory of nationalism through which understand every single case in world history.[27] For the most part, modernist explanations accept nationalism as 'modern' and as a 'political' response 'to the political dimension of modernisation'.[28] It is necessary to discuss these theoretical arguments in detail in order to build a solid ground for understanding Turkish nationalism and its transition to modernity.

I argue that the emergence of Turkish nationalism can be explained by modern theories of nationalism for three main reasons.[29] First, the need to belong to a separate Turkish nation was a result of the erosion of the traditional 'Ottoman', 'Islamic' identity through the collapse of the Ottoman Empire. 'The concept of being a "Turk", as used in modern parlance, was alien to the Ottoman elites, who saw themselves as Ottomans (Osmanli) rather than "Turks"; the latter seems to have implied "uneducated peasants" until the end of the nineteenth century.'[30] There was no conscious idea of Turkification before the twentieth century – the issue was Ottomanisation. The equation of these two terms only became apparent when nationalism emerged in the twentieth century.[31]

Second, the emergence of Turkish nationalism also coincides with the needs of modernisation in the Ottoman Empire in the nineteenth century. As will be examined in detail later, the Turkish transition to modernity was a long historical process which did not occur in just a few years after the Kemalist regime came to power in the 1920s. On the contrary, it spans over two hundred years which commenced with the declaration of Sened-i İttifak (Document of Agreement) as 'the Magna Carta of the Ottomans' in 1808 and it is still an unfinished project.[32] During this transition, the Ottomans invented their Turkishness under the influence of nationalist ideas from the West.

Third, and, more importantly, Turkish nationalism was not purely based on primordialist ties and ethno-symbols. The pre-modern Ottoman identity was based on the *millet* system that was characterised by religious communities rather than ethnic communities or language.[33] Within this system, there was a differentiation between Muslim and non-Muslim subjects but no official differentiation among the Muslims by language or ethnicity. In terms of ethnic ties, 'ethnicity' was not a determining factor *per se*. For instance, many grand vezirs and high officials originated with Albanian, Muslim Slav or other Muslim subjects. In the Ottoman system, the concept of the 'slave élite' (the ruling official class) and the 'devşirme' system (recruitment of Christian boys to be trained as Janissaries) worked against an 'ethnically pure' governing class. In terms of language ties, the state language was *Osmanlıca* (Ottoman Turkish) which was a mixture of Turkish, Arabic and Persian.[34] The multi-national character of the Ottoman system did not make it easy to use ethnic and language ties for the invention of the modern Turkish nation.

Consequently, it is the task of the next section to examine the relationship between the Ottoman modernisation and the emergence of Turkish nationalism. The analysis will be expanded upon in a broad historical framework within which political modernity has been considered a useful concept for understanding the social and political changes of the Islamic Ottoman Empire.

The rise of nationalism and modernisation in the Ottoman period

The Turkish experience has been accepted by both Turkish and Western scholars as a good example of modernisation theory.[35] In one of his last books, Ernest Gellner argued that Turkey deserves the special attention of anyone who is interested in the future of liberal societies, economic development or Islam. Among the Asian states, Japan, India and Turkey, with their success in constitutionalism and genuine elections, provide optimism for Western liberals. Within this trio Turkey differs for two reasons: it had a longer tradition of constitutional government and while never colonised it bordered Europe. Gellner also argued that Turkey's commitment to modern political ideas was a result of an endogenous development rather than being an alien imposition. Turkey achieved political modernity by choosing its own destiny. Yet, there is a dilemma arising from Gellner's analysis because he argued that Turkish commitment to modernisation of the polity and society had both an Ottoman and a Koranic quality.[36] In this case, one can question why Turkish society preferred the Western type of modernisation and the construction of a modern nation, to the Ottoman system and the religious communities of Islam.

It seems to me that this dilemma can be eliminated with further clarification: Turkish commitment to modernisation should be seen as a paradoxical relationship. While it was inevitable for Ottoman modernisation to adopt some aspects of the Western experience, Turkish modernisation, was by definition, opposed to the *Ottoman–Islamic identity* and accepted Westernisation as a totality. Moreover, as explained with reference to five dimensions of transitional foreign policy, the transition to modernity was accepted as a dialogue between past and present. In the Turkish context, the Ottoman and Islamic characteristics of the empire became the past when the modernisation of the empire in accordance with the progress of European modernity represented the present. Yet although Turkish modernisation aimed to cut its ties with the Ottoman past and Islamic identity, it could not so easily destroy the pre-modern – religious – characteristics of the empire. Probably, that is why Gellner argued that the Turkish modernisation had both an Ottoman and an Islamic quality. If the transition to modernity is a complex process as a dialogue between past and present, the paradoxical character of the Turkish experience in transition to modernity requires further elaboration of its historical phases and socio-political changes: the reformation period during the Young Ottomans, the revolution of the Young Turks and the emergence of Turkish nationalism.[37] The scrutiny of these historical periods will help us not only to understand the essence of historical and social changes during Turkey's engagement with European modernity, but also show the possibility of alternative modernities in an Islamic context.

The Young Ottoman movement: reformation

There is a general agreement that the Ottoman Empire's aim to integrate into the European system initiated its reformation or modernisation in the nineteenth century. The Ottoman Empire had an ambiguous status in the European system since it never really became a part of this system. From the European perspective, the Ottoman Empire was officially recognised as the first non-European member of the European state system, since its independence and integrity was seen as vital to the 'Peace of Europe'.[38] From the Ottoman perspective, it was unnecessary to be part of the European system during the climax of the empire because Ottoman civilisation was believed to be superior to that of the Europeans. But, when the empire started to decline during the eighteenth century, either the decaying structure of the Ottoman system or the superiority of European military technology had to be questioned.[39]

Sultan Mahmud II (1808–1839) deserves to be labelled as the first reformist monarch in Ottoman history.[40] Although the military technology and institutions were the first area of Ottoman reform, the emphasis here is on the modernisation of political institutions and the empire's social structure. On 7 October 1808, under the leadership of the grand vezir Bayraktar Mustafa Pasha, the notables and provincial governors forced the Sultan to sign a Document of Agreement (*Sened-i İttifak*) which recognised the Ottoman provincial notables as a new social resource to challenge the Sultan's authority.[41] The agreement did not last long, but it challenged the Ottoman notion of sovereignty. For the first time, the gradual separation of the Ottoman state from the Sultan was introduced legally.[42] The distinction between the government and the Sultan as well as the attempts to delimit his sovereign powers with respect to taxes were interpreted as steps toward constitutionalism. Some scholars accept the *Sened-i İttifak* as the 'Magna Carta of the Ottomans', an agreement which could serve as a written constitution.[43] However, 'unlike the Magna Carta, the Document of Agreement was not subsequently used to further the cause of constitutionalism in the Ottoman Empire'.[44] The first Ottoman constitution would be accepted in 1876 but the *Sened-i İttifak* had a symbolic impact on Ottoman history as the first milestone of the Turkish transition to modernity (See Table 1).

Conversely, Sultan Mahmud II's reforms signalled the beginning of the decay of a multi-national empire, which had to accept the independence of Greece, and an autonomous Serbia and Egypt in the nineteenth century.[45] This was the first signal of the emergence of nationalism within the empire, as a non-European, Islamic entity. The Ottoman Empire's social structure, better known as the *millet* system, was based on the religious and cultural autonomy of different groups. This system was functional for several centuries because nationalist doctrine was unknown.

In the Ottoman Empire, nationalism broadly meant religion. The Ottoman Sultan was accepted as the head of the Muslims, the Caliph, the successor of the prophet Mohammed.[46] As a consequence of this belief, 'Ottomanisation' signified the inevitable 'Islamisation'. Meanwhile, political and economic changes of the European international system during the nineteenth century triggered the political and economic restructuring of the Ottoman system.

In general, the nineteenth century can be characterised as a century of national unification and the expansion of foreign trade to non-European markets. The fruits of these changes were seen in the Ottoman Empire through the interaction between the Ottomans and the European states. It is interesting to note that after the British became the major trade partner with the Anglo-Turkish Convention of 1838,[47] the *Gülhane Hatt-ı Hümayunu* (Imperial Decree of the Rose-Chamber) of 1839 was declared, which opened a new era in Ottoman history.[48]

Thus, the *Gülhane Hatt-ı Hümayunu* had become the second milestone of Turkish modernisation. The period from 1839 to 1876 is known in Turkish historiography as the period of the *Tanzimat* – the era of modern reform – that modernised the Ottoman state and society.[49] The most important international event during this era was the signature of the Treaty of Paris in 1856. It was after this treaty that *Bab-ı Ali* (Sublime Porte) had to develop close economic, political and ideological relationships with the European powers in order to preserve the empire's *status quo* in the international system. At the same time, the empire had to accept the three main requirements of this system. First, the Treaty of Paris forced the Sublime Porte to repudiate the Islamic character of the state.[50] By doing so, arguably, the empire started acting more like a secular dynastic state on the European model of the international system.[51]

The repudiation of the empire's Islamic character was interpreted by the Sublime Porte as accepting all the subjects of the empire, of whatever religion, as equal, and ensuring that it should be so regarded by others in domestic politics. Second, in relation to the first requirement, the Sublime Porte had to accept modern arguments on the principle of nationality, or of national self-determination. This created a paradox in Ottoman politics since the acceptance of these principles would put the empire's integrity in danger by leading to the disintegration of the *millet* system. Statesmen started using modern secular arguments on the legitimacy of the existing Ottoman regime. This meant the usage of the Western law of nations because that law tended to support the *status quo* which the Sublime Porte wanted to preserve. Third, if the empire wanted to be part of the European system on equal terms, it had to observe European international law. In specific terms, the principles of '*pacta sunt servanda*' and 'non-intervention' by other powers in domestic affairs became particularly important for the Ottoman Empire after the Treaty of Paris.[52]

Meanwhile, the *Islahat Fermanı* (Reform Decree) of 1856 as the third milestone in the Turkish transition was a reflection of these requirements in domestic politics. The document emphasised full equality for all subjects.[53] The non-Muslim subjects of the empire were entitled to determine their own internal affairs. While the *Tanzimat* era failed to make non-Muslims loyal to the empire, how did it affect the Muslim subjects?[54]

The movement of the Young Ottomans (1865–1876) emerged as being specifically opposed to the *Tanzimat* reforms. According to Kedourie, this opposition was an outcome of the *Tanzimat* itself.[55] 'They were the first organised opposition group from the Ottoman intelligentsia to use the ideas of the Enlightenment and attempt to synthesise modernisation with Islam. They were also the first Ottoman group to use the media as means of spreading their ideology.'[56] The Young Ottomans' criticism focused on both the pioneers of the *Tanzimat* movement and the ideology of Westernisation itself. The Young Ottomans believed that the *Tanzimat* movement did not have a solid ideological or ethical basis; instead the solution could be found in Islam. For the first time they emphasised the importance of mobilising the 'Ottomans' as a conscious group.[57] Although the Young Ottomans did not know the meaning of modern nation and nationalism, they opened the first discussions on this phenomenon, with consequences for the process of nation-creation in Turkey in four ways.[58] For the first time in Ottoman history the concept of *vatan* (homeland) was used. If one considers that the new loyalty in non-European societies, especially in the Middle East, appeared in the form of 'patriotism' not 'nationalism', the importance of *vatan* becomes clear.[59] Second, they suggested that it was possible to save the empire by delinking themselves from the West. Third, they questioned the extensive authority of the sultan. Lastly, they had an important impact on another group, the Young Turks, who were the forefathers of Turkish nationalism.

During the last period of the Young Ottoman era (1870–1876), the solution to saving the empire appeared to be 'Islamism'.[60] Their main argument was based on the criticism of the *Tanzimat* – that this movement meant the dissolution of the Ottoman Empire. A change in policy from the *Tanzimat* ideas occurred when Sultan Abdulhamid II (1876–1909) took power and used the policy of pan-Islamism (favouring Islam at the expense of the empire's other religious communities) to unite the empire against external and internal threats.[61] Although he was an authoritarian monarch he ordered the establishment of a commission to draft a constitution.

The *Kanun-i Esasi* (the first Ottoman constitution), which was proclaimed on 23 December 1876, became the fourth milestone of Turkey's engagement with modernity.[62] It was not really a Western-style constitution but 'provided for separation of powers much more in form than fact, and the institutional changes reflected evolution rather than a radical departure from past experience'.[63] In specific terms, Article 3 of the Constitution referred to the 'high Islamic Caliphate' of the empire for two reasons: that the Ottoman *reaya* (people) should be united under the flag of 'Islam', and that all other Muslims outside of the empire should be united under the Caliphate.[64] The new emphasis on Sultan as Caliph and protector of all Muslims throughout the world was actually a foreign affairs bluff.[65]

Despite its authoritarian character, the penetration of Western-style national ideas had their impact on Ottoman society during Abdulhamid's regime. The reformation of the state schooling system, which commenced during the *Tanzimat* era, and that of language by the compulsory use of demotic Turkish aimed to make the empire more homogenous. Western concepts such as the influence of the press and the emergence of public opinion became noticeable. While the press began to discuss the concept of being a 'Turk', public opinion perceived Anatolia as the central part of homeland. The basic features for the construction of a modern nation were invoked: language, education, press, public opinion and homeland. In addition, the growth of Armenian and Greek nationalism in Anatolia became a catalyst for the raising of Turkish consciousness. The notion of being a Turk was seen as compatible with the concepts of Ottomanism and Islamism. Interestingly enough, Abdulhamid identified himself as a Turk even if this view was connected with his use of pan-Islam.[66] The end of the Abdulhamid regime in 1908 was itself a sign of new developments in Ottoman history.

The last milestone of the Turkish transition before the emergence of nationalism was the Young Turk revolution.[67] In July 1908, during Abdulhamid's reign, a small number of young officers in Salonika, the headquarters of the third army corps, rebelled and declared themselves the Committee of Union and Progress (CUP), representatives of enlightenment and revolution. They were proposing to rescue the empire once and for all from despotism, military weakness and economic and social backwardness.[68] In practice, they became the political organ of the Young Turks, who believed that a new policy against the *status quo* had to be implemented. The Young Turk revolution in 1908 had the characteristics of Ellen Triemberger's 'revolution from above' thesis.[69] The transformation of the Turkish society was carried out as 'a result of changes in the composition of elites' rather than as 'a result of mass-based revolts from below'.[70] The next section will examine the importance of the revolution of 1908 during Turkey's engagement with modernity.

The Young Turk Revolution in 1908

The Young Turk movement, like that of Young Italy and Young Egypt, was a sign of the breakdown in the transmission of political habits from one generation to the next. According to Smith, the use of the word 'young' was not a coincidence.[71] These nationalist movements were not only opposed to foreign dominators but also to their own ancestors. In Turkey, they were opposed to both European and Ottoman imperialism. They emphasised the meaning of 'Turkism' instead of the previous policies of pan-Ottomanism and pan-Islamism. However, the concept of 'Turk' in their usage did not have any connotation with the notion of modern nation at that time. The Young Turk movement did not rely on any single element of Turkism but on an amalgamation of different elements which can be encapsulated in a quotation from the Turkish poet, Mehmet Emin (Yurdakul): 'I am a Turk, my religion and my race are noble.'[72] Clearly, the first element to differentiate between Muslims and non-Muslims within the empire was religion. The definition of 'race' had different connotations. For many Young Turks, the idea of 'Turan' in defining the Turkish people became a valid inspiration before the First World War. The Turkish sociologist Ziya Gökalp used the concept of 'Turan'. Although 'Turan' was originally an Iranian word, which described the mythical enemy of the Iranians and the united homeland of the Turkic people, it was used by the Young Turks to develop the ideology of pan-Turanism.[73]

The idea of pan-Turanism was a desperate solution to 'to unite the Ottomans, the Azerbaijan Turks, the Crimean Turks, the Uzbek, the Kipchaks, the Kirghiz, and all the other sundered fragments of Turkism into one Turanian nation'.[74] How could they unite with the Turkic people of the Russian Empire while the Ottoman Empire itself was in the process of dissolution?[75] This idea could not go beyond being a utopia. Ziya Gökalp himself shifted the focus from Turan on to the notion of a modern nation and became the main ideologue of Turkish nationalism.[76] The Young Turks aimed to homogenise the Muslim subjects of the empire through changing the *millet* system and having a Western representative-type constitution.[77] The new alternative of a Turkish national consciousness as opposed to the Ottoman '*ümmet*' (umma – religious community) consciousness of the *millet* system became widespread after 1908.[78]

When the Westernised CUP officers decided to revive the Ottoman Empire by revolution on 23 July 1908, they did not plan to form 'a nation-state on the approved occidental nineteenth-century model'.[79] Their main aim was to convince the ignorant masses that a constitution was desirable.[80] Although Sultan Abdulhamit II remained in power for another year, the CUP 'carried on its reform agitation on the lines of the integrity and unity of the Ottoman Empire, [and] brought about the downfall of Palace tyranny after years of arduous struggle'.[81] In this respect, the 1908 revolution set up the era of the CUP, which aimed to establish an Ottoman patriotism among the different ethnic, linguistic and religious divisions of the empire on the basis of the secular values of the Enlightenment.[82] Their most difficult task was to explain what the notions of 'constitution', 'liberty' and 'equality' meant to the uneducated masses.[83] Clearly, the new order had a different meaning for different parts of the empire. For example, while the new order was introduced as a truce to an intolerable blood-feud in Albania, for the Turkish population in Anatolia it meant saving the fatherland from the Europeans.[84]

In reality, the revolution of 1908 accelerated the collapse of the Ottoman Empire. The revolutionaries started a new era with the liberal constitution and parliamentary system, which were the main characteristics of the European bourgeois countries. They had a restricted sense of revolution that did not aim to reform the socio-economic structure of the empire. However, its effects would be felt in the long term. As Lenin wrote in *Pravda* on 1 March 1913, the revolutions in Turkey, Persia and China followed the example of the Russian revolution in 1905. Their 'repercussions' were felt in Europe in the era of the storms before the First World War.[85] The importance of the revolution of 1908 is three-fold in our understanding of the Turkish transition to modernity in order to further argue this transition's influence on foreign policy-making.

First, Turkish nationalism had developed as an unintended consequence of the modernisation of the Ottoman state. As stated earlier, the Young Ottomans found the solution in pan-Islamism to provide an alternative as a stabilising factor among all the Muslim subjects during the empire's attempts at modernisation. Following its failure, the Young Turks focused after 1913 on pan-Turkism, which emphasised national values and campaigned 'for an alliance of all Turkish/Turkic groups, within the empire and outside it'.[86] Afterwards, nationalism became a major ideology of the Young Turks and the basis of a national movement under the leadership of Mustafa Kemal as their successor.[87] The suitable environment for the establishment of a nationalist ideology was created during the Young Turk period. The most influential aspects can be summarised as follows: the acceptance of the freedom of the press, which emphasised the existence of print capitalism; the political parties became the major actors of the empire's political structure; and the enforcement of the use of the Turkish language in schools.[88] Although the CUP leadership prepared the domestic conditions for the rise of Turkish nationalism, they could not complete them. After the First World War, the Kemalist group eventually 'brought this process to a logical end, having also profited from the mistakes of its predecessors'.[89] The nationalist group did not aim to reform the administrative and military institutions of the empire, as had its predecessors, but to transform its political, economic and social structures.

Second, the role of the CUP leadership in the revolution of 1908 as a 'revolution from above' leads us to rethink the dialectical relationship between social structure and its agents. The CUP triumvirate – Enver Pasha (1881–1922), Talat Pasha (1874–1921) and Cemal Pasha (1872–1922) – were the main policy-makers of the Ottoman Empire after 1913. In particular, Enver Pasha 'had the most definite ideas in favour of pan-Turkism and its crucial future role as an expansionist policy and he was the one largely responsible for its adoption as a state policy'.[90] It must be emphasised at this juncture of the analysis that, thinking through FPA, the 'structure and agency' relationship requires more than a simplistic acceptance of heroic leaders or blaming them for failed policies. At this point, Theda Skocpol's analysis helps us. The political leadership involved in revolutions is mainly concerned with state sovereignty. 'This may sound obvious, but it is not the usual way in which political leaderships in revolutions are analysed.'[91] If political leaderships in revolutionary periods are struggling to maintain state sovereignty, their activities must be taken more seriously than their social backgrounds.[92] 'In sum, the backgrounds of the revolutionary leaderships that came to the fore during the French, Russian and Chinese Revolutions are congruent with the perspective advanced here, that these were state-building leaderships.'[93] It is argued here that the same analysis can be applied to the Turkish case.

In particular, Mustafa Kemal became a modern state-building leader by inheriting the previous group's historical concern to preserve state independence and modernise its socio-political structure. The modernisation of the state structure had become the main concern of the different political groups, the Young Ottomans the Young Turks and later the nationalists. 'Devlet [state] was a primary focus of legitimacy.'[94] The Young Turks maintained this idea until 1918. Thus, the orthodox understanding of Mustafa Kemal's role in the Turkish transition can be challenged by arguing that the CUP leaders had already started the process in 1908.

Third, during the Turkish transition as a dialogue between past and present, the nationalists also inherited certain characteristics of the Ottoman Empire.

Of these, Islam was central. It not only determined the Muslim subjects' belief system but also the political and social structure of the Ottoman Empire. Suffice it to emphasise here that religion is the element of any society most able to resist a radical change throughout human history. The succeeding Kemalist group inherited the ambivalent nature of the 1908 movement that not only intended the return of a state according to Islamic principles but also the creation of a parliament based on secular representation. Mustafa Kemal shared the Young Turks' ideas that the liberation of the Ottoman state would be succeeded by the adaptation of European political institutions and social customs, and that the *ancien régime* of the empire had to go.[95] But he did not give any impression that the Islamic identity of the state would be transformed into a secular nation and identity. Possibly, he took into consideration the Young Turks' prudence about the conservative elements of Turkish society.

In conclusion, there is a historical continuity between the nationalist movement and its predecessors, which commenced with the Turkish transition through reformation in 1808 and revolution in 1908. The Ottoman Empire had an alien character within the European system with its different mode of organisation and different religion. The establishment of a parliamentary system in 1876 and the secularisation of politics with new political parties after the revolution of 1908 were the unintended outcomes of the Ottoman Empire's engagement with European modernity. Despite the variances of the suggested policies of the Young Ottomans and the Young Turks the main question remained the same: what was to be done to modernise the Ottoman state? The national solution was a result of the previous failed experiences. The emergence of Turkish nationalism, in general, was potentially an immediate solution to the erosion of traditional Ottoman identity at the end of the First World War.

The emergence of Turkish nationalism and its influence on foreign policy

The idea of 'nationality' appeared dialectically as an anti-thesis of the multinational Ottoman Empire in its historical context. Political loyalty and identity were shaped as 'patriotism', especially in the Middle East, and as 'nationalism' in the modern world. The time was ripe for the Ottoman Empire to change its form of patriotism to nationalism at the end of the First World War. The new patriotism meant the loyalty of citizens to their country where 'nationhood' and 'statehood' were successfully combined.[96] Thus, a new form of 'nation' had to manifest itself through the creation of a 'nation-state' on the basis of the approved European model. It was to be the solution to the problem of identity formation, as it was the main feature of the European style of nation-building. The implications of the idea of European nationalism were that a separate Turkish nation had to be constructed. The invention of Turkish nationalism had no popular roots and the notion of national identity had to be constructed from scratch.[97]

In the early stages of modern Turkish nationalism, one was recognised as a Turk as long as s/he spoke Turkish, shared Turkish values and called her/himself a Turk within the boundaries of the sovereign Turkish state. The Turkish nation was not based on race and religion as discussed earlier in relation to the arguments of primordialism and ethno-symbolism. On the contrary, the Turkish nation was defined as a 'nation' with *de facto* territorial sovereignty.[98] The nationalist elites focused on the nation-state's interests and abandoned the concern for Turks living outside the determined boundaries of the state, a preoccupation which was at the core of previous ideologies, i.e. pan-Islamism, pan-Turanism and pan-Turkism. The construction of the Turkish nation within the limited boundaries of nation-state necessitated the rejection by the nationalists of an expansionist policy in the pan-ideologies of their predecessors. This was an important influence in the emergence of Turkish nationalism, which indicated a radical change in Turkish foreign policy.

The South Caucasus had been the first area to test the radical change in Turkish foreign policy during the transition from an empire to a nation-state. I will briefly summarise the history of imperial foreign policy towards the region in order to further analyse in the next chapter those aspects of nationalist foreign policy between 1918 and 1921 that differed from the previous policies. The first contact between the regional states and the Ottoman Empire was established as a result of a new Ottoman policy to protect the Caucasian Muslims from around 1600, after Yavuz Sultan Selim became 'Caliph' of all Muslims.[99] Although the authority of the Caliph was limited to religious issues, Ottoman strategic and military interests extended to those areas for two main reasons over the following two centuries.

First, countries in the east had been the major arena of a power struggle between the Ottoman and Russian Empires. In relation to the Ottoman Empire's decline towards the end of the eighteenth century, its north-eastern frontier, the Caucasus, became the 'soft spot' of the empire at that time under the dominance of the Russian Empire. When Russia invaded Georgia in 1801, the Ottoman Empire explicitly accepted the dominant role of Russia in the region.[100] However, the region maintained its military importance for the Ottomans. For instance, the Caucasian Muslims collaborated with the Ottoman army during the Ottoman–Russian wars of 1781–1792, 1806–1812 and 1828–1829.[101]

Second, the forbidding Caucasus mountain range strategically formed the land frontier between the two empires in the east. The policy of natural frontiers was based on determining the Turkish–Russian border. In particular, the Ottoman–Russian war of 1877–78 was a turning point in the history of the region. After the Ottoman Empire ceded the provinces of Kars, Ardahan and Batum (*Elviye-i Selase*) to Russia according to the terms of the Treaty of Berlin, the entire Transcaucasian region was incorporated in 1878.[102] Following this loss, regaining these three districts would be the main preoccupation of the Young Turks. Ottoman expansionist foreign policy towards the region during the nineteenth century was mainly shaped by its Islamic universalist ideology, which manifested itself in the pan-Islamism of the Young Ottomans.

At the beginning of the twentieth century, the pan-Turanist and pan-Turkist policies of the Young Turks determined Ottoman foreign policy towards the Caucasus before the emergence of Turkish nationalism. In retrospect, the CUP leaders' expansionist policy towards the Muslims of the East was a sign of a desperate attempt to change the empire's predictable dis-unification during the First World War. The Ottoman Empire became involved in the First World War for three main reasons: to recover from the disastrous effects of the Balkan Wars, to find a new European ally since the British Empire had abandoned its traditional policy as protector of the Ottoman Empire against Russia, and finally to find financial support for the crumbling empire. Germany became its main financial supporter during the war.[103] The Ottoman Empire's participation in the First World War on the German side opened a new era in the history of the Middle East and the Caucasus.

In particular, the Caucasian front became the first war arena between the two empires when Russia declared war on the Ottoman Empire on 2 November 1914. The Ottoman Empire's participation in the war against Russia and its Western Allies was a result of a decision made by the CUP leaders, especially Enver Pasha, the Supreme Commander of the Ottoman armed forces, whose miscalculations influenced their decision. In Enver's plans, the Ottoman–German alliance during the war period could be utilised to realise two important aims in the Caucasian region.

First, as Haley emphasises, what Enver wanted from the Germans was money for the Ottoman Empire, 'what the oil in Baku provided and what he would have taken from anyone' under the right circumstances.[104]

Second, with German help Enver would have the opportunity to eradicate Russian power in the Caucasus in order to capture the Turkic-speaking lands of the Russian Empire, especially Azerbaijan and Turkestan.[105] Consequently, taking command of the Ottoman third army on 21 December 1914, Enver attacked the Caucasus plateau. Following his catastrophic defeat at Sarıkamış in 1915, Russia invaded Eastern Anatolia in 1916. Despite the weak position of the empire, Enver continued to dream of creating a Turkish Empire in the East which would extend through the Caucasus into the Crimea and Central Asia.[106] This was indeed an irrational foreign policy aim which has to be interpreted as a result of Enver Pasha's adventurist personality.[107] Yet the impact of the Ottoman German alliance became significant in the region when the independent Transcaucasian states had come under at least partial occupation by Ottoman and German armies by September/October 1918.[108]

However, the consequences of the two major events, the First World War and the Russian Revolution, brought new elements into being for a radical change not only in the region's history but also in traditional Turkish–Russian relations. On the one hand, the post-war international relations of the Caucasus brought the clash of imperial interests to the East: Russian and British competition over Afghanistan, Iran and the Caucasus intensified after the war. Britain interfered in the Russian civil war in an indirect way by supporting the establishment of anti-Bolshevik governments in Georgia, Azerbaijan and Armenia.[109] On the other hand, with the final defeat of the Ottoman Empire in October 1918 a new nationalist group took power to regain its sovereignty within secured frontiers. As will be argued later, the main aim of the national group between 1918 and 1921 was to transform the empire into a nation-state. It is, therefore, the task of the case-study to analyse how its transitory character influenced Turkish foreign policy towards the South Caucasus, which was also constrained by the new balance of power in the region.

Concluding remarks

The first aim of this chapter was to explain why the study of nationalism is the third pillar that completes the interdisciplinary approach to the foreign policy of transitional states. Its second aim was to locate the analysis of Turkish foreign policy within a historical structure in order to highlight the historical continuity and change, as the first dimension of foreign policy of a state in transition. The empirical study of the relationship between the Ottoman modernisation and the emergence of Turkish nationalism helped us to grasp the structure of historical and social changes that led to Turkey's engagement with alternative modernity.

The first historical continuity was the need to reform the political and military institutions of the declining Ottoman Empire. While nationalism and modernity both emerged from the middle ages in Europe they only penetrated into Ottoman history in the nineteenth century. The modernisation of the state was the main concern of Ottoman history since the *Tanzimat* era and these attempts initiated Turkey's engagement in European politics, 'where modernity was nationalist', rather than the Arab successor states of the Middle East where it remained traditional and religious until the end of the Second World War.[110]

The second historical factor was related to the continuing erosion of the traditional Ottoman identity. When the Ottoman *millet* system failed to unite different groups, that is Muslim and non-Muslim subjects, each group invoked different elements to provide a sense of belonging. The concept of nation was seen as a way of constructing a new identity. The construction of the Turkish nation was not based on ethnic purity but on the relationship between identity and boundaries. Therefore, any attempt to understand the transformation from 'Ottoman *millet*' to 'Turkish nation' on the basis of ethnic origin is bound to fail, as explained earlier.

The third historical continuity is the close relationship between nationalism and the modern nation-state. The construction of the Turkish national identity manifested itself politically in and through a state. The emergence of Turkish nationalism cannot be separated from the construction of the modern state. When there was an imperial state, the Turks were identified with the Ottoman religious (umma) identity. During the transformation of the Ottoman Empire, the need to construct the 'Turkish' nation arose since sovereignty is taken from the Sultan and given unconditionally to people as a nation in the form of a modern nation-state.[111]

The last historical force behind the Turkish transition to modernity had been the requirements of the international system. The Ottoman Empire had refused to take part in the European system and to observe European international law until it was in decline in the nineteenth century. When the empire was inducted into European international society in 1856, it was no longer in a position to

Table 1. Historical Stages of the Turkish Transition to Modernity, 1808–1924

Early stages of the Turkish transition to modernity in the nineteenth century

Historical events		Political consequences	Agents	Ideologies
1808	*Sened-i Ittifak* (Agreement Act)	'The Magna Carta' of the Ottomans		
1839	*Gulhane Hatt-i Humayunu* (Imperial Decree of Gulhane)	***Tanzimat* (Reformation) Era** (1839–1876)	**The Young Ottomans** (1865–1876)	Westernisation
1856	*Islahat Fermani* (Reform Decree)			Ottomanism Pan-Islamism
1876	*Kanun-i Esasi*	***Birinci Meşrutiyet*** (The First Constitutional Monarchy) (1876–1880)		
1878	The Ottoman *Meclis-i Mebusan* was closed			

Late stages of the transition in the twentieth century

Historical events		Political consequences	Agents	Ideologies
1908	The Young Turk Revolution	***Ikinci Meşrutiyet*** (The Second Constitutional Monarchy) (1908–1922)	**The Young Turks** (1908–1918)	Pan-Turanism Pan-Turkism
1909	Modification to 1876 Constitution			
1918	The Mudros Armistice	**The National Movement** (1919–1923)	**The Turkish Nationalists** (1919–1923)	Turkish Nationalism
1920	The Turkish National Pact The Grand National Assembly			
1921	Acceptance of the First Turkish Constitution by the GNA			
1922	Abolition of the Ottoman Sultanate	End of the Ottoman Dynasty and Empire		
1923	The Declaration of the Turkish Republic	**Modern Turkish Nation-State**		
1924	Abolition of the Caliphate			

enforce its own Islamic rules in external relations. The Ottomans had to accept the requirements of the international system like other major European states. Therefore, it is argued here that by repudiating its Islamic traditions in foreign relations by the Treaty of Paris, in fact the Ottoman Empire 'contributed to the universalization of the states-system'.[112] After 1856, legitimacy of the Ottoman Empire's membership in the European system had depended on changing its anachronistic dynastic characters in order both to survive and to be part of the European system. As discussed earlier, there had been three important requirements of the system: to prove the secular character of the state, to accept modern arguments on the principle of nationality or of national self-determination and to observe European international law.

Consequently, the transformation of the Ottoman socio-political structure to the European model of nation-state was an answer to the modern dilemma of 'identity crisis', which arose through the Ottoman Empire's integration into the European international system in the nineteenth century. The movements of the Young Ottomans and the Young Turks were, in fact, different responses to the 'identity crisis' of the Ottoman state and to the modernisation of the empire. Their proposed ideologies, pan-Ottomanism, pan-Islamism and pan-Turkism, did not in themselves provide an answer to modernising the state in accordance with the European norms. When the ideology of Turkish nationalism manifested itself as the main solution and became the main occupation of the nationalist leaders between 1918 and 1921, the nationalist leaders abandoned the imperial expansionist policies in the South Caucasus in accordance with their major goal of transforming into a modern state.

In the final analysis, the emergence of Turkish nationalism as an unintended consequence of the empire's engagement with European modernity underlines the fact that historical forces were largely beyond the control of leaders in certain circumstances. These factors also influence the goals of both domestic and foreign policies. In the Turkish case, the historical analysis has demonstrated that there were two main continuing goals of the different political groups in the domestic realm: to preserve the sovereignty of the state and to modernise the socio-political structure of the empire, in order to catch up with the modern European system. When the solution was found in transforming its anachronistic identity to a modern one under the leadership of the Turkish nationalists, these two goals were given priority in their domestic and foreign policies. Thus, the rise of Turkish nationalism in 1919 is accepted as a result of the historical continuity of attempts by different agents between 1808 and 1918 to respond to the forces of the Ottoman Empire's integration into European modernity (See Table 1).

Notes

1 James Mayall, *Nationalism and International Society*, Cambridge, Cambridge University Press, 1990, p. 5.
2 John Breuilly, 'Approaches to Nationalism', in Gopal Balakrishnan, ed., *Mapping the Nation*, London, Verso, 1996, p. 156.

3 Paul James, *Nation Formation: Towards a Theory of Abstract Community*, London, Sage, 1996, p. 128.

4 The dichotomy of traditional/modern has expanded upon the concept of transition. See, for example, 'Walt Rostow who, in *Stages of Economic Growth: A Non-Communist Manifesto*, Cambridge, Cambridge University Press, 1960 suggested an ideologically value-laden, five state evolutionary scheme: (1) traditional, (2) preconditioning, (3) take-off, (4) the drive to maturity, (5) the age of mass-consumption'. James, *Nation Formation*, p. 128, fn. 19. See, Daniel Lerner, *The Passing of Traditional Society: Modernising the Middle East*, London, The Free Press of Glencoe, 1958.

5 Anthony D. Smith, *Nationalism and Modernism: A Critical Survey of Recent Theories of Nations and Nationalism*, London, Routledge, 1998, p. 44.

6 Otto Dann, 'Modernity and the Project of the Modern Nation', in Johannes U. Müller and Bo Stråth, eds, *Nationalism and Modernity*, EUI Working Paper HEC No. 99/1, Florence, European University Institute, 1999, p. 24.

7 Liah Greenfeld, *Nationalism: Five Roads to Modernity*, London, Harvard University Press, 1995, p. 18.

8 Will Kymlicka, 'Misunderstanding Nationalism', in Ronald Beiner, ed., *Theorising Nationalism*, Albany, State University of New York Press, 1999, p. 136.

9 Ibid., p. 137.

10 Charles Taylor, 'Nationalism and Modernity', in John A. Hall, ed., *The State of the Nation: Ernest Gellner and the Theory of Nationalism*, Cambridge, Cambridge University Press, 1998, p. 205.

11 Dann, 'Modernity and the Project of the Modern Nation', pp. 25–27.

12 Hugh Seton-Watson, *Nations and States: An Enquiry into the Origins of Nations and the Politics of Nationalism*, London, Methuen, 1977, p. 1; Shumel Sandler, 'Ethnonationalism and the Foreign Policy of Nation-States', *Nationalism and Ethnic Politics*, 1:2 (Summer 1995), p. 250.

13 Elie Kedourie, ed., *Nationalism in Asia and Africa*, London, Weidenfeld & Nicolson, 1970, p. 29; Mayall, *Nationalism and International Society*, p. 2.

14 Anthony D. Smith, 'State-Making and Nation-Building', in John A. Hall, ed., *States in History*, Oxford, Basil Blackwell, 1986, p. 228.

15 Charles Tilly, 'Reflections on the History of European State-Making', in Charles Tilly, ed., *The Formation of National States in Western Europe*, Princeton, NJ, Princeton University Press, 1975, p. 6.

16 Arthur N. Waldron, 'Theories of Nationalism and Historical Explanation', *World Politics: A Quarterly Journal of International Relations*, 37:3 (April 1985), p. 417.

17 John Breuilly, 'Nationalism and Modernity', in Müller and Stråth, *Nationalism and Modernity*, p. 42.

18 Anthony D. Smith, *Nations and Nationalism in a Global Era*, Cambridge, Polity Press, 1995, p. 149.

19 Breuilly, 'Nationalism and Modernity', p. 42. Although Breuilly takes the idea of a 'core doctrine' from A.D. Smith he modifies Smith's version. Ibid., fn. 8.

20 The primordialists represented by Clifford Geertz, Pierre van den Berghe, Michael Hechter and Walker Connor; the ethno-symbolists represented by John Armstrong, and in particular Anthony D. Smith; and finally, the modernists such as Elie Kedourie, Ernest Gellner, Eric Hobsbawm, Benedict Anderson, John Breuilly, Tom Nairn and Michael Mann.

21 James, *Nation Formation*, p. xiii.

22 In the classical Marxist perception, the nation, as a social formation, was a result of

the process of transition from feudalism to capitalism. Although nationalism was accepted as a bourgeois phenomenon alien to Marxism it is sometimes accepted as rational by classical Marxists. Ephraim Nimni, *Marxism and Nationalism: Theoretical Origins of a Political Crisis*, London, Pluto Press, 1991, pp. 13–16; Horace B. Davis, *Toward a Marxist Theory of Nationalism*, New York, Monthly Review Press, 1978, p. 22.

23 John Breuilly, 'Reflections on Nationalism', *Philosophy of the Social Sciences*, 15:1 (March 1985), p. 65; Nimni, *Marxism and Nationalism*, p. 16; Breuilly, 'Approaches to Nationalism', p. 158.

24 James Mayall, 'Nationalism in the Study of International Relations', in A.J.R. Groom and Margot Light, eds., *Contemporary International Relations: A Guide to Theory*, London, Pinter, 1994, p. 183.

25 Ibid., p. 168.

26 David L. Adamson, *Class, Ideology and the Nation: A Theory of Welsh Nationalism*, Cardiff, University of Wales, 1991, p. 74.

27 John A. Hall, 'Nationalisms, Classified and Explained', in Sukumar Periwal, ed., *Notions of Nationalism*, Budapest, Central European University Press, 1995, p. 8; Waldron, 'Theories of Nationalism and Historical Explanation', p. 420.

28 Breuilly, 'Nationalism and Modernity', p. 39.

29 Ayla Göl, 'Imagining the Turkish Nation through "Othering" Armenians', *Nations and Nationalism*, 11:1 (2005), p. 121.

30 Hugh Poulton, *Top Hat, Grey Wolf and Crescent: Turkish Nationalism and the Turkish Republic*, London, Hurst & Company, 1997, p. 43.

31 Anthony D. Smith, *Theories of Nationalism*, London, Duckworth, 1971 p. 56; Kemal H. Karpat, *The Politicization of Islam: Reconstructing Identity, State, Faith and Community in the Late Ottoman State*, Oxford, Oxford University Press, 2001, p. 13.

32 Stanford J. Shaw and Ezel Kural Shaw, *History of the Ottoman Empire and Modern Turkey, Vol. II – Reform, Revolution and Republic: The Rise of Modern Turkey, 1808–1975*, Cambridge University Press, 1995, p. 3.

33 The Ottoman Empire was a multi-national empire but the usage of '*millet*' (nation) is totally different from the modern usage. The definition of nation was based on religion in its *millet* system. Thus, the separation was between Muslims (Turks, Kurds, Laz, Alevis), Christians (Armenians, Greeks) and Jews in the empire. The number of *millets* changed throughout the Ottoman history. New *millets* were created as a consequence of pressure from the great powers. 'By 1875 there were nine recognised *millets*, of which six were fairly large, by 1914 there were seventeen.' See also, Kemal K. Karpat, *An Inquiry into the Social Foundation of Nationalism in the Ottoman States: From Social Estates to Classes, from Millets to Nations*, Princeton, NJ, Princeton University Press, 1973, pp. 88–98 in Poulton, *Top Hat, Grey Wolf and Crescent*, p. 52.

34 Ibid., p. 44.

35 See Suna Kili, *Atatürk Devrimi: Bir Cağdaşlaşma Modeli*, Ankara, 1995; Şerif Mardin, *Türk Modernleşmesi*, İstanbul, 1991; R.E. Ward and D.A. Rustow, eds, *Political Modernisation in Japan and Turkey*, Princeton, NJ: Princeton University Press, 1964.

36 Ernest Gellner, *Encounters with Nationalism*, Oxford, Blackwell, 1994, pp. 81–83.

37 Fatma Muge Göcek, *The Transformation of Turkey: Redefining State and Society from the Ottoman Empire to the Modern Era*, London, I.B. Taurus, 2011, p. 62.

38 Iver B. Neumann and Jennifer M. Welsh, 'The Other in European Self-definition:

An Addendum to the Literature on International Society', *Review of International Studies*, 17 (1991), p. 333.

39 Mardin, *Türk Modernleşmesi*, p. 12.

40 Karpat, *An Inquiry into the Social Foundation of Nationalism*, pp. 92–94.

41 Sina Akşin, 'Siyasal Tarih (1789–1908)', in Sina Akşin *et al.*, ed., *Türkiye Tarihi 3: Osmanlı Devleti, 1600–1908*, İstanbul, Cem Yayınevi, 1995, pp. 94–95. For the details of the seven clauses in the agreement, see Shaw and Shaw, *History of the Ottoman Empire and Modern Turkey, Vol. II*, p. 2.

42 Fatma Müge Göcek, *Rise of the Bourgeoisie, Demise of Empire: Ottoman Westernisation and Social Change*, New York, Oxford University Press, 1996, p. 65.

43 Yet some Turkish scholars do not interpret *Sened-i İttifak* as the 'Magna Carta of the Ottomans'. See Ali Kazancigil, 'Türkiye'de Modern Devletin Oluşumu ve Kemalizm', in Ersin Kalaycıoğlu ve Ali Y. Sarıbay, eds, *Türkiye'de Politik Değişim ve Modernleşme*, İstanbul, Alfa, 2000, p. 145.

44 Shaw and Shaw, *History of the Ottoman Empire and Modern Turkey, Vol. II*, p. 3.

45 Robert Matran, ed., *Osmanlı İmparatorluğu Tarihi, Vol. II*, İstanbul, Cem Yayınevi, 1995, p. 27.

46 E.J. Hobsbawm, *The Age of Empire: 1875–1914*, London, Abacus, 1994, p. 278.

47 Donald Quataert, 'The Age of Reforms, 1812–1914', in Halil İnalcık and Donald Quataert, eds, *An Economic and Social History of the Ottoman Empire, Vol. II: 1600–1914*, Cambridge, Cambridge University Press, 1997, p. 764.

48 It was a statement of intent on the part of the Ottoman governments, promising in effect four basic reforms:
'The establishment of guarantees for the life, honour and property of the sultan's subjects; An orderly system of taxation to replace the system of taxfaming; A system of conscription for the army; and Equality before the law of all subjects, whatever their religion (although this was formulated somewhat ambiguously in the document)'. Erik J. Zürcher., *Turkey: A Modern History*, London, I.B. Taurus, 1995, p. 53.

49 Shaw and Shaw, *History of the Ottoman Empire and Modern Turkey, Vol. II*, p. 55.

50 Robert H. Jackson, *Quasi-states: Sovereignty, International Relations and the Third World*, Cambridge, Cambridge University Press, 1990, p. 63.
In Article VII of the Treaty of Paris (1856), the signatory states solemnly 'declare the Sublime Porte admitted to participate in the advantages of the Public Law and System of Europe'.

51 In relation to the empire's secular character and its *millet* system, it is crucial to note that non-Muslim subjects, Christians and Jews, were never overtly forced to convert to Islam. Therefore, this point forces us to think about the Islamic character of the empire. Although Islam was the major determining element of the Ottoman identity distinguishing it from the European identity, it did not have the same function within the Ottoman system itself since it was identified with the Arabs and their culture.

52 Roderic H. Davison, 'The Westernisation of Ottoman Diplomacy in the Nineteenth Century', in Edward Ingram, ed., *National and International Politics in the Middle East: Essays in Honour of Elie Kedourie*, London, Franc Cass, 1986, pp. 56–59.

53 There are two different interpretations of the *Islahat Fermanı*: one accepts that this new reform decree was elaborating the promises made in *Gülhane Hatt-ı Hümayunu* of 1839. It was dictated by the Western powers, especially Britain and France, in order to coincide with the Treaty of Paris of 1856. See Zürcher, *Turkey*, p. 57; Elie Kedourie, *Politics in the Middle East*, Oxford, Oxford University Press, 1992, p. 37. The second interpretation, by mainly Turkish and French Ottoman specialists, argues

that the *Islahat Fermanı* was more than the confirmation of the promises of 1839 although it was dictated by the Western powers. Akşin, 'Siyasal Tarih (1789-1908)', p. 132; Robert Mantran, 'Mustafa Kemal Atatürk', in Olivier Roy, ed., *Turkey Today: A European Country?*, London, Anthem Press, 2004, pp. 110–113.

54 Poulton, *Top Hat, Grey Wolf and Crescent*, p. 54.
55 Kedourie, *Politics in the Middle East*, p. 50.
56 Poulton, *Top Hat, Grey Wolf and Crescent*, p. 55. See also Serif Mardin, *The Genesis of Young Ottoman Thought*, Princeton, NJ: Princeton University Press, 1962.
57 Mardin, *Türk Modernleşmesi*, p. 89.
58 Baskın Oran, *Atatürk Milliyetçiliği: Resmi İdeoloji Dışı Bir İnceleme*, Ankara, Bilgi Yayınevi, 1993, p. 50.
59 Bernard Lewis, *The Shaping of the Modern Middle East*, Oxford, Oxford University Press, 1994, p. 75.
60 Tim Jacoby, *Social Power and the Turkish State*, London, Routledge, 2004, p. 73.
61 Jacob M. Landau, *The Politics of Pan-Islam: Ideology and Organisation*, Oxford, Clarendon Press, 1994, pp. 9–10.
62 Kemal Ciftci, *Tarih, Kimlik ve Elestirel Kuram Baglaminda Turk Dis Politikasi*, Ankara, Siyasal Kitabevi, 2010, p. 82.
63 Shaw and Shaw, *History of the Ottoman Empire and Modern Turkey, Vol. II*, p. 175.
64 Mardin, *Türk Modernleşmesi*, pp. 92–94.
65 Poulton, *Top Hat, Grey Wolf and Crescent*, p. 58.
66 Ibid., pp. 61–63.
67 M. Sukru Hanioglu, 'Turkism and the Young Turks, 1889–1908', in Hans-Lukas Kieser, ed., *Turkey Beyond Nationalism: Towards Post-National Identities*, London, I.B. Taurus, 2006, p. 4.
68 Kedourie, *Politics in the Middle East*, p. 73.
69 Ellen K. Trimberger, *Revolution From Above: Military Bureaucrats and Development in Japan, Turkey, Egypt and Peru*, New Jersey, Transaction Books, 1978, p. 3.
70 Fred Halliday, *Revolution and World Politics: The Rise and Fall of the Sixth Great Powers*, London, Macmillan, 1999, p. 48.
71 Smith, *Theories of Nationalism*, p. 33.
72 Ziya Gökalp, *The Principles of Turkism*, Leiden, 1968, p. 5.
73 '[Turan] first identified with groups to south-east later ascribed to Turkic elements on northeast frontier'. John A. Armstrong, *Nations before Nationalism*, Chapel Hill, The University of North Carolina Press, 1982, p. xx; *Örnekleriyle Türkçe Sözlük, Vol. IV*, Ankara, Milli Eğitim Bakanlığı Yayınları, 1996, p. 2928; Pan-Turanism aimed to unite all peoples whose origins were extended back to Turan, 'an undefined Shangrai-La-like area in the steppes of Central Asia'. Jacob M. Landau, *Pan-Turkism: From Irredentism to Cooperation*, London, Hurst & Company, 1995, p. 1.
74 Kedourie, *Nationalism in Asia*, p. 51.
75 The term 'Turkic people' historically refers to a broad range of ethno-linguistic people geographically stretching from Anatolia in Turkey to north-western China via Central Asia.
76 See Uriel Heyd, *Foundations of Turkish Nationalism: The Life and Teachings of Ziya Gökalp*, The Harvill Press, 1950; Niyazi Berkes, 'Ziya Gökalp: His Contribution to Turkish Nationalism', *The Middle East Journal*, 8: 4 (Autumn 1954).
77 H. Luke, *The Making of Modern Turkey: From Byzantium to Angora*, London, Macmillan, 1936, p. 131.
78 Trimberger, *Revolution From Above*, p. 86.

79 Hobsbawm, *The Age of Empire*, p. 284.
80 Noel Buxton, 'The Young Turks', *The Nineteenth Century*, Vol. LXV, January 1909, p. 21.
81 Halil Halid, 'The Origin of the Revolt in Turkey', *The Nineteenth Century*, Vol. LXV, May, 1909, pp. 756–757.
82 Hobsbawm, *The Age of Empire*, p. 284.
83 Edwin Pears, 'The Turkish Revolution', *Contemporary Review*, 94 (1908), p. 298.
84 Buxton, 'The Young Turks', p. 21.
85 V. I. Lenin, *The National Liberation Movement in the East*, Moscow, Progress Publishers, 1980, p. 58.
86 Landau, *The Politics of Pan-Islam*, p. 9.
87 Masami Arai, *Jön Türk Dönemi Türk Milliyetçiliği*, İstanbul, İletişim Yayınları, 1992, p. 20; Erik J. Zücher, *The Unionist Factor: The Role of the Committee of Union and Progress in the Turkish National Movement, 1905–1926*, Leiden, E. J. Brill, 1984, p. 23.
88 Shaw and Shaw, *History of the Ottoman Empire and Modern Turkey*, Vol. II, p. 279; Bowles, pp. 756–757; Buxton, 'The Young Turks', p. 21.
89 Mardin, *Türk Modernleşmesi*, p. 201.
90 Landau, *Pan-Turkism*, p. 51.
91 Theda Skocpol, *States and Social Revolutions: A Comparative Analysis of France, Russia and China*, Cambridge University Press, 1979, p. 164.
92 Ibid., p. 165.
93 Ibid., p. 168.
94 Şerif Mardin, 'The Ottoman Empire', in Karen Barkey and Mark Von Hagen, eds, *After Empire – Multiethnic Societies and Nation-Building: The Soviet Union and the Russian, Ottoman and Habsburg Empires*, Oxford, Westview Press, 1997, p. 117.
95 Kedourie, *Politics in the Middle East*, p. 96.
96 Lewis, *The Shaping*, p. 75.
97 Çağlar Keyder, 'The Dilemma of Cultural Identity on the Margin of Europe', *Review*, 16:1 (Winter 1993), p. 24.
98 Smith, *Theories of Nationalism*, p. 189.
99 Cemal Gökçe, *Kafkasya ve Osmanlı İmparatorluğunun Kafkasya Siyaseti*, İstanbul, Has Kutulmuş Matbaası, 1979, pp. 23–26.
100 Ibid., p. 89.
101 Ibid., p. 248.
102 Public Records Office, Kew, London, FO371/6269/E8378/8378/58, Outline of Events in Transcaucasia from the beginning of the Russian Revolution in the summer of 1917 to April 1921, May 31, 1922.
103 Sina Akşin, *Ana Çizgileriyle Türkiye'nin Yakın Tarihi*, Ankara, İmaj Yayınevi, 1996, p. 81.
104 Charles D. Haley, 'The Desperate Ottoman: Enver Pasa and German Empire: II', *Middle Eastern Studies*, 30:2 (1994), p. 236.
105 David Fromkin, *A Peace to End All Peace: Creating the Modern Middle East, 1914–1922*, London, Penguin Books, 1989, p. 313.
106 Mete Tunçay, 'Siyasal Tarih (1908–1923)', in Sina Akşin, ed., *Türkiye Tarihi 4: Çağdaş Türkiye (1908–1980)*, İstanbul, Cem Yayınevi, 1995, p. 50; Shaw, *History of the Ottoman Empire and Modern Turkey*, Vol. II, p. 325.
107 Although it is difficult to decide whether Enver was a passionate man, or an adventurist, or a Turkish Napoleon. His personality was, perhaps, a combination of all these elements. Enver believed that he had a great mission in history. However, he did

not have the qualities of a great military commander but rather was a man of action and organisation. He miscalculated generally the changes of history and the role of geopolitics.
Şevket S. Aydemir, *Makedonya'dan Ortaasya'ya Enver Paşa, Vol. III*, İstanbul, Remzi Kitabevi, 1992, p.652.

108 Bülent Gökay, 'Turkish Settlement and the Caucasus, 1918–20', *Middle Eastern Studies*, 32:2 (April 1996), p.54.
109 Ömer Kürkçüoğlu, *Türk-İngiliz İlişkileri: 1919–1926*, Ankara, Siyasal Bilgiler Fakültesi Yayınları, 1978, p.64.
110 Gellner, *Encounters with Nationalism*, p.89.
111 Selim Deringil, 'The Ottoman Origins of Kemalist Nationalism: Namık Kemal to Mustafa Kemal', *European History Quarterly*, 23 (1993), p.172.
112 Jackson, *Quasi-states*, p.62.

4
Challenges of nationalist foreign policy

The Ottoman defeat in the First World War by the signature of the Armistice of Mudros with Britain, representing the other Allied powers, on 30 October 1918, had been a turning point in deciding the future of an Islamic empire. The international conjuncture surrounding the empire undermined its anachronistic social, economic and political structures at the end of the First World War. As argued in Chapter 2, the Ottoman state had implicitly accepted the validity of European modernity when it had been accepted as a member of the European system with the Treaty of Paris in 1856. The main question in 1918 was how to restructure the disintegrating state in order to preserve its sovereignty and take its place in the modern international system.

Drawing from the findings of the previous chapter, there are two main theoretical concerns of the empirical analysis of this chapter: First, the determining structure of Ottoman socio-political change, which is the creation of the nation-state as an integral part of modernity, must be taken into account while analysing the driving forces behind Turkish foreign policy towards its eastern neighbours. Second, Turkish foreign policy towards the South Caucasus between 1918 and 1921 played an important role in determining its new borders in the most problematic region of the Ottoman Empire. This paved the way for the first step to becoming a modern state since in the modern era nation-states are territorial political units. The previous chapter showed the historical continuity and change as the first dimension of transitional foreign policy. Following from this, the aim of this chapter to explain the role of the decision-makers within the historical structure of state transformation based on the second dimension of transitional foreign policy. This chapter will begin by recognising the geostrategic significance of the South Caucasus in Turkish–Bolshevik relations.

The geostrategic significance of the South Caucasus in Turkish–Russian relations

The background factors in Turkish foreign policy were: the legacy of geo-strategy, the Turkish identity crisis and the traditional Ottoman–Russian animosity. These factors had direct consequences on Eastern affairs. Ottoman–Russian relations were based on traditional animosity as a consequence of the clash of imperial interests in the two strategically important regions: the Turkish Straits and the Caucasus. In general terms, 'the existence of the two marine basins lying one on either side of the Caucasian isthmus – the Black Sea and the Caspian Seas' determined Ottoman–Russian relations and the Caucasus became the epic scene of battlefields during the nineteenth century.[1] When the First World War brought an end to the Ottoman Empire the CUP leaders, especially Enver Pasha, implemented an expansionist foreign policy towards the region in order to liberate the Muslims inside the Russian Empire and to secure the most disputed eastern frontiers of the Ottoman Empire. However, as discussed earlier, these last desperate attempts to save the empire did not prevent its disintegration, which was accelerated by its participation in the First World War.

Despite the fact that the Bolshevik Revolution introduced a radical change in Russian foreign policy towards the Ottoman Empire, the determination of the Turkish–Russian border remained an obstacle, not only in establishing friendly relations but also in achieving territorial integrity. Ottoman foreign policy towards the region during the First World War was based on attempts to regain the three districts of *Elviye-i Selase* (Kars, Ardahan and Batum), which had been ceded to Russia in 1878, and the Turkish nationalists continued to pursue this aim. The next section will show that the South Caucasus continued to be important in Turkish–Bolshevik relations, despite the changes in Russian foreign policy after the Bolshevik Revolution.

Persistent Russian and Turkish concerns

The ideological foundation of the Bolshevik regime had an immediate effect on two issues of foreign policy: the revelation of the secret treaties of the Russian Empire, and the signature of the Treaty of Brest-Litovsk. The new Commissar for Foreign Affairs, Leon Trotsky, declared that 'the victorious revolution' would not seek to establish diplomatic relations with capitalist regimes or request recognition of the new Soviet regime by them. 'In a fiery speech to the astounded employees of the newly formed Foreign Commissariat, he announced his intention to publish the secret treaties with the imperialist governments, print revolutionary pamphlets, and then "[shut up] shop" and dismiss them.'[2]

With respect to the first change, the Bolsheviks published the secret treaties in relation to the partition of the Ottoman Empire between the tsarist regime and the capitalist European powers.[3] In a statement on the publication of the secret treaties on 22 November 1917, Trotsky argued that the abolition of 'secret diplomacy' was the primary condition for a democratic policy and that the new government was determined to implement this policy.[4] In the 'Appeal to the Council of People's Commissars to the Moslems of Russia and the East' on 3 December 1917, it was announced that the Bolsheviks repudiated Russia's rights which were given by the secret treaties. Not only was the treaty for the partition of the Ottoman Empire null and void, but also the new regime also indicated that they did not have any interest in controlling Constantinople. In the same appeal, they declared that the Armenians would be, guaranteed the right to determine their political destiny when military operations ended in the region.[5] However, this statement did not mean that the Bolsheviks were ready to employ the right of national self-determination.

Although the new regime abandoned the tsarist rights regarding the Ottoman Empire, this policy was not applied to the Russian borderlands – the Ukraine, Belorussia and the Caucasus. Soviet Russia would be cut off from sufficient food, fuel and raw materials in the event of losing its borderlands. The question which confronted the Bolsheviks under the leadership of Lenin 'was how to reconcile the slogan of national self-determination with the need of preserving the unity of the Soviet state'.[6]

In relation to the second change in Russian foreign policy, the Treaty of Brest-Litovsk was signed between Russia and the Central Powers on 3 March 1918. None of the Bolshevik leaders wanted to 'put their name to a treaty which was seen throughout Russia as a "shameful peace"'.[7] But negotiations had been going on since December 1917 and Lenin stressed to the Bolsheviks the priority of the peace since they had always denounced the war as capitalistic. From the Bolshevik point of view, the Treaty of Brest-Litovsk was a peace which was not based 'on the voluntary agreement of the peoples of Russia, Germany, Austria-Hungary, Bulgaria and Turkey' but was an imposed peace by capitalist states.[8] The peace treaty had a double-edged influence on Russian foreign policy: when Russia lost significant territories in Europe, 'in economic and territorial terms, it had been reduced to a status on a par with seventeenth-century Moscovy'.[9] Its terms also forced the Bolsheviks to maintain diplomatic relations with the Central Powers.[10]

During the Brest-Litovsk negotiations the Soviet government was obliged to make a final concession: the Ottoman Empire was to be represented during the final minutes of the negotiations.[11] The main treaty between Russia, Germany, Austria-Hungary, Bulgaria and Turkey contained a provision in article 4 for the cession of *Elviye-i Selase* to the Ottomans in the negotiation of which the Transcaucasian republics had had no part.[12] In addition to this article, supplementary to the Treaty of Brest-Litovsk a separate Ottoman–Russian agreement of 3 March 1918 determined the conditions and details of this exchange.[13] The Bolsheviks had to 'accept the return of Kars, Ardahan and Batum to the Ottomans as a consequence of German support for the Ottoman demands', despite the fact that the two former districts were claimed by Armenia and the latter by Georgia.[14]

For the Ottomans, the treaty was a diplomatic success on three issues: a peace was established with Russia in the Caucasus; the Ottomans gained possession of *Elviye-i Selase*; and all agreements signed with Russia before the war became null and void.[15] I would like to emphasise the two important implications of these Ottoman concerns for the successor nationalist foreign policy: the establishment of peace with the Bolsheviks had always been related to Caucasian affairs, and the question of *Elviye-i Selase* was given priority during the transition of the Turkish state.[16] The importance of Kars and Ardahan was due to their utility in a defensive strategy relating to both Anatolia and the Caucasian frontier.[17]

In the final analysis, the Treaty of Brest-Litovsk had a negative effect on the international relations of the South Caucasus by intensifying the conflict of interests among the regional states and the external powers. On the one hand, after the Treaty of Brest-Litovsk, Russia retreated from the continent of Europe and there was no real prospect of the revolution spreading to the West. Thus, the Bolsheviks were forced to look towards the East.[18] On the other hand, the nationalist feelings of the Transcaucasian states, upheld by Wilsonian and Leninist attitudes towards national self-determination, prevented a solution to the regional disputes.

Elements of instability in the east

The indirect consequence of the Treaty of Brest-Litovsk was the proclamation of an independent Transcaucasian Federal Republic on 22 April 1918. There were two possibilities for the peoples of the region: either to stay as an integral part of Russia, which would bring the possibility of a foreign invasion, at that time from the Ottoman Empire; or to proclaim political independence, which might provide the region's security and integrity.[19]

The Transcaucasian states tried the first possibility after the Bolshevik Revolution. The main direct result of the revolution in the region was the establishment of a temporary government under the name 'Transcaucasian Commissariat' at Tiflis in November 1917. The task of the commissariat was to maintain order until a new government for the entire Russian state was established. Afterwards, the 'Council of the Transcaucasian Peoples' (Transcaucasian Diet) was established as a legislative organ. Despite the emergence of an executive organ (Commissariat) and a legislative body (Diet) at the beginning of February 1918, Transcaucasia did not display the separatist tendencies needed to claim independence from Russia.[20] The new political organs of local self-rule were not able to protect the entire region from Ottoman invasions. In fact, an armistice was signed in Erzincan in December 1917 to bring about the cessation of hostilities between the Russian and Ottoman armies in the region.[21] Both sides agreed to demarcate a border in the Caucasus which would not be violated by either the Russian or the Turkish armies.[22] After the Erzincan Armistice, the last Russian armies were withdrawn from the Turkish front. During the Brest-Litovsk negotiations, Enver Pasha ordered Vehip Pasha, the commander of Third Ottoman Corps, to march on the pre-war Ottoman–Russian borders: Erzincan, on 13 February 1918, and Erzurum, on 12 March 1918, were taken over.[23] Clearly, neither the Erzincan Armistice nor the establishment of a *de facto* independent Transcaucasian government with its own army had secured the region from the Ottoman threat.

Consequently, the second possibility, the creation of the independent Transcaucasian Federal Republic was the only solution. It was actually a vain attempt to place the region outside the operation of the terms of the Treaty of Brest-Litovsk. The new republic consisted of the Transcaucasian provinces of the tsarist regime apart from those areas ceded to the Ottoman Empire by the Treaty of Brest-Litovsk, and Baku in which a Bolshevik government, under the name of the Baku Commune with the leadership of Stephan Shaumyan, an old

Bolshevik and also Lenin's friend, was established.[24] They gained support mainly from the Armenians, who were afraid of the Turkophile Azerbaijani population of the hinterland.[25] However, the Ottoman armies continued their occupation of the Caucasian territories without taking into consideration the fact that Transcaucasia was now an independent state. The Ottomans entered Batum on 14 April and Kars on 25 April 1918.[26] The easy success of Ottoman advances in the region convinced Enver Pasha that time was ripe to implement his pan-Turanian policy: 'the conquest of Baku and the annexation to the Ottoman Empire of both Caucasian and Persian Azerbaijan'.[27]

Subsequently, Enver extended the Ottoman demands beyond the Brest-Litovsk provisions to include a number of districts defined by the borders of 1828, when a peace conference between the Russians, the Ottomans and the Transcaucasian republics was held at Batum on 11 May 1918.[28] However, Enver could not easily get away with these demands since Germany and Britain were also interested in taking over the area, specifically the Baku oil and Georgian mineral reserves. On the one hand, the German preference was for taking the Ottoman side against Britain in that Enver Pasha had to keep 'his forces in eastern Anatolia against the possibility of British advances in Iraq and Syria'.[29] On the other hand, the Ottoman presence in Batum was seen as a danger to German economic and military interests. On 23 May 1918, the Germans gave an ultimatum to the Ottomans for the 'immediate evacuation of the Caucasus'.[30]

At that time, the Bolsheviks were not indifferent to Caucasian affairs. The Transcaucasian Federal Republic was seen as a secessionist movement and denounced by Moscow. This repudiation, together with the above-discussed Ottoman offensive attacks and the interference of Germany, aggravated internal problems among the three Transcaucasian states and led to the dissolution of the Federal Republic on 26 May 1918. On the same day Georgia, with the help of Germany, was the first of these states to declare its independence and form a national government. Two days later Azerbaijan and Armenia followed suit and became separate independent states.[31] The Georgians took advantage of Ottoman–German rivalry for control of the region and gained Germany's protection, preventing the Ottomans from imposing harsh peace terms. Germany signed a peace treaty with Georgia and recognised its independence.[32] The Ottoman government signed peace agreements with independent Azerbaijan, Armenian and Georgia on 4 June 1918.[33] The border between the Ottoman Empire and the three Transcaucasian states was re-defined to the situation, as it had existed before the Ottoman–Russian War of 1877–78 (See Map 1: The Turkish–Russian Borders). The Ottomans promised military and financial assistance to Azerbaijan.[34] While the German–Georgian and the Ottoman–Azeri rapprochement took place, the Armenians found themselves diplomatically isolated since they had nothing to offer either strategically or economically to gain the support of any great power. They attempted to gain German protection by making territorial concessions to the Ottomans, but Berlin was not interested.[35] They even considered accepting an US mandate over Armenia, a subject to which I shall return later.

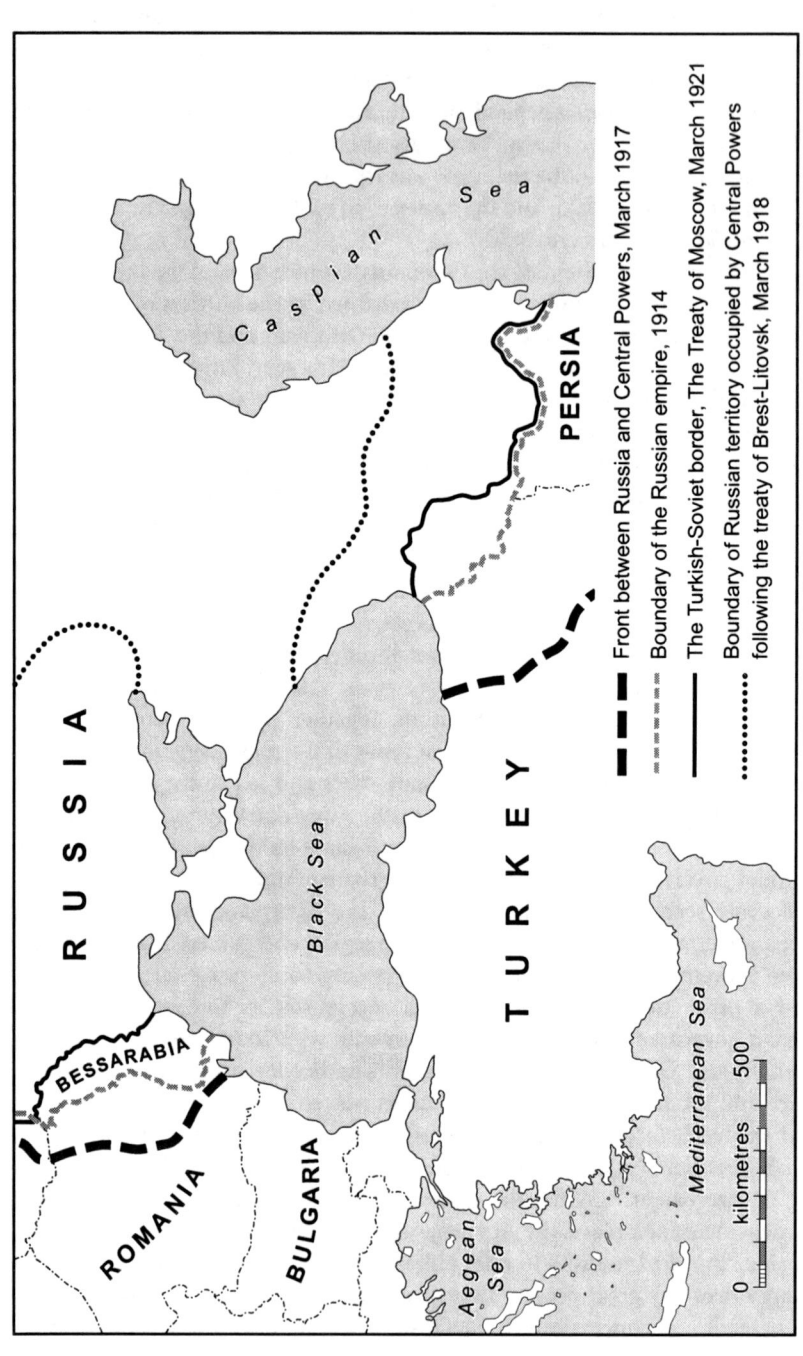

Map 1. The Turkish–Russian borders, 1914–1921

Legend:

- Front between Russia and Central Powers, March 1917
- Boundary of the Russian empire, 1914
- The Turkish-Soviet border, The Treaty of Moscow, March 1921
- Boundary of Russian territory occupied by Central Powers following the treaty of Brest-Litovsk, March 1918

RUSSIA

Caspian Sea

PERSIA

Black Sea

TURKEY

BESSARABIA

ROMANIA

BULGARIA

Aegean Sea

Mediterranean Sea

0   500
kilometres

The proclamation of the three independent states did not bring order but rather political instability to the region, for three main reasons:

1. *The British involvement*: The establishment of German, Ottoman and British power in the region was a consequence of the absence of a Russian role since the October Revolution. Although the geographic location of Transcaucasia was an advantage in isolating the states from the Russian Civil War behind the Caucasus mountains, it turned out to be a disadvantage in luring Great Britain to fill the vacuum in the region.[36] The main British concern was to secure the Caucasian region as a strategic corridor *en route* to India and to control Baku oil.[37] On 4 August 1918, the British forces, under the command of General Dunsterville, arrived at Baku from Mesopotamia, via Persia and the Caspian.[38] Actually, this was part of a British plan to replace German and Ottoman power in the region as a consequence of its military campaign in Mesopotamia, which was only now coming to fruition.[39]

2. *The intensification of border disputes*: The Transcaucasian states had experienced economic, political and administrative unity as an integral part of the Russian Empire for over a century. Not only the establishment of separate national economies, political organs and military forces but also the determination of boundaries was particularly difficult. The main source of the problem was the complex ethnic configuration of the Transcaucasian peoples. There were three major border disputes which were inherited from the administrative divisions of the Russian Empire and the Russian–Ottoman agreements in the nineteenth century (See Map 2 The borders in dispute in the South Caucasus). The first dispute, between Armenia and Georgia, over the districts of Akhalkalak and Lori, was solved comparatively more easily than the other two. According to Armenian scholars, although these two districts had a solid Armenian majority and were part of historic, Armenia they had been part of the Tiflis (Tbilisi) Province and were claimed by Georgia as part of its new republic. 'The dispute led to minor military conflicts between the two Christian states, which were resolved by a compromise, whereby Armenia took control of half of Lori, with the other half becoming a neutral zone, and Georgia retained control of Akhalkalak'.[40] The second border problem was between Armenia and Azerbaijan over Karabagh and Zangezur, the solution to which proved difficult.[41] Each side made a firm claim to these two districts which even today has not been resolved. The third dispute, the Ottoman–Armenian frontier, was especially troublesome due to both sides' claims on the six provinces in Eastern Anatolia, as will be discussed later.

3. *The desperate policies of the Ottoman Empire*: For Enver Pasha, the main decision-maker of the expansionist Ottoman foreign policy, the unstable Caucasus provided the best opportunity to undertake his ambitious plans. If Russia's weak position in the region continued, the Ottomans would expand their power to Transcaspia and Turkestan and then they would manipulate the pan-Islamic

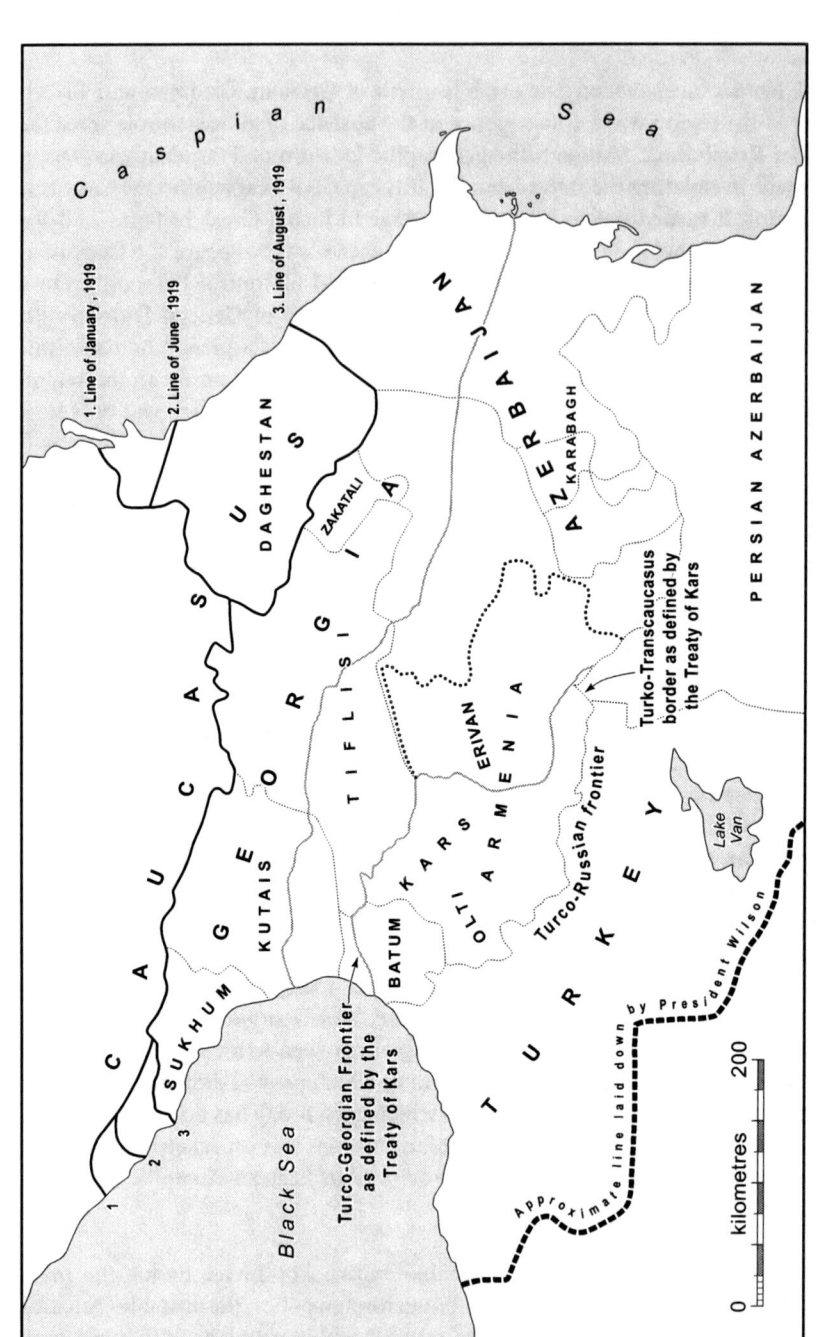

Map 2. The borders in dispute in the South Caucasus, 1919–1921

revolt against the British in Afghanistan, Persia and India. In accordance with the provisions of the Ottoman-Azeri agreement (4 June 1918), Enver organised the 'Army of Islam' on the Caucasian front and appointed Halil Pasha, his uncle, as its commander.[42] He was specifically obsessed with the conquest of Baku, and this task was given to Halil Pasha. In Enver's plans, a Kars–Baku railway was the key to penetrating Central Asia. The arrival of the British brigade in Baku in August provoked Enver's actions. The Ottomans captured Baku on 15 September and the city became the new capital of the Azerbaijani Republic. The occupation of Derbent, in Daghestan, on 6 October 1918 was the next step in his plans. Enver's final goal was to establish a 'Turkish-Islamic state' under the confederation of Ottoman, Azerbaijani and Daghestani states.[43] However, not only were these ambitious schemes irrational, but also Enver's victories in the Caucasus were gained at the expense of the other Ottoman fronts in the Balkans and Syria. While the British forces were advancing into the heartland of the empire from the south, the Allies blockaded the Dardanelles.[44] Thus, the expansionist foreign policy of the CUP leaders towards the region had an ever-increasing influence on the collapse of the Ottoman Empire.[45]

On 20 September, Chicherin sent a note to the Ottoman government relating to Turkish violations of the Treaty of Brest-Litovsk. He emphasised that the Ottoman government, by invading Baku, had indicated that the treaty was no longer in force and that the Ottomans, in fact, had destroyed the peaceful relations established by the treaty.[46] However, the Ottomans could not stay long in the region. The Armistice of Mudros between the Allies and the Ottoman Empire on 30 October 1918 provided for the evacuation of the Transcaucasian territory by Ottoman troops. The armistice of 11 November between the Allies and Germany required a similar evacuation by German troops. Acting on behalf of the Allies, a British occupation of Transcaucasia now began in order to ensure the execution of the terms of both armistices. The signing of the Armistice of Mudros not only forced the Ottomans to hand over all their gains in the region to the Allies but also brought the empire itself to an end. A new era of Turkish history, in its transition to modernity, was about to begin.

The end of the Ottoman Empire: the impact of the Armistice of Mudros

The Ottoman Empire was in complete turmoil and authority was on the wane in Istanbul following the Allied occupation and cabinet changes. The day after the armistice was signed, 1 November 1918, the main decision-makers – the CUP leaders: Enver, Talat and Cemal Pashas – left the country on a German cruiser, and the era of the CUP was over. When the Istanbul government agreed to sign the armistice, the expectation was that the Ottoman territories, apart from the Dardanelles Straits, would not be occupied by the Allied powers.[47] However, a squadron under the command of Admiral Calthorpe entered the Dardanelles under the British flag on 12 November and landed at Istanbul.[48] When the Allied forces entered the Ottoman Empire, their authority would not be limited only to military issues but would also include the civil and social aspects of the empire's domestic affairs.[49] As a result of the loss of civil and military authority to the Allies, the Istanbul government became a shadow of its former self. There were two important implications of the armistice for Turkish state transformation: an authority vacuum in domestic politics which led to the emergence of the Turkish nationalist movement and the direct connection between the Anatolian and Caucasian settlements. These two implications will help us understand the relationship between the Turkish state transition and the inclination of nationalist foreign policy towards the Bolsheviks in the East.

Therefore, the armistice not only affected the future of Anatolia but also that of the South Caucasus. The armistice consisted of twenty-five articles of which three directly related to the South Caucasus.[50] Britain was in a strong position to impose its own interests on the region during the negotiations at Mudros. It was important for the British military position to keep all key locations in the South Caucasus under its control. In particular, Batum was connected to the oil fields around Baku with its rail and pipeline routes, and also the Batum-Baku railway line had to be secured to prevent the spread of Bolshevism southwards.[51] With the Mudros Armistice, the Ottomans were not only compelled to withdraw from these two provinces but the Transcaucasian railways were also put under Allied control, according to article XV.[52] As noted earlier, three days after the Ottomans left Baku the British forces entered the city, starting an occupation which would last until the end of 1919. The War Office announced that British policy in the Caucasus in 1919 was to ensure that the Turks complied with the terms of the armistice and that there would be independent states in Georgia, Daghestan and Azerbaijan. More importantly, the question of an independent Armenian state was not decided since Britain was not sure whether to favour consolidation of the Armenian state near Erivan or to foster a greater Armenia stretching down to Cilicia.[53]

Britain's dominant position in the problematic regions of the dying Ottoman Empire – i.e. the Ottoman lands in Thrace, Anatolia and the Caucasus – has been interpreted by Turkish scholars as evidence that the Turkish war of liberation had, in essence, come to be against Britain.[54] In this struggle, the Bolsheviks had become a natural ally of the Turkish nationalists but the Armenian question was the main obstacle in establishing relations. As stated earlier, the demarcation of borders is one of the most important conditions of modern state construction. The most problematic region of the Ottoman Empire was its north-eastern borders, due to Armenian claims on the six provinces, and this is described as the eastern affairs historically. It was evident that the newly emerging Turkey's eastern affairs could not be solved without the consent of Moscow.

The alternative solutions for reconstruction of the Ottoman state

When Ottoman territory was under Allied occupation in October 1918, the main question was to decide what was to be done after its final disintegration. Specifically, Ottoman territory had united various cultural and ethnic groups in Europe, Anatolia and the Middle East and the emergence of more than one new nation-state was almost inevitable. As the Balkan peoples in Europe and the Arabic peoples in the Middle East are not the subject of this study, I shall only focus on those proposed solutions for Anatolia, which affected mainly the Turks, Kurds, Greeks and Armenians.[55] The national struggle between these four peoples would be based on their various claims on Anatolian territory. Despite the cultural and linguistic differences, the religious tie between Turks and Kurds, that is Islam, united them against the 'others' – the Armenians and the Greeks. Deciding how many new states would be created after the disintegration of the Ottoman Empire became the crux of the 'state question' in Anatolia.[56] It was a crucial period in determining the future of the Turkish transition to modernity. An analysis of the two main solutions – the Ottoman solution and the opposed social movement as the Anatolian solution – will be carried out in accordance with the main requirements of modern statehood in Turkey's engagement with modernity.

The Ottoman solution: a US mandate

After the Armistice of Mudros, the Ottoman government in Istanbul believed that the disintegration of the empire could be prevented with the help of a foreign power, the United States of America.[57] The main consideration was to protect its Sultanate and the Caliphate rather than transforming the empire into a sovereign state. At that time, the US mandate had seemed to be the most attractive option, since it rested on President Wilson's Fourteen Points. Article 12 of these 'points' promised the Turkish areas of the empire secure sovereignty. The Turkish people interpreted this article very positively since both the rights of national self-determination and national sovereignty were recognised. The creation of a Turkish state where the majority of people were Turkish would be possible.[58] However, the US mandate would have connotations very different from the Wilsonian right of self-determination.[59]

There were other possibilities as in May 1919 Damad Ferid Pasha, the Ottoman prime minister, announced his decision to put Turkey under the protective assistance of one of the great powers: Britain, France or Italy.[60] Some members suggested a British protectorate while others argued for a US mandate.[61] It can be argued that the idea of a US mandate became a counter-weight for those Turkish intellectuals who were against British protection.[62]

In terms of the main features of statehood – namely sovereignty, territoriality, legitimate authority, military force and nationality – the discussions on the US mandate indicated that the Istanbul government was not a sovereign power and did not have a clear notion of the principle of territoriality in order to exercise its authority. While Istanbul wanted to keep the Arab countries and peoples within the empire, they did not show the same concern to keep Anatolian territory as a whole. Istanbul was even ready to surrender part of Eastern Anatolia in order to eventually form an Armenian state and to secure the US mandate.[63] For instance, Grand Vizier Tevfik Pasha, in relation to the minority question, declared on 12 February 1919 that the Armenians would either return to their homeland or to greater Armenia, which included some eastern Vilayets in Anatolia.[64] As a result, during the Paris Peace Conference negotiations the Ottoman representative insisted on claims over the Arab territories, Western Thrace, Cyprus and even Egypt and, in return, abandoned Ottoman claims over Kars, Ardahan and Batum.[65] Moreover, although the grand vizier accepted the principle of Armenian autonomy, the frontiers of Armenia were not defined. Interestingly enough, the Ottoman government's 'attempt to negotiate with Armenia, promising the Turkish Armenians autonomy within the Turkish state, and proposing to effect an exchange of populations in some areas where tension was especially acute' was rejected by the Armenians.[66] However, the autonomy granted to Armenia bewildered the Turkish population of the eastern provinces.

The nationalist movement would later use this issue against the Ottoman government's solution. Mustafa Kemal subsequently explained that the broad autonomy being suggested for Armenia and the acceptance of a foreign protectorate by the Ottoman government did not represent the national will.[67] But the concept of having a separate Turkish nation did not exist in the Ottoman government's plans at all. In sum, the Ottoman government's solution was based on the protection of imperial interests and failed to meet the requirements of the transition to modernity. In contrast, the 'Anatolian solution' brought these requirements together. Although the acceptance of a US mandate due to its connection to the right of national self-determination found some supporters among the nationalists, Refet Bey and Halide Edip Adıvar in particular among Mustafa Kemal's friends, it was rejected at the congresses of Erzurum and Sivas in September 1919.[68]

The Anatolian solution: the local congresses

This book argues that the creation of a modern Turkish state as an integral part of the transition to modernity from the nineteenth century onwards was a result of complex historical process which should not be reduced to a single factor and/ or a single leader. Chapter 2 identified the means of Ottoman integration into the capitalist international system. But in addition to the external factors, an examination of Turkish internal affairs will show that there was a 'prelude' to the emergence of the Turkish nationalist movement. It is argued here that the emphasis should be on social movements in the form the local congresses, including the most important congresses in Erzurum and Sivas, between 1918 and 1920, which aimed to solve the 'state and the sovereignty question' through the initiatives of Muslim peoples in Anatolia.[69] Although these congresses had a regional character, they were to play a vital role in the rise of the national liberation movement.[70]

On a theoretical level, in relation to the idea of modern statehood, the social movements of these local congresses differed from the Ottoman solution. The emphasis of these congresses was on the five main characteristics of the modern state: territory, nation, sovereignty, legitimate authority and military force. First, the idea of national territory or homeland was very clear in these programmes. The protection of the empire's territorial integrity was decided at the four different local congresses. This decision became the main dictum of the Erzurum Congress, one of the milestones in the national movement. After the Armistice of Mudros, local congresses were organised in the different regions which were in danger of being handed over to the Greeks and the Armenians. They focused mainly on saving the geographical core of the empire, since the disintegration of the Ottoman Empire as a whole was extremely probable.[71]

Second, despite their regional character they believed in the principle of nation and national unity. The words 'Türklük' (Turkism), 'Türkler' (Turks) and 'Türkiye' (Turkey) were used often by these societies, especially in the eastern provinces (*Elviye-i Selase*) where the first civil organisation in Anatolia was initiated. This terminology is a clear indication of how they defined their identities in the eastern provinces (Kars, Ardahan, Batum). The local movements were conscious of the 'Turkish nation' and 'national will-power'. The definition of society was based on 'nation' rather than 'umma' (religious community).[72]

Third, the principle of sovereignty meant in theory that all could be under the control of the Istanbul government, but in practice against it and adopting the principles of national-democratic sovereignty since the local movements wanted to break away from the Ottoman Empire's rule. Among these movements, the organisations in the eastern provinces developed differently. In particular, the 'Defence of the National Rights of the Eastern Provinces Union' planned to ensure the free exercise and development of the religious and political rights of the inhabitants. It would also defend the historical and national rights of the Muslims of these provinces if it should become necessary. In 1919, the *Cenub-i Garbi Kafkas Cumhuriyesi* (The South-Western Caucasian Republic) was declared. There are two important implications of this republic: (a) before the Turkish Republic there was an attempt to establish a new nation-state in the eastern part of the Ottoman Empire; (b) in their laws they stated that they would be part of the military and civilian organisation of the new state; although the name of the state was not 'Turkish State' (*Türkiye Devleti*) but 'Ottoman State' (*Devlet-i Osmaniye*) and the country was not called 'Turkey' (*Türkiye*) but 'Ottoman' (*Memalik-i Osmaniyye*).[73]

Fourth, the foundations of a legitimate authority for the nationalist cause were established by the principles of the Amasya Proclamation (18–22 June 1919), and the decisions of the Erzurum and the Sivas Congresses. More crucially, a 'Representative Committee' (*Heyet-i Temsiliye*) was appointed at the Erzurum Congress, which also formed the basis of a National Pact (*Misak-i Milli*), a subject to which I shall return later.[74] Afterwards, the legitimate authority of the national movement was consolidated through the power of the *Heyet-i Temsiliye*.

The fifth principle of statehood, military force, was also in progress of being formed, although it was in a premature condition in 1919. The national forces (*Kuvay-i Milliye*) were organised by the local militias after the Greek occupation of İzmir (Smyrna) on 15 May 1919. The first *Kuvay-i Milliye* was established at Ödemiş on the night of 29/30 May.[75] The other armed forces were organised by local people in the Aegean region of Anatolia.[76] In conclusion, the local congresses not only rejected the Istanbul government's solution but also established the socio-political conditions for the creation of a nation-state under the leadership of Mustafa Kemal.

One cannot separate any leader from his particular historical context. In this case, the organisation of local congresses indicates the spontaneously initiated

Anatolian movements of creating the sovereignty and territorial integrity of the Turkish state. Therefore, in relation to the examination of the impact of structure on decision-makers – which is, as described in Chapter 1, one of the five dimensions of transitional foreign policies – the goals of both domestic and foreign policies had to be shaped and implemented in accordance with this question of statehood. The Anatolian people's will to find a solution to the Turkish state question manifested itself through the local congresses, and the nationalist group under the leadership of Mustafa Kemal became the agency of this struggle to gain independence. This book aims to analyse the socio-historical dimension of the Turkish transition. As discussed in Chapter 3, the pre-conditions of the emergence of Turkish nationalism and its transition to modernity, on-going since the nineteenth century, must not be disregarded. The aim of the nationalists was indeed to gain the sovereignty and the territorial integrity of the state from the Allies but there was no military resistance against the Istanbul government. The struggle between the two sides was in the political and social arena, and based on the striving of each to gain authority in domestic politics and to consolidate power as the only representative of the Turkish nation in foreign affairs. The most important point to emphasise is that there was no legal civil-political authority behind the Anatolian solution until September 1919. Therefore, the next question to answer is how the national movement consolidated its power in internal affairs and found a leader to represent itself in foreign affairs, which in turn brought about the transition of the empire's socio-political structure into modernity and modern statehood.

Domestic sources of nationalist foreign policy

Having discussed the two possible solutions to the Ottoman state question, it is legitimate to ask: 'Was the creation of a Turkish nation-state inevitable?'[77] In the light of the alternative approach of this book, I advocate that the sources of the Turkish state transition lie as much in domestic factors as they do in the operation of the international system. If the actions of human agencies are the product of certain historical conditions, what kind of solution could Mustafa Kemal find other than that of leading the already initiated national movement to create a nation-state? In specific terms, the role of local congresses in internal affairs indicated that there was no way of finding a solution to the 'state question' in Istanbul through the acceptance of a US mandate and that the solution lay in Anatolia. Both the army and the Muslim people there were ready to save the homogenous heartland of the Ottoman Empire in Anatolia through the means of a national cause, engineered by the wave of feeling for national self-determination at the end of the First World War.

When British forces landed at Samsun on 9 March 1919, they informed the Istanbul government that there was a local civil war between the Turkish and Greek inhabitants of the region. If Istanbul was incapable of taking control of the situation, the Allied powers would take the necessary precautions. The Sublime Porte decided to take action, but it was impractical to control the situation from

Istanbul. A special commission was given to an Ottoman officer to investigate the situation in the region. The Minister of War, Şakir Pasha, had a meeting with Mustafa Kemal in which Kemal was informed that he was being appointed to investigate the situation in the region.[78] But following Mustafa Kemal's appointment as Inspector-General of the Ninth Army on 30 April 1919, the empire went through a disastrous period: İzmir was occupied by the Greeks on 15 May 1919 and the Turkish resistance to the Greeks was the first sign of an 'Anatolian revolt'.[79] In the orthodox Turkish historiography, the day on which Mustafa Kemal landed at Samsun, 19 May 1919, has come to be understood as the starting date of the national movement.[80] However, it is important to emphasise that the landing at Samsun was only the symbolic beginning of a complex transitional period on a certain day with a single leader. It is important to place the individual factor in context since its mythology has become a significant variable itself in Turkish history. Such an interpretation of history disregards the role of societal factors.

For instance, Mustafa Kemal was not the only leader who recognised the desire of the local congresses to have an independent nation-state. When Kazim Karabekir Pasha, the commander of the Fifteenth Army Corps on the Caucasian front, met Mustafa Kemal on 11 April 1919 before departing for his post in Erzurum, Karabekir proposed that Kemal join him in the establishment of a 'national government' in Eastern Anatolia. According to Karabekir's testimony, Kemal's answer was ambiguous, in that he merely accepted this as one possible way forward.[81] If this is true, we must assume that Mustafa Kemal was still hesitating over the future of the country at that time, but did not fail to recognise the societal factors.[82] At this stage, the analysis requires two important questions to be answered in relation to the role of a single leader in a crucial period: why Mustafa Kemal had risen above other Turkish nationalist leaders and what role he played in the creation of the Turkish state. The rest of this chapter will answer these questions in order to understand the domestic sources of nationalist foreign policy and then it will examine how these developments in Turkish internal affairs influenced its foreign policy towards the South Caucasus.

The importance of charismatic leadership

As stated in Chapter 1, charismatic leadership can act as a revolutionary force during the transitional period that becomes the third dimension of transitional foreign policy. Moreover, the charismatic leader was considered an 'intermediate phenomenon who is neither traditional nor bureaucratic, but a linking or bridging phenomenon who can be – or at least be seen to be – both traditional *and* modern at the same time'.[83] The characteristics of the transitional process can be manifested to his followers in the personality of a charismatic leader who moulds society's perception of a new order. The concern in repudiating the past and transcending traditional constraints and in institutionalising a new order, which 'is called the 'routinisation' of charisma' becomes even more important during the transition period.[84] In the Turkish context, the routinisaton of Mustafa Kemal's charisma proceeded while the national movement was manifested during the local congresses. The rise of Kemal over other national leaders was dependent on the support of his fellow army officers and the will power of the Anatolian peoples during these congresses. A new stage would commence in Turkish history when Mustafa Kemal, Kazım Karabekir, Rauf Orbay and Ali Fuad Cebesoy – who were also loyal to the national cause and well-educated Ottoman soldiers – gathered in Amasya on 21–22 June 1919. In an undeclared secret clause of the Amasya Proclamation on 22 July 1919, they decided to create the first framework of a 'national government'. The leader of this organisation would be Mustafa Kemal.[85]

There were two main reasons behind the assertion of Kemal's leadership: First, Kemal had actual military achievements during the Gallipoli campaign.[86] During this campaign, the efforts of a single division commander influenced not only the course of battle but also the fate of a nation. On the one hand, the Allied failure at the Dardanelles caused a momentary psychological reawakening among the Turkish people. The Turks had won a victory, for the first time within living memory, against a European power, the British. On the other hand, his successes during the campaign created myths which had made him known to the Anatolian peoples.[87] He was 'the only Turkish commander without a defeat to his name' from four long disastrous years of war.[88] The long-awaited national leader would be identified with the heroic personality of Mustafa Kemal. Consequently, on a theoretical level, three components of charismatic authority would come together: a large uneducated population, a society undergoing transformation and the leaders enjoying the glory of newly won independence.[89]

The second reason is that Kemal had the support of his fellow officers for carrying the national cause to a successful end. One important event in Turkish domestic politics, which is not emphasised enough by both Turkish and Western scholars, was the resignation of Mustafa Kemal from the Ottoman Army on the night of 8/9 July 1919.[90] This had to be a very difficult decision for Mustafa Kemal since he was aware that military authority had been influential in Turkish politics. He was not as popular as Enver Pasha and the other CUP leaders among the Anatolian people until after the Gallipoli victory. After Mustafa Kemal went to Samsun, the Ottoman Minister of War, on a demand from British General Headquarters, ordered Kemal to return to Istanbul in June 1919. When he did not obey, he was declared an outlaw by the Ottoman government.[91] Mustafa Kemal was not sure, therefore, how his colleagues, especially Kazım Karabekir Pasha, would interpret his resignation and whether they would place him in the nationalist movement. Karabekir's decision was a turning point in the establishment of Kemal's leadership: Karabekir did not arrest Kemal, believing that the Ottoman government was incapable of exercising its authority in the country, especially in Eastern Anatolia. More importantly, Karabekir declared that he himself was still under the command of Mustafa Kemal even if he was not an Ottoman soldier any more.[92] Thus, on Kemal's part, the first trial of the consolidation of his power was concluded.[93] Thereafter, the foundations of his legitimate authority were secured by Karabekir and other nationalist leaders.

Subsequently, there were three crucial events which asserted Kemal's leadership in domestic politics. In the first instance, Kemal was appointed chairman of the Erzurum Congress on 23 July 1919.[94] In the second instance, the congress was to select a 'Representative Committee' (*Heyet-i Temsiliye*) which would work to establish national unity.[95] The details of the establishment of this committee were determined at the Sivas Congress.[96] Mustafa Kemal's authority was confirmed since he would sign further communications on behalf of the Representative Committee. In the third instance, Kemal's leadership became unquestionable when he was selected chairman of the Grand National Assembly (GNA) on 23 April 1920, as will be discussed in the next section. Afterwards, even when his charisma reached its highest, Mustafa Kemal was 'fully absorbed in perfecting [his] organisations' and the new set of norms.[97]

In relation to the second question, namely the role of Mustafa Kemal as a charismatic leader in the creation of the Turkish state, it is argued here that Mustafa Kemal's role should not be imposed on history by virtue of his inherent greatness or charisma. On the one hand, the very existence of charisma depends upon the presence of certain historical permissive conditions along with the presence of a determined political actor who possesses enough resources to exploit these conditions in accordance with an overall strategy.[98] On the other hand, as Carr writes, in reference to Hegel's classic description: 'The great man of the age is the one who can put into words the will of his age, tell his age what its will is, and accomplish it. What he does is the heart and essence of his age; he actualises his age.'[99] In this case, if charisma depends on a set of permissive conditions and the great man represents existing forces, Mustafa Kemal's role cannot be an exception. He was a product and agent of determination of both the Turkish military officers and the Muslim Anatolian peoples to protect the sovereignty of the state against invading forces.[100] More importantly, his role in the Turkish transition as related to the existence of his charisma cannot be analysed separately from the determination and belief of a collective nation, which acknowledges the role of an impersonal mass, i.e. the Muslim majority of Anatolia. The establishment of Kemal's cult was also a response to the desire of creating a hero of a nation which had been oppressed by the West for two hundred years and had lost its self-confidence. Although this an ahistorical assumption, if Kemal had died before the declaration of the Turkish Republic, another nationalist leader, probably Kazim Karabekir, would have continued the struggle to the end.[101] In addition, if an analysis claims 'a decisive role for the individual will, which is independent or autonomous from society', the counter argument would be that the view which takes the '*isolated*' leader as its starting point disregards the historical and societal factors.[102]

During the nation-state building process, the role of charismatic leader becomes crucial in foreign policy-making and national unification. There is no doubt that each charismatic leader has been an 'historically unique phenomenon insofar as ... the *extent* to which he can transcend limits over time and structural space are bound to vary with circumstances'.[103] More importantly, the role of the charismatic leader and the role of socio-historical factors reinforce each other in a mutual way. The combination of these two elements can be particularly important in pursuing the goals of transitional foreign policy, which are primarily nation-state building and the legitimisation of authority in domestic and foreign policies.

Mustafa Kemal's significant role in the Turkish transition cannot be denied but a single leader cannot accomplish such a complex task without the support of society's will power and the existence of appropriate historical circumstances. It is the task of the next section to identify the reciprocal relationship between the leader and the socio-historical factors.

The establishment of national authority

Although the nationalist movement had found a heroic leader, the Istanbul government was still the only centre to exercise authority in domestic and foreign policies. There were two important events which had a direct influence on the establishment of national authority in internal affairs: the declaration of a 'National Pact' and the occupation of Istanbul by the Allies.

It was explained earlier that there was an authority vacuum after the signing of the Mudros Armistice. The Ottoman Chamber of Deputies (*Meclis-i Mebusan*) was closed between 23 December 1918 and 12 January 1920 and during this period without an assembly decisions were taken by legal decrees.[104] Meanwhile, the spontaneous local reactionary congresses manifested the desire of the Anatolian peoples to secure the independence of the state. One of the decisions taken at Sivas Congress was to re-open the assembly. The Istanbul government did not stay indifferent to the Anatolian solution any longer. At a secret meeting of the Ottoman *Meclis-i Mebusan*, which was also its last meeting, on 12 January 1920, a new group, namely 'the Group of the Liberation of the Homeland' (*Felahi Vatan Grubu*), was established.[105] They decided to support the Anatolian liberation movement and drafted a 'National Pact' (*Misak-ı Milli*) according to decisions made at the Sivas and Erzurum congresses, and declared it on 28 January 1920.[106] The National Pact presented the democratic and national aims of the nationalist program to domestic and foreign public opinion. The pact consisted of six articles which expressed the determination of the Anatolian solution to regain the full national integrity and independence of the Turkish people.[107]

Arnold J. Toynbee described the document as 'a Declaration of Independence of the Turkish nation'.[108] Elaine Smith gives an interesting interpretation of the National Pact, seeing it as a declaration similar to the United States Declaration of Independence.[109] The declaration of the rights of the Turkish people signalled the desire to built up the superstructure of a modern Turkish state on a Western pattern.[110] The pact clearly spelled out five major goals: to liberate Ottoman territory from foreign invasion; to unite *Elviye-i Selase* (Kars, Ardahan and Batum) with the Turkish homeland; to gain control of Istanbul; to protect the rights of Muslim minorities in neighbouring states; and to secure the complete sovereignty of the country.[111] It not only became a key document of modern Turkish history but also laid the basis of nationalist foreign policy, which would be implemented under the leadership of Mustafa Kemal.

The final step for replenishing the authority vacuum was an unexpected consequence of the Allied occupation of Istanbul on 16 March 1920. The natural reaction of the nationalists to the occupation was to convene a new assembly and to found a new government centre in Ankara.[112] On 18 March 1920, Mustafa

Kemal sent a telegram to the commander in Sivas saying that it was necessary to convene a national assembly in Ankara.[113] The occupation constituted a fatal blow to Ottoman sovereignty and became a catalyst for the establishment of national authority in internal affairs. The GNA, declaring the establishment of the Ankara government, was opened in Ankara on 23 April 1920. This immediate link between the occupation of Istanbul and the opening of the GNA has been neglected by many scholars.[114]

The direct consequence of the opening of the GNA was the consolidation of the power of the new nationalist government in Ankara.[115] The GNA, the only legal institution in Anatolia, declared that there was no power above the GNA in Ankara for the following reasons: the GNA was the legislative and the executive power, and it was a people's government, based on the principle of the sovereignty of the Turkish people.[116] When the Ankara government had established its authority, the sultan, after being emancipated from foreign pressure, would take his power back within the constitutional system according to a decision made by the GNA. In fact, these principles laid the basis for the first constitution of the new Turkish state in January 1921.[117]

Moreover, the authority of the GNA was not limited to domestic politics. On 26 April 1920, three days after the opening of the assembly, Mustafa Kemal 'sent a note to the Soviet government expressing "the desire to enter into regular relations with it and to take part in the struggle against foreign imperialism which threatens both countries"'.[118] The occupation of Istanbul, therefore, had two unexpected impacts on Turkish politics. On the one hand, the nationalists consolidated their authority in domestic policy with the opening of the GNA; on the other, the establishment of relations with the Bolsheviks became the new foreign policy orientation of Ankara.

The opening of the GNA meant the establishment of a national authority in domestic politics. However, this consolidation did not mean that Ankara had become the only channel of foreign relations, since the nationalists were not recognised by either the Allies or the Bolsheviks at that time. The Istanbul government and the former CUP leaders abroad were still in contact with both the Allies and the Bolsheviks. The crucial test for the replacement of the Istanbul government by the Ankara government would take place in foreign relations, given the importance of international recognition to both statehood and the legitimacy of a government. As will be argued in the next chapter, the two consequences reveal the close relationship between the spheres of domestic and foreign policies during the Turkish model of constructing a modern state. In order to understand the establishment of relations with the Bolsheviks, the next section will analyse the actors' goals and their problems in the South Caucasian region.

State-building and nationalist foreign policy

As the next dimension of transitional foreign policy, the close interrelation between Turkish domestic and foreign policies, the main of this section is to identify the goals of the nationalist leadership, in particular that of Mustafa Kemal and Kazım Karabekir, which influenced the decisions on the establishment of relations with the Bolsheviks. The nationalists had two main goals: providing the maximum realistic conditions for independence, and territorial integrity, within the proclaimed borders of the National Pact. In this respect, Ankara's Eastern affairs in the Southern Caucasus was vital for two reasons: (a) the existence of the Allies or the Allied-dominated states on the eastern front would threaten Turkish power in Eastern Anatolia; (b) the loss of the region would obstruct any material aid from the Bolsheviks to the revolutionary movement in Anatolia. If the South Caucasian countries in the east allowed the Allied powers to encircle Turkey completely by cutting military and financial Bolshevik assistance to Turkey, the main strength of the nationalist resistance would collapse altogether.

Thus, Turkish nationalist foreign policy had to prevent at all costs the Caucasian barrier in the east, which would mean 'absolute annihilation' for Turkey. How could they implement a good neighbour policy towards the Bolsheviks based on common interests in the east? The ideological foundation of the Bolsheviks was the main reason for hesitation: would they collaborate with the Anatolian national movement? If so, under what conditions and to what end? The major problems were the determination of the Turkish–Armenian frontier and the pan-Islamic tendency of the Istanbul government towards Azerbaijan. While the next section aims to find the answers to these questions, the analysis of the new foreign policy orientation of Ankara also will help us to understand the impact of state transition as part of historical structure on foreign policy-making.

The principle of the South Caucasian 'buffer' between Ankara and Moscow

While the Turkish nationalists intended to establish relations with the Bolsheviks, Moscow was also intensely interested in the future of Anatolia and the East. It was argued here that the geographic location of Anatolia between the Balkans, the Middle East and the Caucasus established a role for the Turkish territories as a 'principal buffer' in this area. The Russians have been concerned with the international and internal orientations of their 'southern tier', countries – Turkey, Iran, Afghanistan and China – since the nineteenth century.[119] After the First World War, the new Soviet regime was afraid that the Western powers would turn their attention to destroying them. British control in Turkey, the Caucasus and Persia at the end of the war intensified its suspicions about the Allied plans. With the signing of the Armistice of Mudros in 1918, Lenin became more fearful that the British attack on Russia could come from the south through the Dardanelles. The British-controlled Greek occupation of Asia Minor in May 1919 was regarded as a direct threat not only to the future of the Turkish state but also to that of the Soviet regime. In Moscow's opinion, a powerful Greece extending into Asia Minor would obstruct Soviet access to the Mediterranean in the long term.[120] More importantly, the Bolsheviks would be deprived of raw materials in the South Caucasus if the British also controlled the Baku region with the intention of strangling them.[121] In 1919, the interests of the two new regimes overlapped on the protection of Anatolia and the South Caucasus from Allied expansion. However, the main obstacle was the Armenian question, which created difficulties in establishing a stable border between the two newly emerging regimes.

The Turkish–Armenian territorial dispute

Armenian territorial demands on the six Ottoman provinces (Erzurum, Van, Bitlis, Diyarbekir, Harput, Sivas), which had been named 'Turkish Armenia' by the Armenians and the Europeans, were the main bone of contention.[122] Specifically, after the massacre and deportation of the Armenians from these provinces by the CUP leaders in 1915, the 'Armenian question' became a thorny issue in Turkish politics. The Turkish nationalists had to overcome it while establishing relations with the Bolsheviks.

The Ottoman Empire regained these provinces and *Elviye-i Selase* from Russia with the Treaty of Brest-Litovsk. Three months later, in June 1918, the Batum Agreement determined the Turkish–Armenian border as that of the former Ottoman–Russian border of 1877–78 and Armenia renounced all claims to the six provinces.[123] As soon as the Ottomans signed the Armistice of Mudros, the Armenians repudiated the Batum Agreement and resumed their demands.[124] When an independent Armenia was proclaimed in the South Caucasus in May 1918, a new hope emerged among Armenians that developments in 'Eastern (Russian) Armenia would soon touch upon the desolate provinces of Western (Turkish) Armenia'.[125] For the Armenian leaders, the security and survival of the new Armenian Republic could not be achieved without uniting with 'Turkish Armenia'. The Armenians explored different channels through which to achieve their aim.

The first international arena was the Peace Conference that gathered in Paris on 18 January 1919, which was seen as an opportunity by the Armenians to invest their faith in the justice of the Allies.[126] In specific terms, the Armenians believed that the Peace Conference signalled a willingness to accommodate their territorial claims against the defeated Ottoman Empire.[127] A telegram from Lord Derby to Lord Curzon in January 1919 presented the Armenian attitude towards the Allies: the only solution to confirming the rights of the Armenian people was to form one 'great Armenia' by uniting the former Russian and Turkish Armenian provinces from the Black Sea to the Mediterranean under the protection of the Allies or the League of Nations. The United States should be the 'guardian of this new Armenia'.[128]

The Armenians were represented at the conference by two delegations. Avetis Aharonian, a Dashnak activist, represented the first delegation from the republic; the second rival delegation, the so-called 'Armenian National Delegation', or 'Delegation of Turkish Armenia', represented by Boghos Nubar Pasha, arrived in Paris in January 1919.[129] However, the two leaders 'decided to work together in a single joint delegation and present a single list of demands to the peace conference' rather than clashing with each other's claims.[130] Thus, Boghos Nubar Pasha presented an official joint memorandum to the Paris Peace Conference in February 1919. This memorandum included the following territorial demands:

(1) Seven eastern vilayets of Turkey (instead of the traditional six): Van, Bitlis,
     Diarbekir, Kharput, Sivas, Erzurum and Trebsiond.
(2) The four Cilician sanjaks: Marash, Khozan, Jebel Bereket and Adana with the
     town of Alexandretta.
(3) All the territory of the Armenian Republic of the Caucasus, including the
     entire province of Erivan, the southern portion of the former government of
     Tiflis the southern part of the government of Elisavetpol and the district of
     Kars, with the exception of the area north of Ardahan.[131]

Aharonian also brought the following points to the attention of the Peace
Conference: (a) By signing the Treaty of Brest-Litovsk, which abandoned Kars
and Ardahan to Turkey, Russia had severed the ties which united them with
Armenia. (b) Armenia claimed an equal status at the conference with newly
formed countries since it had participated in the war on the side of the Allies.[132]
During the peace conference, the Armenian demands set out an Armenian state
stretching from Transcaucasia, including the Black Sea, to the Mediterranean.
The provinces of Trabzon and Cilicia, Van, Bitlis, Diyarbakır, Kharput, Sivas,
Erzurum, Maraş, Adana, Kars, Karabagh, Zangezur and Erivan were part of this
territory. As Ronald Suny rightly points out, most of these provinces, such as
Trabzon, had never belonged to the Armenians nor did the Armenians constitute
a majority of the population, but the Armenian claims over these provinces were
justified for security or commercial reasons.[133] The Allies were also aware that
these provinces consisted of a mixed population – Armenian, Kurdish, Turkish
and Greek. Arnold J. Toynbee, who worked in the Foreign Office Section of the
British Delegation to the peace conference in Paris, argued in January 1919 that
'to make the Armenians dominant over a large Turkish and Kurdish majority
would be in the interest neither of the country as a whole nor of the Armenians
themselves'.[134] The Ottoman government in a memorandum on 12 February 1919
informed the US, British, French, and Italian commissioners in Istanbul that
'nearly 80 percent of the inhabitants in the six eastern vilayets were Muslims, "the
Armenians being everywhere in a small minority"'.[135]

There were a number of complainants regarding the Armenian territorial
claims at the peace conference. During the partition of the territories of the
Ottoman Empire, 'Turkish Armenia' was divided between France and Russia.
While France was awarded Cilicia and three western vilayets (Sivas, Harput and
Diyarbakır), the eastern vilayets (Van, Erzurum, Bitlis together with Dersim and
Trabzon) would be placed under Russian control.[136] Both France and Russia
therefore complained since their situation was not clear concerning western
Armenia. In addition, there was also a Kurdish majority in the territory claimed
by the Armenians.[137] In the Allies' opinion, the solution to the Armenian question
could be satisfactory without fully taking the Kurds into account. A report in May
1919 from the British High Commission in Istanbul argued that there were geographical, ethnic, economic and political arguments against the formation of any
Armenian state, and few in favour of it.[138] These counterarguments did not affect
the general tendency in Paris to challenge the right of the future Armenian state

to incorporate the six eastern Ottoman provinces. For instance, France was ready to abandon claims to Cilicia if the United States took the Armenian mandate. The determination of Armenia's permanent boundaries was accepted by nearly all US and European representatives in Transcaucasia.[139] Meanwhile, the Armenian delegations continued to demand more Allied support. They suggested returning Armenian refugees from the deportation in 1915 to create an Armenian majority in Eastern Anatolia.

In addition to the use of diplomacy during the peace conference, on 28 May 1919 the Erivan government declared the Act of United Armenia, which claimed national restoration by uniting the two parts, the Armenian territories of Transcaucasia and those of the Ottoman Empire, in 'historic Armenia'.[140] The Armenians knew that immediate unification was impossible but they 'justified the act as a symbolic gesture and as a legal basis for making representations on behalf of an integral Armenia and the western Armenian refugees'.[141] The consequences of the act were not foreseen. Its aim of creating a combined independent political Armenian identity failed since it led to the dissolution of the coalition cabinet in Erivan. More importantly, the reaction of the Turkish nationalists to this declaration was drastic: the Turks regarded the annexation of Turkish Armenia as a declaration of war.[142] The Kemalist 'leadership was equally certain that national integrity was inconceivable without the eastern Anatolian highlands – Turkish Armenia. The arena was thus prepared for mortal combat.'[143]

The Turkish nationalists could not take any action in May 1919 since they were preoccupied with the consolidation of their authority in internal politics. Their first reaction was to organise the military forces on the eastern front against the possibility of a 'united Armenia'. Kazim Karabekir was appointed to command the XV Army Corps, which would control the provinces of Van, Erzurum and Trabzon in April 1919.[144] When General Karabekir arrived at Erzurum, the headquarters of the XV Army Corps, on 3 May 1919, he was determined not to abandon Erzurum to the Armenians and to carry the struggle forward as long as a small portion of Ottoman territories remained free.[145] He argued that the Ottoman Empire would not only retrieve the three sanjaks of Kars, Ardahan and Batum, but would also occupy Armenia, to be used as a pawn to secure the Turkish position in the favourable peace settlement with the Allies which they so strongly desired.[146]

At that time, Britain changed its traditional policy in the region by transferring some of its responsibilities to another Allied power since the British burdens in the East were already too heavy. The Allies, especially Britain, had publicly expressed sympathy for the Armenians, but in practice diminished their support for the extensive Armenian demands. First, it was suggested in May 1919 that Italy would take Britain's place in the region. However, after the Italians had abandoned their intentions of going to the Caucasus, Britain and France suggested that the United States take the place of British troops.[147] In fact, they all knew that an independent Armenian state could not be established in the region unless a great power undertook mandate for Armenia.[148] As a result, President Wilson decided to send two investigative commissions to the Middle East: one to Syria under the leadership of H. C. King and C. Crane and the other to Anatolia under Major General J. G. Harbord.[149] In the summer of 1919, Harbord led an investigation into conditions in Anatolia and the Armenian question. In September 1919, he had a meeting with Karabekir, who had one clear aim in mind: gaining the neutrality of the United States on the Armenian question.[150] Karabekir presented an extensive report to the Harbord commission on 25 September.[151] Afterwards, in October 1919, General Harbord prepared a report for President Wilson in which he explained the fact that 'Trans-Caucasia and the whole of the former Turkish Empire, less Syria, Palestine and Mesopotamia, would be included in the terms of a single mandate.'[152] His report was unfavourable to the idea of a separate Armenian mandate.[153]

In the meantime, although the Allies *de facto* recognised the Republic of Armenia, in January 1920, this recognition would not prejudice the question of the eventual frontiers of that state.[154] The question of the Armenian mandate and the determination of borders between Armenia and Turkey were the most difficult problems while establishing relations between Ankara and Moscow, as will be discussed in Chapter 5.

The establishment of an area of security in the east

Both Ankara and Moscow were suspicious of an Allied plot in the east after the *de facto* recognition of Azerbaijan, Armenia and Georgia by the Allies.[155] The Soviet regime was interested in re-establishing an area of security in its southern tier.[156] Given the fact that the Bolsheviks were confronted with foreign attacks in 1918–20, there was an ideological reason behind this concern: 'the belief that the capitalist world would like to weaken and, if possible, destroy the Soviet system'.[157] From the points of view of Ankara and Moscow, if the Caucasus had been under the control of the Allies, have it would have negatively affected the two newly, emerging regimes. In order to prevent an Allied plot, both Ankara and Moscow concluded that any direct communication between the two regimes could only take place through the Caucasian route. Therefore, the South Caucasus, which had been an area of battlefields between the Ottoman and Russian empires, would provide a buffer zone between the two newly emerging regimes. However, neither side represented a united front when it came to establishing relations between them. On the one hand, the Bolshevik leaders remained divided and uncertain whether to support the Turkish national movement. The main issue was the class character of the movement, even if its struggle against the Allies was worthy of support.[158] As will be discussed in Chapter 7, the Baku Congress in September 1920 indicated that the Bolsheviks considered Turkey their only ally in the East, despite the bourgeois character of the Anatolian movement.

On the other hand, the Turkish nationalists could not clearly define whether the Caucasus would be a barrier or a bridge between Ankara and Moscow. The reason for forming a barrier in the Caucasus against the Bolsheviks was the fear of communism, which could spread to Anatolia. This idea found some advocates among the nationalists in Istanbul. At a meeting on 11 February 1920, Rauf Bey, a leading nationalists, asked Fevzi Pasha, the Minister of War, to negotiate with the British as regards the Caucasian question. The suggestion was that the Turks could influence Caucasian affairs and stop the Bolsheviks in the northern part of the Caucasian mountains if the British supported Turkish independence.[159] On the contrary, some leading nationalists supported the co-operation with the Bolsheviks to stop the formation of a barrier in the Caucasus.[160]

The examination of correspondence between the two nationalist leaders, Kemal and Karabekir, shows that they carefully considered the two arguments. For instance, Kemal stated in his telegram to Karabekir on 6 February 1920 that the Caucasus was the only possible front on which to initiate a counter attack against the Allies. He argued that the Allied powers had planned to cut the ties between the Turks and the Bolsheviks by recognising the South Caucasian republics. If the Allies constituted a barrier in the east against the Turks, the establishment of an independent Turkish state would be in real danger. Therefore, the Turks should do everything to stop this plan in the Caucasus and co-operate with the Bolsheviks.[161]

Karabekir replied to Kemal's telegram five days later. After meeting with Rawlinson, the British High Commissioner in Istanbul, on 11 February 1920, Karabekir informed Ankara that there was no possibility of establishing a Caucasian barrier between the Turks and the Bolsheviks.[162] Karabekir's own conclusion was that the British had neither a clear policy nor the military power in the region to support their offers. However, Karabekir preferred to be cautious about the Bolsheviks and to follow a policy of 'skilful neutrality'. He argued that if Turkish–Bolshevik co-operation was established, the Allies would eliminate Turkey.[163] New developments in Turkish politics, especially the increased British coercion in Istanbul and the initiatives of the CUP leaders in the Caucasus, would change Karabekir's opinion. He sent a telegram to Mustafa Kemal on 5 March 1920 informing him that the Allied plans had forced the Turkish nationalists to co-operate with the Bolsheviks. The Bolsheviks would help them only by controlling the South Caucasus without the Turks taking any responsibility.[164]

The crucial event which pushed the Turkish nationalists towards the Bolsheviks had been the occupation of Istanbul by the Allies on 16 March. The same day, Kemal sent a telegram to Karabekir to explain that he agreed with Karabekir's decision to establish co-operation with the Bolshevik regime in Batum and its environs. He suggested that Karabekir had to establish the necessary contacts in order to implement this decision.[165] In a subsequent telegram on the same day, he asked Karabekir's opinions on the right time and conditions for a military attack on the eastern front.[166] The new nationalist foreign policy was to establish immediate contact with the Bolsheviks for a united front in the Caucasus. Moreover, on the day following the occupation of Istanbul, 17 March 1919, a circular was sent to the entire Islamic world. Mustafa Kemal described the occupation as an insult to the Muslim people of Azerbaijan, the Caucasus, Turkestan, Afghanistan, Iran and Indochina. The whole Muslim world would have to unite against this action which was the last attempt of crusaders against the Caliphate.[167] In this case, the Muslims of the Caucasus and the East were considered to be providing a common ground to bring Ankara and Moscow together.

While the Turkish nationalists decided on co-operating with the Bolsheviks the British government was considering increasing its influence in the region. In the summer of 1920, Commander Luke, the British representative in Tiflis, suggested to the British Foreign Office 'to keep British policy in the Trans-Caucasia to the principle of Trans-Caucasian "buffer", i.e., to support of the three republics as independent'.[168] Control of the South Caucasus became crucial in relation to Turkish–Russian co-operation and for the interests of the British, who were opposed to this policy. Since the Armenian question was the biggest obstacle in Turkish–Bolshevik relations, the Turks had, at least, to be on good terms with Azerbaijan and the Georgians.[169] In particular, the establishment of Soviet control in Azerbaijan was the crucial event to test each other's intentions towards the other. Given the fact that the CUP leaders had implemented a pan-Islamist policy towards the region, how would the nationalist leaders react to the Sovietisation of Azerbaijan? Thus, the next chapter will examine why the South Caucasus came to reflect a radical change in the foreign policies of two transitional regimes.

Concluding remarks

Having identified the first dimension of transitional foreign policy – historical continuity and change – in the previous chapter, this chapter, in particular, explained why the South Caucasus had been a major arena of expansionist policies of the Russian, Ottoman and British Empires, for strategic, ideological and economic reasons. After 1878, the determination of the border between the Ottoman and the Russian Empires was the main issue which the new regimes inherited as one of the important priorities of their foreign policies. The Armenian question would become even more important during the creation of a new Turkish state after 1919. Yet despite the continuing geopolitical problems in eastern affairs, the new regimes had to implement policies different from those of their predecessors as a consequence of their transitional character. The sphere of foreign policy became the first arena to test each other's intentions. The new dynamics of the international system after the First World War imposed the elements of change in Turkish domestic politics, which influenced its foreign policy towards the South Caucasus. The Turkish nationalists in accordance with the requirements of modern state-building abandoned the expansionist imperial policies and limited their goals to the determination of settled national borders. Thus, the new understanding between Ankara and Moscow in the east indicated a radical change in their foreign policies.

This chapter further contextualised the second dimension of a transitional foreign policy in Turkey with reference to the relationship between the historical structural and decision makers as agencies of change. On the one hand, the two possibilities for restructuring the state are examined in relation to the main features of modern statehood in order to place the rise of the Turkish nationalist movement within the broader socio-historical structure of the Ottoman transition since the *Tanzimat* era. On the other hand, the construction of the modern Turkish state has been accepted as a consequence of Ottoman modernisation and the expansion of the international capitalistic system, as argued in Chapter 2. Therefore, the role of a single leader is analysed as an integral part of the domestic society which was influenced by this historical process. In particular, the role of the organisation of local congresses and the will power of the Anatolian Muslim peoples are emphasised in the context of the state-building question.

Therefore, the role of a charismatic leader during the transition – the third dimension of transitional foreign policy – has also been related to the matrix of socio-historical conditions that brought forth the rise of Mustafa Kemal, rather than examining his cult of personality. The establishment of his authority in domestic affairs was examined in relation to the Anatolian solution's applicability to the creation of a modern nation-state. The opening of the Grand National Assembly in Ankara meant the filling of the authority vacuum that had been created by the Armistice of Mudros and the occupation of the Ottoman capital. On the foreign policy level, the direct result of the occupation of Istanbul was the establishment of relations with Moscow. Having identified the internal causes of initiating relations with the Russian Bolsheviks, the next chapter will show the fourth dimension of transitional foreign policy that there is a close relationship between the spheres of the foreign and the domestic during the transformation from an imperial state to a modern state.

Notes

1 W.E.D. Allen and Paul Muratoff, *Caucasian Battlefields: A History of the Wars on the Turco-Caucasian Border, 1828–1921*, Cambridge, The University Press, 1953, pp. 9–10.
2 Gabriel Gorodetsky, 'The Formulation of Soviet Foreign Policy: Ideology and *Realpolitik*', in Gabriel Gorodetsky, ed., *Soviet Foreign Policy, 1917–1991: A Retrospective*, London, Frank Cass, 1994, p. 31.
3 J.C. Hurewitz, *Diplomacy in the Near and Middle East: A Documentary Record: 1914–1956, Vol. II*, Princeton, NJ, Van Nostrand, 1956, pp. 18–22.
4 Jane Degras, ed., *Soviet Documents on Foreign Policy, Vol. I: 1917–1924*, London, Oxford University Press, 1951, p. 8.
5 E.H. Carr, *The Bolshevik Revolution: 1917–1923, Vol. III*, London, Macmillan, 1961, p. 235; Degras, *Soviet Documents on Foreign Policy, Vol. I: 1917–1924*, pp. 16–17.
6 Richard Pipes, *The Formation of the Soviet Union: Communism and Nationalism, 1917–1923*, Cambridge, MA, Harvard University Press, 1954, p. 108.
7 Orlanda Figes, *A People's Tragedy: The Russian Revolution, 1891–1924*, New York, Penguin Books, 1998, pp. 547–548.
8 Degras, *Soviet Documents on Foreign Policy, Vol. I: 1917–1924*, p. 48.
9 Figes, *A People's Tragedy*, p. 548.
10 Vernon V. Aspaturian, 'Soviet Foreign Policy', in Roy C. Macridis, ed., *Foreign Policy in World Politics: States and Regions*, Englewood Cliffs, Prentice Hall, 1992, p. 212.
11 Carr, *The Bolshevik Revolution, Vol. III*, p. 51.
12 According to article 4: 'Russia will do all within her power to ensure the immediate evacuation of the provinces of Eastern Anatolia and their lawful return to Turkey. The Districts of Ardahan, Kars, and Batum will likewise and without delay be cleared of Russian troops. Russia will not interfere in the reorganisation of the national and

international relations of these districts, but leave it to the population of these districts to carry out this reorganisation in agreement with the neighbouring States, especially with Turkey.' Akdes N. Kurat, *Türkiye ve Rusya*, Ankara, Sevinç Matbaası, 1990, p. 488 (Turkish version) and see the English translation in Degras, *Soviet Documents on Foreign Policy, Vol. I: 1917–1924*, p. 53; R.G. Hovannisian, 'Armenia's Road to Independence', in R.G. Hovannisian, ed., *The Armenian People from Ancient to Modern Times, Vol. II: Foreign dominion to Statehood: The Fifteenth Century to the Twentieth Century*, New York, St. Martin's Press, 1997, p. 288.

13 Stefanos Yerasimos, *Türk-Sovyet İlişkileri: Ekim Devriminden Milli Mücadele'ye*, İstanbul, Gözlem Yayınevi, 1979, Doc. 5, pp. 44–49.

14 Kurat, *Türkiye ve Rusya*, p. 383.

15 Uygur Kocabaşoğlu and Metin Berge, *Bolşevik İhtilali ve Osmanlılar*, Ankara, Kebikec Yayınları, 1994, p. 132.

16 Deciding on the future of the three districts continued to be a problem in Turkish–Soviet relations not only during the rapprochement between the nationalists and the Bolsheviks but also in later years. When Stalin wanted to expand his sphere of influence to the Near East after the Second World War, he used diplomatic pressure on Turkey for the return of Kars and Arhadan (Batum was left to the Bolsheviks in 1921) to the Soviet Union in 1946. Bruce R. Kuniholm, 'The Origins of the Cold War in the Near East', in Gabriel Gorodetsky, ed., *Soviet Foreign Policy, 1917–1991: A Retrospective*, London, Frank Cass, 1994, p. 139.

17 Allen and Muratoff, *Caucasian Battlefields*, p. 114.

18 Figes, *A People's Tragedy*, p. 550.

19 Pipes, *The Formation of the Soviet Union*, p. 107.

20 Public Records Office, Kew, London, FO371/6269/E8378/8378/58, Outline of Events in Transcaucasia from the beginning of the Russian Revolution in the summer of 1917 to April 1921, 31 May 1922; Pipes, *The Formation of the Soviet Union*, p. 103.

21 Fahri Taş, *Erzincan Mütarekesi ve Brest-Litovsk*, Ankara, Özyurt Matbaacılık, p. 29.

22 Yerasimos, *Türk-Sovyet İlişkileri*, p. 38, Doc. 2.

23 Kurat, *Türkiye ve Rusya*, p. 467; Allen and Muratoff, *Caucasian Battlefields*, pp. 462–463.

24 For a detailed analysis of the Baku Commune which existed from 13 April to 25 July 1918 see Ronald G. Suny, *The Baku Commune, 1917–1918: Class and Nationality in the Russian Revolution*, Princeton, NJ, Princeton University Press, 1972.

25 Carr, *The Bolshevik Revolution, Vol. I*, p. 346.

26 Kurat, *Türkiye ve Rusya*, p. 473.

27 Allen and Muratoff, *Caucasian Battlefields*, pp. 467–468.

28 Stanford J. Shaw and Ezel Kural Shaw, *History of the Ottoman Empire and Modern Turkey, Vol. II – Reform, Revolution and Republic: The Rise of Modern Turkey, 1808–1975*, Cambridge University Press, 1995, p. 326.

29 Ibid.

30 Şevket S. Aydemir, *Makedon'dan Ortaasya'ya Enver Paşa, Vol. III*, İstanbul, Remzi Kitabevi, 1992, p. 414.

31 Pipes, *The Formation of the Soviet Union*, pp. 194–195.

32 Public Records Office, Kew, London, FO371/E8378/8378/58, Outline of Events in Transcaucasia from the beginning of the Russian Revolution in the summer of 1917 to April 1921, 31 May 1922.

33 Kurat, *Türkiye ve Rusya*, p. 477.

34 *Osmanlı Devleti ile Azerbaycan Türk Hanlıkları Arasındaki Münasabetlere Dair Arşiv*

Belgeleri: Karabağ, Susa, Nahçıhan, Baku, Gence, Sirvan, Seki, Revan, Kuba, Hay, Ankara, T.C. Başbakanlık Devlet Arşivleri Genel Müdürlüğü, Yayın No. 9, 1993, pp. 226–229.

35 Pipes, *The Formation of the Soviet Union*, pp. 208–209.

36 D. Cameron Watt, ed., *British Documents on Foreign Affairs: Reports and Papers from the Foreign Office Confidential Print [BDFA], Vol. I*, University Publications of America, 1984, pp. 46–50, Doc. 6.

37 Stefanos Yerasimos, *Milliyetler ve Sınırlar: Balkanlar, Kafkasya ve Orta-doğu*, İstanbul, İletişim Yayınları, 1994, p. 315.

38 Public Records Office, Kew, London, FO371/6269/E8378/8378/58, Outline of Events in Transcaucasia from the beginning of the Russian Revolution in the summer of 1917 to April 1921, 31 May 1922.

39 Briton C. Busch, *Mudros to Lausanne: Britain's Frontier in West Asia, 1918–1923*, New York, State University of New York Press, 1976, pp. 23–29.

40 George A. Bournoutian, *A History of the Armenian People*, Costa Mesa, Mazda Publishers, 1994, p. 138.

41 Public Records Office, Kew, London, FO371/3662/72735, Secrets Reports on Transcaucasia, dated 25 April 1919. See the further articles on Karabagh issue: Stephan H. Astourian, 'The Nagorno-Karabakh Conflict: Dimensions, Lessons, and Prospects', *Mediterranean Quarterly: A Journal of Global Issues*, 5:4 (Fall 1994), pp. 89–105; Richard G. Hovannisian, 'The Armeno-Azerbaijani Conflict Over Mountainous Karabagh, 1918–1919', *The Armenian Review*, 24:2–94 (1971), pp. 3–39; Suante E. Cornell, 'Turkey and the Conflict in Nagorna Karabakh: A Delicate Balance', *Middle Eastern Studies*, 34:1 (January 1998), pp. 51–72.

42 Allen and Muratoff, *Caucasian Battlefields*, p. 468.

43 Kurat, *Türkiye ve Rusya*, pp. 535–540.

44 Shaw and Shaw, *History of the Ottoman Empire and Modern Turkey, Vol. II*, p. 327.

45 A.M. Samsutdinov, *Mondros'tan Lozan'a Türkiye Ulusal Kurtuluş Savaşı Tarihi, 1918–1923*, İstanbul, Doğan Kitap, 1999, p. 22.

46 Degras, *Soviet Documents on Foreign Policy, Vol. I: 1917–1924*, p. 110.

47 Mete Tunçay, 'Siyasal Tarih (1908–1923)', in Sina Akşin, ed., *Türkiye Tarihi: Çağdaş Türkiye, 1908–1980, Vol. IV*, Istanbul, Cem Yayınevi, 1995, p. 55.

48 David Fromkin, *A Peace to End All Peace: Creating the Modern Middle East, 1914–1922*, London, Penguin Books, 1989, p. 373.

49 Kemal Ciftci, *Tarih, Kimlik ve Elestirel Kuram Baglaminda Turk Dis Politikasi*, Ankara, Siyasal Kitabevi, 2010, pp. 113–114.

50 Seha L. Meray and Osman Olcay, *Osmanlı İmparatorluğunun Çöküş Belgeleri (Mondros Bırakışması, Sevr Andlaşması, İlgili Belgeler)*, Ankara, Siyasal Bilgiler Fakültesi Yayınları, 1977, pp. 1–5.
The three articles relating to Transcaucasia were as follows: The Turkish troops agreed to evacuate a part of Transcaucasia earlier; if necessary, the evacuation of the rest of the region would be put into effect after a review of the situation in the east by the Allies (Article 11). The Allied occupation of Batum would be accepted and the Ottoman Empire would not resist the Allied occupation of Baku (Article 15). Finally, the Allies reserved the right to occupy any part of the six eastern provinces in the event of any disorder in them (Article 24).

51 Public Records Office, Kew, London, FO371/3661/41025, Interdepartmental Conference on Middle Eastern Conference, 14 March 1919.

52 Meray and Olcay, *Osmanlı İmparatorluğunun Çöküş Belgeleri*, p. 3.

53 Public Records Office, Kew, London, FO371/3661/41025, Interdepartmental Conference on Middle Eastern Conference, 14 March 1919.

54 Ömer Kürkçüoğlu, *Türk-İngiliz İlişkileri: 1919-1926*, Ankara, Siyasal Bilgiler Fakültesi Yayınları, 1978, p. 3.

55 Fatma Muge Göcek, *The Transformation of Turkey: Redefining State and Society from the Ottoman Empire to the Modern Era*, London, I.B. Taurus, 2011, p. 38.

56 Bülent Tanör, *Türkiye'de Kongre İktidarları (1918-1920)*, Istanbul, Yapı Kredi Yayınları, 1998, p. 15.

57 Mine Erol, *Türkiye'de Amerikan Mandası Meselesi: 1919-1920*, Giresun, İleri Basımevi, 1972, p. 41.

58 Doğan Avcıoğlu, *Milli Kurtuluş Tarihi: 1838'den 1995'e*, Vol. I, Istanbul, Tekin Yayınevi, 1993, p. 257.

59 Falih Rıfkı Atay, *Cankaya*, Istanbul, Pozitif Yayinlari, 2004, p. 209.

60 See details of the discussions on the British, French and Italian mandates in Osman Özsoy, *Saltanattan Cumhuriyet'e Giden Yolda Kurtuluş Savaşı'nın Perde Arkası*, Istanbul, Aksoy Yayıncılık, 1999, pp. 225-228.

61 Zeki Sarıhan, *Kurtuluş Savaşı Günlüğü (Açıklamalı Kronoloji)*, Ankara, Türk Tarih Kurumu Basımevi, 1993, p. 278.

62 Tanör, *Türkiye'de Kongre İktidarları*, p. 77.

63 Mustafa Kemal Atatürk, Speech delivered at Angora, 15-20 October 1927, English Translation, Leipzig, 1929, p. 87; Tanör, *Türkiye'de Kongre İktidarları*, p. 79; Erol, *Türkiye'de Amerikan Mandası Meselesi*, p. 96.

64 Sina Akşin, *Istanbul Hükümetleri ve Milli Mücadele*, Vol. I: *Mutlakıyete Dönüş (1918-1919)*, Ankara, Türkiye İş Bankası Kültür Yayınları, 1998, p. 166.

65 Ibid., pp. 408-409; Tanör, *Türkiye'de Kongre İktidarları*, p. 29.

66 Firuz Kazemzadeh, *The Struggle for Transcaucasia (1917-1921)*, New York, 1951, p. 214.

67 Atatürk, Speech delivered at Angora, p. 29.

68 Şevket S. Aydemir, *Tek Adam: Mustafa Kemal*, Vol. II, 14th edn, Istanbul, Remzi Kitabevi, 1997, pp. 122-123.

69 See Appendix 2: The list of the local congresses.

70 İhsan Güneş, *Birinci TBMM'nin Düşünce Yapısı (1920-1923)*, Türkiye İş Bankası Kültür Yayınları, 1997, p. 110; Erik J. Zürcher, *Turkey: A Modern History*, London, I.B. Tauris Publishers, 1995, p. 141.

71 Atatürk, Speech delivered at Angora, p. 10.

72 Tanör, *Türkiye'de Kongre İktidarları*, pp. 35-40.

73 Ibid., pp. 42-44.

74 Salahi Ramadan Sonyel, *Turkish Diplomacy, 1918-1923: Mustafa Kemal and the Turkish National Movement*, London, Sage, 1975, p. 16.

75 Alev Coşkun, *Kuvayi Milliye'nin Kuruluşu: En Uzun 15 Gün, Ödemiş Direnişi*, 3. Baskı, Istanbul, Cumhuriyet Kitapları, 1998, p. 193.

76 Sabahattin Selek, *Milli Mücadele: Ulusal Kurtuluş Savaşı*, Vol. I, 2nd edn, Istanbul, Orgun Yayınları, 1982, pp. 211-218.

77 Çağlar Keyder, 'The Ottoman Empire', in K. Barkey and M. V. Hagen, eds, *After Empire – Multiethnic Societies and Nation-Building: The Soviet Union and the Russian, Ottoman and Habsburg Empires*, Oxford, Westview Press, 1997, p. 36.

78 Ünsal Yavuz, *Atatürk: İmparatorluktan Milli Devlete*, Ankara, Türk Tarih Kurumu Basımevi, 1990, pp. 42-43. Kemal was suggested by the Acting Minister who believed

that his opposition to Enver had prevented him from receiving major command appointments during the war. Fromkin, *A Peace to End All Peace*, p. 406.

79 Menter Şahinler, *Atatürkçülüğün Kökeni, Etkisi ve Güncelliği*, Istanbul, Çağdaş Yayınları, 1998, p. 47.

80 Mehmet Gönlübol et al., *Olaylarla Türk Dış Politikası, 7*. Bası, Ankara, Alkım Kitabevi, 1989, p. 8.

81 Kazım Karabekir, *İstiklal Harbimiz, Vol. I*, Istanbul, Emre Yayınları, 1993, p. 55.

82 Zürcher argues that the combination of different factors constrained his decision to go to Samsun in May: pressure from his fellow army officers, the Anatolian peoples' will-power, the fear of being arrested and an agreement with the *Karakol Cemiyeti* (Outpost Society). Erik J. Zürcher, *The Unionist Factor: The Role of the Committee of Union and Progress in the Turkish National Movement, 1905-1926*, Leiden, E. J. Brill, 1984, p. 111.

83 Philip G. Cerny, 'Foreign Policy Leadership and National Integration', *British Journal of International Studies*, 5 (April 1979), p. 79.

84 Cited in Max Weber, 'The Routinisation of Charisma', in Amitai Etzioni and Eva Etzioni, eds, *Social Change: Sources, Patterns and Consequences*, New York, 1964, chapter 9, in Cerny, 'Foreign Policy Leadership', pp. 79-80.

85 Sina Akşin, 'Mustafa Kemal'in İktidar Yolu', in Ömer C. Sarc et al., *Çağdaş Düşüncenin Işığında Atatürk, 2*, Baskı, Istanbul, Dr. N.F. Eczacıbaşı Vakfı Yayınları, 1986, p. 71.

86 In February 1915, Kemal was appointed to reorganise and command the Nineteenth Division in Thrace. He established the headquarters of this division at Maydos, in Çanakkale (Chanak) in order to direct operations against the Allied naval attack on the Dardanelles and the Turkish Straits. The Allied military landings on the Gallipoli peninsula in the spring of 1915 were confronted with Kemal's Nineteenth Division at Arıburnu (the Cape of Bees), Anafartalar and Conkbayırı (Chunuk Bair). As a result of the successful Turkish defence, the Allies had to evacuate the peninsula in January 1916. Muzaffer Özsoy, 'Askerlik Bilimi ve Strateji Açısından Atatürk', in Sarc et al., *Çağdaş Düşüncenin Işığında Atatürk*, pp. 93-98.

87 Patrick Kinross, *Atatürk: The Rebirth of a Nation*, London, Weidenfeld, 1993, p. 96.

88 Ibid., p. 129.

89 Christopher Hill, 'Theories of Foreign Policy-making for the Developing Countries', in Christopher Clapham, ed., *Foreign Policy-Making in Developing States: A comparative Approach*, Westmead, Saxon House, 1977, p. 6.

90 Aydemir, *Tek Adam, Vol. II*, p. 101.

91 Public Records Office, Kew, London, FO371/3659/117547, Report on Situation in Erzerum, dated 16 August 1919.

92 Karabekir, *İstiklal Harbimiz, Vol. I*, p. 108.

93 Aydemir, *Tek Adam, Vol. II*, p. 105.

94 Karabekir, *İstiklal Harbimiz, Vol. I*, p. 118.

95 Ibid., p. 141.

96 Ibid., pp. 247-248.

97 Cited in Dankward A. Rustow, 'Atatürk as Founder of a State', *Daedalus*, iiic, 1968, p. 797, in Cerny, 'Foreign Policy Leadership', p. 80.

98 Ibid., pp. 77-78.

99 Cited in Hegel, *Philosophy of Right* (English tranl., 1942), p. 295 in E. H. Carr, *What is History?*, 2nd Edition (edited by R. W. Davies), London, Penguin Books, 1990, p. 54.

100 Tarık Z. Tunaya, 'Tarihin Yolu Nasıl Keşfedilir? Atatürk ve Osmanlı Mirası', in Sarc

et al., *Çağdaş Düşüncenin Işığında Atatürk*, pp.7–8; Adnan Nur Baykal, *Yöneticiler İçin Yeni Bir Bakış: Mustafa Kemal Atatürk'ün Liderlik Sırları*, Istanbul, Sistem Yayıncılık, 1999, p.165.

101 Kazım Karabekir 'was the only nationalist commander whose prestige could rival Mustafa Kemal's, but he was slow to put it to political use'. Andrew Mango, *Atatürk*, London, John Murray, 1999, p.295 It is also an ahistorical question to consider whether Karabekir would carry the struggle to the end successfully.

102 Carr, *What is History*, p.167.

103 Cerny, 'Foreign Policy Leadership', p.81.

104 Tanör, *Türkiye'de Kongre İktidarları*, p.97.

105 Fahrettin Çiloğlu, *Kurtuluş Savaşı Sözlüğü*, Istanbul, Doğan Kitap, 1999, p.155.

106 Kemal Melek, *Doğu Sorunu ve Milli Mücadelenin Dış Politikasi*, Istanbul, Der Yayınları, 1985, p.50.

107 See Appendix 3: The National Pact.

108 Arnold J. Toynbee and Kenneth P. Kirkwood, *Turkey*, London, Ernest Benn Limited, 1926, p.85.

109 Elaine D. Smith, *Turkey: Origins of the Kemalist Movement and the Government of the Grand National Assembly (1919–1923)*, Washington, DC, Judd & Detweiller Inc., 1959, p.25.

110 Toynbee and Kirkwood, *Turkey*, p.85.

111 Kemal H. Karpat, *The Politicization of Islam: Reconstructing Identity, State, Faith and Community in the Late Ottoman State*, Oxford, Oxford University Press, 2001, p.345.

112 Aydemir, *Tek Adam, Vol. II*, p.188.
    The decision to go to Ankara on 27 December 1919 was not a coincidence. The local people in Ankara had a quality which attracted the attention of the nationalist leaders: they rebelled against the Ottoman bureaucrats and believed in a national-democratic movement. Sina Akşin, *Ana Çizgileriyle Türkiye'nin Yakın Tarihi*, Ankara, İmaj Yayıncılık, 1996, p.123.

113 *Atatürk'ün Tamim, Telgraf ve Beyannameleri [ATTB], Vol. IV*, Atatürk Kültür, Dil ve Tarih Yüksek Kurumu, Atatürk Araştırma Merkezi, Ankara, Türk Tarih Kurumu Basımevi, 1991, pp.272–274, Doc. No: 257.

114 See Bülent Gökay, *A Clash of Empires: Turkey between Russian Bolshevism and British Imperialism, 1918–1923*, London, Tauris Academic Studies, 1997, p.198, fn. 95.

115 During the Turkish national struggle, between the signing of the Armistice of Mudros in 1918 and the declaration of the Turkish Republic in 1923, in Turkish history there were two government centres, one in Istanbul and one in Ankara. The *de jure* Istanbul government would become the *de facto* government with the opening of the GNA in 1920. Meanwhile a *de facto* government of Ankara would establish its authority as a *de jure* government with the abolition of the Ottoman Sultanate by the GNA in 1922. See Appendix 4: List of cabinets and their chief ministers in Istanbul and Ankara.

116 Atatürk, Speech delivered at Angora, p.380.

117 Emre Kongar, *21. Yüzyılda Türkiye: 2000'li Yıllarda Türkiye'nin Toplumsal Yapısı*, Istanbul, Remzi Kitabevi, 1998, p.90.

118 *ATTB*, p.318, Doc. 305; Yerasimos, *Türk-Sovyet İlişkileri*, p.232, Doc. 39. There is a reply by Chicerin dated 2 or 3 June 1920. Carr, *The Bolshevik Revolution, Vol. III*, p.250; *Atatürk'un Milli Dış Politikası (Cumhuriyet Dönemine Ait 100 Belge: 1919–1923) [AMDP], Vol. I*, Ankara, T.C. Kültür Bakanlığı Yayınları, 1994, pp.160–161, Doc. 24.

119 Fred Halliday, *Threat from the East? Soviet Policy from Afghanistan and Iran to the Horn of Africa*, Middlesex, Penguin Books, 1982, pp.43–44.

120 Gökay, *A Clash of Empires*, p.64.

121 Ibid., p.57.

122 Kurat, *Türkiye ve Rusya*, pp.203–204.
     Turkish historians do not refer to these provinces as 'Turkish Armenia'. The number
     of provinces also are different. For instance, Kurat argues that the number is either
     five or six and he gives only four provinces, Erzurum, Van, Bitlis and Diyarbekir.
     However, the six provinces were called '*Vilaya-i Sitte*' in the Ottoman administrative
     structure. See Karabekir, *İstiklal Harbimiz, Vol. II*, p.520.
     According to the Armenians, historic Armenia had been divided between the
     Ottoman Empire and the Russian Empire after the first quarter of the nineteenth
     century 'with Armenians living in Western or Turkish (Ottoman) Armenia and
     Eastern or Russian Armenia'. Manoug J. Somakian, *Empires in Conflict: Armenia and
     the Great Powers, 1895–1920*, London, I.B. Tauris Publishers, 1995, p.1.

123 See Appendix 1: Chronology: Turkey and the South Caucasus, 1918–1921.

124 Kazemzadeh, *The Struggle for Transcaucasia*, p.286; Kurat, *Türkiye ve Rusya*, p.477.

125 Richard G. Hovannisian, *The Republic of Armenia: From Versailles to London, 1919–
     1920, Vol. II*, Berkeley, CA, University of California Press, 1982, p.1.

126 Kazemzadeh, *The Struggle for Transcaucasia*, p.253.

127 Vahakn N. Dadrian, *The History of the Armenian Genocide: Ethnic Conflict from the
     Balkans to Anatolia to the Caucasus*, Oxford, Berghahn Books, 1995, p.362.

128 Public Records Office, Kew, London, FO371/3657/9846, Telegram from Lord Derby,
     No. 116, dated 16 January 1919.

129 Public Records Office, Kew, London, FO371/3657/13693, Telegram from Calthorpe,
     No. 165-Urgent, dated 25 January 1919.

130 Ronald G. Suny, *Looking Toward Ararat: Armenia in Modern History*, Bloomington,
     Indiana University Press, 1993, p.128.

131 Kazemzadeh, *The Struggle for Transcaucasia*, pp.255–256; Cemil Hasanlı, *Azerbaycan
     Tarihi: Türkiye Yardımından Rusya İşgaline Kadar (1918–1920)*, Ankara, Azerbaycan
     Kültür Derneği Yayınları, 1998, p.258.

132 Kazemzadeh, *The Struggle for Transcaucasia*, p.259.

133 Suny, *Looking Toward Ararat*, pp.128–129; Public Records Office, Kew, London,
     FO371/E553/134/58, Liberation of Armenia, from Boghos Nubar, dated 23 February
     1920.

134 Public Records Office, Kew, London, FO371/3657/13595, Subject: Future administra-
     tion of Armenia, from Balfour to Curzon, dated 22 January 1919.

135 Richard G. Hovannisian, *The Republic of Armenia: The First Year, 1918–1919, Vol. I*,
     Berkeley, CA, University of California Press, 1971, p.421.
     During the exchange of telegrams between Mr Balfour and Mr Gerard in February
     1920, both sides would emphasise the fact that the inhabitants of the six Turkish
     eastern vilayets were predominantly Turkish in race and religion. Therefore, if the
     future 'Greater Armenia' held these provinces it would be entirely dependent on
     military support without which the Armenians could not hope to exist at all as a
     nation. Public Records Office, Kew, London, FO371/4952/E625/134/58, Telegrams
     on Armenian Question, From Mr. Balfour, dated 16 February 1920.

136 Public Records Office, Kew, London, FO371/4952/E446/134/8, Claims of Armenia in
     Turkish Settlement, from Mr J.A. Malcolm to Mr. Vansittart, dated 22 February 1920.

137 Bournoutian, *A History of the Armenian People*, p.136.

138 Public Records Office, Kew, London, FO371/3658/75852, Armenian Questions, From
     Admiral Caltorpe, dated 3 May 1919.

139 Hovannisian, *The Republic of Armenia, Vol. II*, p. 4.
140 Public Records Office, Kew, London, FO371/4965/E15106/134/58, Communication by League of Nations, No. 20/40/56E, dated 26 November 1920.
141 Hovannisian, *The Republic of Armenia, Vol. II*, p. 1.
142 Kazemzadeh, *The Struggle for Transcaucasia*, p. 286.
143 Hovannisian, *The Republic of Armenia, Vol. I*, p. 447.
144 Karabekir, *İstiklal Harbimiz, Vol. I*, p. 54.
145 Ibid., p. 59; Taner Akçam, *İnsan Hakları ve Ermeni Sorunu: İttihat ve Terakki'den Kurtuluş Savaşı'na*, Ankara, İmge Kitabevi, 1999, p. 499.
146 Karabekir, *İstiklal Harbimiz, Vol. I*, p. 60; Hovannisian, *The Republic of Armenia, Vol. I*, p. 426.
147 Public Records Office, Kew, London, FO371/3668/124999, minutes, dated 2 September 1919.
148 Public Records Office, Kew, London, FO371/3662/115213, Secret Report on Situation in Caucasus, from D.M.I B.I/4881(M.I.2), dated 11 August 1919.
149 Shaw and Shaw, *History of the Ottoman Empire and Modern Turkey, Vol. II.*, p. 331.
150 Karabekir, *İstiklal Harbimiz, Vol. I*, pp. 321–323.
151 Ibid., pp. 323–331.
152 *Papers Relating to the Foreign Relations of the United States [PRFRUS], 1920, Vol. III*, Washington, US Government Printing Office, p. 784.
153 Hasanlı, *Azerbaycan Tarihi*, p. 313.
154 *PRFRUS, Vol. III*, p. 778.
155 *BDFA, Vol. II*, p. 30, Doc. 39.
156 R. D. McLaurin, *The Middle East in Soviet Politics*, Lexington, MA, Lexington Books, 1975, p. 17.
157 Halliday, *Threat from the East*, p. 36.
158 Walter Z. Laqueur, *The Soviet Union and the Middle East*, New York, Frederick A. Praeger, 1959, p. 27.
159 Yerasimos, *Milliyetler ve Sınırlar*, p. 120.
160 Gökay, *A Clash of Empires*, p. 73.
161 Karabekir, *İstiklal Harbimiz, Vol. I*, pp. 474–475.
162 Ibid., p. 475.
163 Ibid., p. 476; Yerasimos, *Milliyetler ve Sınırlar*, p. 121.
164 Karabekir, *İstiklal Harbimiz, Vol. I*, p. 519; Yerasimos, *Milliyetler ve Sınırlar*, p. 122.
165 Mustafa Onar, ed., *Atatürk'ün Kurtuluş Savaşı Yazışmaları [AKSY], Vol. II*, Ankara, G.U. Teknik Eğitim Fakültesi Matbaası, 1995, p. 34, Doc. 684.
166 Ibid., p. 41, Doc. 695.
167 *ATTB*, pp. 271–272, Doc. 256; *AKSY, Vol. II*, p. 45, Doc. 704.
The new tendency towards the East would be strongly noticeable in the following actions of the nationalists. It was not a coincidence that the opening day of the GNA on 23 April 1920 was chosen after prayer on Friday, the holy day of Muslims.
'As it will be opened on a Friday, the solemn character of this day will be profited by for offering solemn prayer, before the opening, in the Hadji Beiram Mosque', Atatürk, Speech delivered at Angora, p. 372.
168 Public Records Office, Kew, London, FO371/4945/E10727/1/58, Telegram from Commander Luke, Confidential, No. 257/60, dated 12 August 1920.
169 Sonyel, *Turkish Diplomacy*, pp. 21–22.

5

New rules of engagement between Ankara and Moscow in the East

As stated in the previous chapter, after the final defeat of the Ottoman Empire in October 1918, the Turkish nationalists proceeded to establish their authority in 1919 and determined the main goals of the nationalist movement in the National Pact of April 1920. In this document, the eastern provinces of *Elviye-i Selase* (Kars, Ardahan and Batum) were accepted as an integral part of the Turkish state. While this goal was inherited from the previous CUP policies, a radical break with these policies occurred in relation to Azerbaijan as opposed to the Ottoman imperial foreign policy, which was designed by Enver Pasha to annex both Russian and Persian Azerbaijan during the First World War.[1]

Therefore, the main empirical concern of this chapter is to explain the new rules of engagement in the East between Ankara and Moscow. The first section will explain why the region became a test arena through the following guiding questions: how did the Turks react to the establishment of Soviet control in Azerbaijan, and why did the Armenian question obstruct the progress of relations in the east? The second section will draw our attention to the use of modern diplomacy between Ankara and Moscow. On the one hand, the correspondence between the two newly emerging regimes helps us to understand the main concerns of the two sides. On the other hand, Kemal's correspondence with Kazım Karabekir, the commander of the Fifteenth Army Corps on the Caucasian front, and Bekir Sami, Minister for Foreign Affairs, demonstrates the process of decision-making in Turkish foreign policy. The third section critically explores the consequences of the Treaty of Sèvres on Turkish foreign policy as a catalyst for Turkish–Bolshevik co-operation against the West. The chapter concludes by explaining why the Turkish nationalists chose the Armenian theatre to show their determination to reject the treaty. The overall theoretical concern of the chapter is to understand how domestic and foreign policies are closely intertwined under the conditions of state transformation.

Stabilisation of the eastern front between Ankara and Moscow

The main question in analysing Turkish foreign policy towards Azerbaijan is why the Turkish nationalists had little interest in preventing the Sovietisation of Azerbaijan in April 1920. According to Azeri historian Musa Qasimov, relations between Azerbaijan and Turkey in this period have not been investigated in detail either by Russian, Turkish or Azeri scholars.[2] Relations between Azerbaijan and Turkey were very complicated between 1918 and 1921 for two main reasons: first, the pan-Turkic and pan-Turanian policies of the CUP at the end of the First World War found advocates in Azerbaijan, which affiliated them with Ottoman expansionist designs. Second, the power struggle between the Turkish nationalists and the former CUP regime was more pronounced in Azerbaijan while subdued in Anatolia.[3] Thus, the examination of Turkish foreign policy towards Azerbaijan will help us to understand the reasons behind abandoning the expansionist designs of the Ottomans towards the region.

The Sovietisation of Azerbaijan

When an independent Azerbaijan was declared on 28 May 1918 it was gained through the support of Ottoman policies.[4] Although the independent government of Azerbaijan, led by the Musavat Party (officially called the Turkish Federalist Musavat Party), was basically centrist and nationalist in orientation, like other independent Transcaucasian states the establishment of its independence would be for a limited period, for both external and internal reasons.[5] External factors, such as the formation of a Soviet government in Russia and the British occupation of Baku after the withdrawal of Ottoman forces, and internal conflicts both within the Musavat Party itself and between the different political groups contributed to the instability of the new government when the British evacuated the region.[6]

The full independence of Azerbaijan began when the British troops left Transcaucasia, with the exception of Batum, in August 1919. Under these circumstances, the Azerbaijani Republic realised the danger of the Red Army establishing Soviet control and tried to gain some support from the Allied powers. The British leaders, especially Lloyd George, were aware that a 'reunited Russia' would leave British interests in the region in danger. In Lloyd George's opinion, the British Empire was destined to help Denikin's cause against the Bolsheviks. However, this policy turned out to be a disappointment when Denikin was defeated as the Red Army advanced in early 1920.[7] Denikin's failure had rapid effects on Caucasian affairs. As stated in the previous chapter, the Allied Supreme Council unexpectedly decided to recognise the *de facto* independence of Azerbaijan, Georgia and Armenia in January 1920.[8] By this sudden recognition, the Allies – or Britain – hoped to strengthen their position in regard to Soviet Russia after the defeat of Denikin's White Armies. According to British documents, the most important development in Russian policy at this stage was its approach to the Turkish nationalists. At the end of 1919, the two regimes 'had various aims in common: they had the same enemies; they were both in political, military and economic isolation; each was capable of giving invaluable assistance to the other'.[9] Therefore, the Allies also hoped to prevent a Turkish–Bolshevik rapprochement by this recognition. However, its consequences would be different from Allied expectations.

In the meantime, a new decision was taken by the Moscow government. 'On January 3, 1920, the Politburo decided that in order to combat chauvinism and advance the socialist revolution in the Caucasus there should be separate Communist parties in the states controlled by the "factually created governments" and that these autonomous bodies would be linked at the regional level with the Russian Communist party.'[10] In Azeri internal affairs, the first action was the formation of the Communist Party of Azerbaijan by the first congress of Bolshevik organisations in Azerbaijan on 11–12 February 1920. The Azerbaijani Communist party was a 'multinational, territorial unit under the jurisdiction of the regional committee of the Russian communist party'.[11] This was the first sign of the Bolshevik take-over process in Azerbaijan and the final step took place in April 1920.

A government crisis occurred in Azerbaijan on the night of 26–27 April, while the first Red Army forces were advancing towards Baku. On that night, the government of the Musavat Party was replaced by the Provisional Azerbaijani Military-Revolutionary Committee (Azrevkom).[12] At 11 p.m. on 27 April, just one hour before the deadline of the Communist ultimatum, the Parliament of Azerbaijan agreed to withdraw from power. The parliament declared that an independent Azerbaijani state had come to an end and the Azerbaijani Soviet Socialist Republic was proclaimed on 28 April.[13] When a treaty of military and economic union was signed between Russia and Soviet Azerbaijan, the Great Powers, apart from the British, hardly noticed the disappearance of Azerbaijan from the international scene.[14] Did the Turkish nationalists remain indifferent to these developments?

The Turkish nationalists did not bring about an independent Azeri state under Turkey's control, nor did they prevent the Sovietisation of Azerbaijan. In December 1919, the Chief British Commissioner, Colonel Stokes, informed the Foreign Office that there were four separate Turkish organisations at work in Azerbaijan: 7000 'Volunteers' under the command of Major Yusuf Ziya Bey, an agent of the CUP; the Turkish Bolsheviks who were in direct contact with the Istanbul government; Nuri Pasha with 15 Turkish officers in Daghestan; and Turkish political propagandists.[15] Among these groups, Nuri Pasha, Enver's brother, and Halil Pasha, Enver's uncle, actively participated in Azeri politics. The Turkish nationalists did not approve of the activities of Nuri Pasha, the Commander of the Caucasian Islamic Army in Azerbaijan, after he escaped from British detention in Batum.[16] However, they also skilfully manoeuvred politics in Azerbaijan with the help of the CUP leaders.

In December 1919, the Turkish nationalists contacted Halil Pasha to secure the strategic corridor (the area between Nakhichevan and Zangezur) linking Anatolia with Azerbaijan for the future flow of Soviet aid, and to this end he joined forces with the volunteers resisting Armenian rule over Nakhichevan.[17] Halil tried to assure Azerbaijani politicians that both Turkey and Azerbaijan would benefit from the advance of the Red Army, while the Reds would march against the rebels of Karabagh and then across Armenia to aid the Turks in Anatolia.[18] According to this understanding, Azerbaijan would be a bridge linking Moscow and Ankara rather than a barrier between the two transitional regimes.[19] The sudden *de facto* recognition of Azerbaijan's independence by the Allies in January 1920 made both sides more suspicious of the Allied plots in the region. In February, the British Foreign Office suspected that either a secret agreement or a military understanding had been made between Turkey and Azerbaijan to protect the independence and territorial integrity of Azerbaijan.[20] Moreover, in March the British political officer at Baku informed London that Mustafa Kemal had reached 'an agreement with Lenin to allow Bolsheviks free hand in North Caucasus and Azerbaijan in order to secure free passage of arms for him'.[21] This was, indeed, an accurate interpretation of the new Turkish policy towards Azerbaijan.

The GNA was ready to establish relations with the Bolsheviks against the Allied powers and to urge the Azerbaijani government to accept the Bolshevik regime.[22] In fact, two days before the Sovietisation of Azerbaijan, on 26 April 1920, 'The First Proposal of the Turkish GNA to the Soviet Government in Moscow', signed by Mustafa Kemal as chairman of the GNA, was sent to the Soviet government. In this letter, the basis of the new Turkish foreign policy towards the Bolsheviks and the South Caucasus was explained. The letter emphasised the following points:[23] (a) The GNA agreed to join the fight of the Bolshevik government against the imperialists for the emancipation of all oppressed peoples. (b) If the Bolshevik forces undertook military operations against Georgia to drive them into union with Moscow, the Ankara government promised to undertake military operations against expansionist Armenia, and to force Azerbaijan to enter into a union with Soviet Russia. (c) In order to protect Turkish national territory from foreign invasion and then to join the common cause against imperialism, the Ankara government had to stabilise its domestic politics. Therefore, they were appealing for Soviet financial aid, ammunition, war materials and medicine.

This letter, according to Gökay, was a 'manifestation of an unqualified guarantee of Turkish support [for] the Bolsheviks' campaign in the Caucasus'.[24] However, the Azeri historians' interpretation is different. They argue that Mustafa Kemal wanted to create a free corridor through Azerbaijan for Bolshevik aid.[25] I submit that Ankara's policy towards Azerbaijan was influenced by a combination of these two factors. It was directed towards putting Azerbaijan under Soviet control in order to gain Bolshevik financial and military assistance for the nationalist movement.[26]

After receiving Karabekir's telegram, which informed them that the Soviet control was established in Azerbaijan, the GNA decided to send a congratulatory telegram to the new Azeri government on 28 April.[27] The acceptance of the Sovietisation of Azerbaijan was a clear indication of new trends in Turkish foreign policy. First, the Turkish nationalists rejected the pan-Turkist, pan-Islamist and pan-Turanist policies of the CUP since these were not compatible with nationalist foreign policy. Their main goal was to secure the integrity of

Anatolian territories within the agreed borders of the National Pact. Second, the government in Ankara decided to transform traditional Ottoman–Russian animosity into regional co-operation. In this respect, the South Caucasus had become the subject of a bigger game, as a means of countering the influence of the Allied powers. Finally, and more importantly, the nationalists would also take advantage of the new understanding between Ankara and Moscow to solve the Armenian question, which had been the main challenge to the determination of Turkey's borders with Russia.

The insoluble Armenian question

In April 1920, a united Turkish–Russian Armenia seemed likely to come about when the Allies reached an agreement on the Armenian question at San Remo, the main points of which were: (a) to address an appeal to the United States government to accept a mandate for Armenia; (b) to ask President Wilson to arbitrate on the boundaries of Armenia whatever the US government decided on the subject of a mandate; (c) to establish the boundary between Armenia and Turkey to include the disputed Ottoman provinces – Erzurum, Trabzon, Van and Bitlis – in order to secure access to the sea for the independent state of Armenia.[28] In addition, the Allies knew that the security and even the existence of the new state would be difficult to maintain without military aid and they did not want to take on additional military responsibilities in the region.

Armenian historians consider the San Remo agreement to have been a 'dead letter' since the Allies did not want to provide military forces to establish Armenian control over such a large territory, given the fact that the Turkish forces in Eastern Anatolia would be a real threat to their existence.[29] In May 1920, the British Foreign Office wrote to Admiral Webb to inform the Armenian government that Britain would supply a certain quantity of arms if Armenia was resolute in maintaining its independence.[30] In addition, in the same month Wilson gladly accepted the request of the Supreme Council of the League of Nations to act as arbitrator for the Armenian borders so as to contribute to the welfare of the Armenian people.[31] Armenia had by this time been *de jure* recognised by the United States, Belgium, France, Britain, Italy, Chile, Argentina, Brazil and several other states.[32] Despite all these promising developments, the question of the American mandate would be invalidated when the US Senate 'rejected the Treaty of Versailles and membership in the League of Nations and refused to accept a Mandate to govern Armenia' in June 1920.[33] Irrespective of the rejection of the mandate, there remained the main consideration of the boundaries of Armenia on which the Allies felt compelled to decide.[34]

The Armenian question had been closely related to the Turkish settlement, and the recently constituted Ankara government was determined not to leave the resolution to the Allies. On 5 May, the first decision of the Ankara government in foreign relations was to send a delegation to Moscow. The official delegation under the leadership of Bekir Sami Bey, Minister for Foreign Affairs, and Yusuf Kemal Bey, Minister of Economy, left Ankara on 11 May 1920. The chief objective of this delegation was to establish diplomatic relations with Soviet Russia in order to gain Soviet recognition of the complete sovereignty and territorial integrity of Turkey as well as financial and military aid.[35]

Among the nationalist leaders, Karabekir was the first to recognise the importance of the eastern borders for the creation of a new Turkish state. He criticised Kemal's instructions to the delegation since the question of eastern boundaries was not mentioned.[36] On 9 May, he telegraphed Mustafa Kemal to urge the delegation to take with it the text of the 1918 treaties of Brest-Litovsk and Batum, which had provided for Turkish possession of Kars, Ardahan and Batum (the Treaty of Brest-Litovsk) and half of the Erivan *guberniia* (Batum treaty). In his opinion, the time was ripe for an offensive against Armenia with the entry of the Red Army into Transcaucasia. Karabekir warned that the establishment of Soviet rule in Armenia before the Turks moved would prevent the recovery of Kars and the other districts lost to the Russian Empire in 1878. In Karabekir's opinion, this possibility would also have negative consequences for the national movement: the Armenian problem would become chronic; the resistance forces in Anatolia would be demoralised; the Kurds would turn against the Turks; and Turkey's bonds with the Turkic and other Muslim peoples of the East would be damaged.[37]

In May 1919, General Osebyan took over Kars from the British forces on behalf of the Armenian government in Erivan.[38] At that time, Mustafa Kemal was not in favour of an early offensive against the Armenians. On 10 and 13 May, Kemal instructed Karabekir to hold the offensive until a definite understanding had been reached with the Bolsheviks. An attack on Armenia would trigger a reaction by the Allied powers. A counter attack by the Allies, especially the British, would be ruinous for the nationalist movement. They could not trust in Bolshevik support since a Turkish–Soviet agreement had not yet been reached. In addition, Kemal argued that the western front against the Greeks, and not the eastern, was the most critical at that moment. He also implied that Karabekir should be prepared to march to the western front.[39] In his reply on 15 May, Karabekir did not agree to transfer the XV Corps to the west and insisted that his forces had to stay in the east in order to protect the region from Armenian expansion and the still unknown real objective of the Bolsheviks. He argued that it would be safe to transfer most of the forces to the west after the Armenians had been crushed.[40] While Karabekir repeated his suggestion in May and June that they should attack Armenia, Mustafa Kemal preferred to await the Allies' proposals in the peace treaty. According to Karabekir, this was a futile policy given the fact that there were signs in Western newspapers that the future peace treaty would give İzmir to the Greeks and the eastern provinces to the Armenians.[41] Indeed, Armenian hopes for the future were high in the summer of 1920. But the Ankara government initiated the first official negotiations with the Moscow government to obstruct the Allied and Armenian plans, as will be discussed in the next section.

The use of modern diplomacy: the first Moscow meetings

The two newly emerging regimes of Ankara and Moscow were brought together by the need to establish stability and security in the South Caucasus. This common interest indicated the abandonment of traditional Russian–Ottoman policies in the east. Since they were aiming to transform the socio-political and economic structures of the imperial entities, they had to replace the principles and practices of the previous regimes in all respects. The arena of diplomacy provided the first signs of this change in Turkish foreign relations. For instance, as stated earlier the Ankara government's first decision was to establish diplomatic relations with Moscow. Given the fact that diplomatic negotiations in politics take place in order to achieve certain objectives, such as the 'identification of common interests and agreement on joint or parallel action in their pursuit; recognition of conflicting interests and agreements on compromise; or, more often than not, some combination of both', the Ankara government's decision reveals the new dimension of its transitional foreign policy.[42] The following analysis of Ankara–Moscow correspondence will show that the diplomatic relations were not only concerned with negotiation but also with the clarification of concerns between governments and the symbolic demonstration of their legitimacy.[43]

The first diplomatic success of Ankara government

In the first stage of correspondence, both sides expressed their interest in establishing negotiations and in agreeing on the general principles of a settlement in the east. As we saw earlier, Mustafa Kemal sent the first letter on 26 April 1920 in which the Turkish nationalists explained their willingness to take part in the struggle against Western imperialism. On 3 June, Chicherin replied to this letter in the following way.[44] Although the Moscow government had become acquainted with the main lines of nationalist policy, there were seven principles in question: (a) the declaration of Turkish independence; (b) the annexation to Turkey of essentially Turkish territories; (c) the declaration of the independence of Arabia and Syria; (d) that the peoples in Armenia, Kurdistan, Lazistan, the Batum area, and those where Turks and Arabs lived together should decide their own future, while refugees and emigrants should be allowed to return to their homes in order to participate in a referendum in these zones; (e) that all the rights which were accorded to minorities in the European states should be conceded to the minorities in the new Turkish territories; (f) that the question of the Turkish Straits should be entrusted to a conference to be held among the governments of the states that bordered upon the Black Sea; (g) that the Capitulations should be abolished.[45]

Clearly, this letter was the first diplomatic success for the Ankara government since the Bolshevik regime had recognised Turkish independence and the legitimacy of the GNA. However, the Turkish leaders were disappointed since there was no word of Russian financial and military aid, and Chicherin had emphasised the importance of other issues. The question of the Turkish Straits was put on the agenda in addition to the border problems between Turkey and Armenia. In a way, Chicherin's suggestion of Soviet mediation in regard to the settlement of Turkish–Armenian and Turkish–Iranian border disputes was a rejection of the Turkish proposal to undertake military operations against Armenia, which had been made to the Soviets in Mustafa Kemal's letter of 26 April 1920.[46]

At the second stage, the details of a settlement were suggested in Kemal's reply on 20 June 1920.[47] First, the GNA had received Chicherin's letter with great pleasure and emphasised that they would continue their struggle against the Allies, which prevented the Turks from implementing the mentioned principles. Second, they also accepted in principle Chicherin's recommendation to determine the Turkish–Armenian and Turkish–Iranian borders through Soviet mediation. Moreover, third, after receiving Chicherin's letter Ankara had postponed the military operations aimed at occupying *Elviye-i Selase* so as to stop the Armenian offensive in the region. Therefore, the Soviet suggestion of mediating in the Turkish–Armenian border dispute had to be put forward immediately. Fourth, the Turkish delegates, who were supposed to have established diplomatic relations with the Bolsheviks were waiting in Erzurum. The Soviet government would have to provide the necessary facilities in order to accelerate this process. Finally, the Turkish nation's continuing struggle against Western imperialism would bring the Russian and Turkish peoples together in a peaceful environment. Mustafa Kemal ended his letter by emphasising the importance of Turkish–Russian relations, which would be based on the security of both sides.[48]

This letter clearly emphasised the importance to Turkey of establishing diplomatic relations with the Bolsheviks. The Turkish Minister of Foreign Affairs, Bekir Sami, wrote the next letter to Chicherin on 23 June 1920. In this letter, Bekir Sami asked the assistance of the Soviet government in order to complete the Turkish delegation's journey to Moscow safely via Armenia. The reason behind this was that the Armenian occupation of transportation routes in the region was obstructing the Turkish delegation's journey to Moscow. The Soviets could send military forces to Nakhichevan and open the Turkish–Azeri railroad.[49] Bekir Sami also underlined the importance of Soviet mediation in solving the border disputes between Turkey, Armenia and Iran. Bekir Sami's delegation was authorised by the GNA to sign a friendship agreement with the Bolshevik government.[50] Therefore the delegation was looking forward to being in Moscow and the Turkish government would be equally glad to receive a Soviet delegation in Turkey.[51] Another letter, from Chicherin to Mustafa Kemal and dated 2 July 1920, indicated that the Soviet government was ready to send an ambassador to Turkey.[52] These letters indicated the willingness of both sides to initiate relations even if they were still hesitant about each other's intentions.

The disharmony of interests in the eastern affairs
Despite the diplomatic correspondence, on 8 July 1920 the GNA debated whether to establish relations with the Bolsheviks. While some members expressed their doubts about Bolshevik aims which, in their opinion, would not be compatible with the aims of the nationalist struggle and Islam, others argued that Bolshevism could be utilised for the service of their common cause against the West. Mustafa Kemal's reply to the two opposing statements was that the Ankara government's aim was to preserve the independence of the country and the people. In order to achieve this aim, they, without questioning the principles of Bolshevism, would co-operate with the Soviet government in order to obtain material help, arms and

money.[53] These debates indicated that co-operation with the Bolsheviks did not mean accepting the principles of communism, but was merely to obtain financial and military support from them by accepting the establishment of Soviet power in the South Caucasus.

The official negotiations between Ankara and Moscow, the first Moscow meetings, began when the Turkish delegation arrived in Moscow on 19 July.[54] The first meeting between the Turkish delegation and Chicherin was held on 24 July. However, at that time the Bolshevik government was preoccupied with preparations for the First Congress of the Peoples of the East that would take place in Baku in September, as will be examined later. While the Turkish delegation was waiting for three weeks before starting negotiations, the Treaty of Sèvres was signed on 10 August 1920.

In the meanwhile, the Turkish delegation had four important meetings with the Bolshevik leaders. The first meeting was with Chicherin on 13 August.[55] The Turkish side proposed to open a direct route between Ankara and Moscow through Armenia. Chicherin told the Turkish delegation that this route could not be opened because of a new agreement between the Armenians and the Bolsheviks. On 10 August 1920, the same day as the signing of the Treaty of Sèvres, an agreement between Soviet Russia and the Republic of Armenia was signed. The Soviet Union admitted full recognition of the independence of the Republic of Armenia as an independent state and both sides agreed that 'after cessation of all military hostilities by the negotiating parties, they must cease to concentrate military forces in the disputed areas or borders now under dispute'.[56] The Turkish side reminded Chicherin that the Armenian route was vital to receiving Soviet aid for the Turkish nationalists and that they would be prepared to open it using Turkish military forces. However, Chicherin rejected the idea.

The second meeting was held with Lenin on 14 August as a result of dissatisfaction with Chicherin's suggestions.[57] In this meeting, Lenin explained that the Bolshevik policy aimed to emancipate the Muslim peoples of the East and the Turkish nation from imperialism. The Turkish delegation expressed similar warm opinions towards the Bolsheviks and reminded Lenin of the importance of their financial aid to the nationalist movement. However, they also expressed their disappointment about the Soviet–Armenian treaty, which gave the 'Nakhichevan–Şahtahtı' railway line to the Armenians.[58] At that time, this was the only railway connecting Ankara and Moscow. Lenin explained why it was necessary to sign an agreement with Armenia, and then interestingly admitted that the Bolsheviks had also realised their mistake in giving this railway line to the Armenians. They were trying to correct it.[59] The minutes of a speech by Yusuf Kemal, a member of the Turkish delegation during the Moscow meetings, at a secret meeting of the GNA confirm this account.[60]

At the third meeting, on 24 August, a Soviet committee and the Turkish delegation prepared the first draft of the Turkish–Soviet friendship agreement and presented it to Chicherin. This laid the basis for the Moscow agreement of March 1921.[61] The fourth meeting took place on 28 August at which Chicherin's suggestions surprised the Turkish side. Chicherin argued that the borders, particularly in the first article, which had been accepted in the National Pact, needed to be re-determined according to the ethnic composition of the region. In specific terms, in accordance with every nation's right of self-determination, the Armenians would be free to decide their future. Moreover, Soviet aid to the Turkish government was dependent on one condition: the old Armenian towns, Van and Bitlis, had to be returned to Armenia. In Bekir Sami's view, these conditions were unacceptable; the Soviet government was treating the Turkish nationalists just as the Allied powers had treated them. Under these conditions, the Turkish delegation could not continue negotiations without consulting the GNA.[62] Although a draft agreement was signed by Bekir Sami with the Bolsheviks on 30 August 1920, the negotiations were cut short.[63] Bekir Sami decided to stay in Moscow and sent Yusuf Kemal to Ankara.

At that time, although Bekir Sami was sending reports to Ankara through telegrams via Trabzon, his reports reached the GNA a few weeks later due to the difficulty of communication. For instance, the Ankara government was informed about the Turkish delegation's meeting with Lenin two weeks after the fact, on 29 August 1920 and about the signing of a draft agreement at the beginning of September.[64] The Treaty of Sèvres played a significant role in deciding the future of relations with the Bolsheviks. Therefore, the next section will aim to understand how this treaty helped to harmonise Ankara and Moscow's interests.

Catalyst for Turkish–Bolshevik rapprochement: the Treaty of Sèvres

The post-war peace settlements, known as the Treaty of Versailles, were imposed upon Germany, the Austro-Hungarian and Ottoman Empires, and Bulgaria.[65] However, the treaty signed in the Hall of Mirrors in the Palace of Versailles on 28 June related only to Germany. 'There were other peace treaties distributed round Paris, until the stock of adjacent palaces was almost exhausted. Neuilly with Bulgaria, and St German with Austria in 1919; Trianon with Hungary, and Sèvres with Turkey in 1920. These are the treaties usually denounced under the heading of "Versailles".'[66] Although the Versailles system was no more than the settlement of details of the various frontiers, it implicitly accepted the emergence of new states. 'Bulgaria was the only one which had a real continuity with the old state of the same name. Austria, Hungary, and Turkey were as much new states as Czechoslovakia, Rumania, or Yugoslavia, though they were treated as enemies.'[67]

The Treaty of Sèvres was signed on 10 August 1920 between Britain, France, Italy, Japan, Armenia, Belgium, Greece, the Hejaz, Poland, Portugal, Rumania, the Serbo-Croat-Slovene state, and Czecho-Slovakia on the one part and Turkey on the other.[68] There was an interesting dilemma in the Turkish case since Turkey was not regarded as a new state. Although the peace treaty was signed with the Istanbul government, the participating side was defined as Turkey not the Ottoman Empire. As stated in Chapter 4, the Ottoman Empire had to sign the Mudros Armistice in 1918 which also named the signing part as Turkey. This implied that Turkey and the Ottoman Empire were regarded as having the same identity by the Western powers, and also that the Allies did not accept the Ankara government as the representative of the new Turkish state. The content of the Treaty, which consisted of 433 articles, is self-explanatory as to what the Allied powers designed for the Turkish state.[69] Because it was such a detailed document, most scholars usually just summarise its political clauses (Article 36 to 139).[70] In sum, the treaty gave south-eastern Anatolia to France, and Thrace and İzmir (Smyrna) to Greece. More importantly, an independent Armenia was established, while an autonomous Kurdish state was created in Eastern Anatolia. A neutral international commission would control Istanbul and the Turkish Straits (see Map 3: Turkey's partition according to the Treaty of Sèvres).

The Treaty of Sèvres was treated by Turkey as null and void from the beginning since it was not ratified by the Istanbul government and rejected by the Ankara government.[71] It had a major influence on Turkish foreign policy, which draws our attention to the close relationship between the question of the Turkish state and foreign policy.

The unintended consequences of Treaty of Sèvres Turkish foreign policy
Domestically, the treaty underlined the importance of finding a solution to the disintegrating Ottoman state question. Despite the Allied powers' expectations of bringing a final solution to the problem of 'the sick of man of Europe', it produced further complications. As a British Foreign Office report which subsequently described the Treaty of Sèvres 'as the origin of Turkish nationalism' suggested, it proved to be the trigger which set off the nationalists towards the Bolsheviks.[72] Thus an examination of the treaty's influence on Turkish politics will highlight the interrelation between domestic and foreign policies. The implications of the Treaty of Sèvres for the Turkish 'state question' were profound.

With respect to the main principles of modern statehood, there would have been no sovereign Turkish state at the beginning of the twentieth century if the Turks had accepted the treaty's conditions. In terms of territoriality, the Turks stood to inherit a small piece of land in the middle of Anatolia if the Allied powers implemented the conditions of the treaty. In addition, according to the Three Party Agreements (*Accord Tripartite*), which were also signed on 10 August 1920 between Britain, France and Italy, two-thirds of Anatolia was to be divided between France and Italy. In specific terms, they defined the troubled areas in order to recognise the special interests of Italy in Southern Anatolia and of France in Cilicia and the western part of Kurdistan bordering on Syria.[73] In this plan, 'New Turkey' consisted of four vilayets (Kastomonu, Sivas, Ankara and Bursa) in Anatolia (see 7 in Map 3). There were no industrial or trade elites in this 'mini state'. The composition of society was based on peasants. If it were necessary to name the new state according to its demographic character, it would have been a 'peasant state'. There was no clear notion of a 'national homeland' for the Turkish people. Thus, the creation of a true Turkish nation-state was not foreseeable in the short term. To the Turks, this policy was a result of the Allied powers' plan to create a 'semi-colonised peasant state'.[74]

As Stanford Shaw and Ezel Kural Shaw ask: 'What of the Ottoman state that was left? Additional provisions made it clear that Turkish sovereignty would

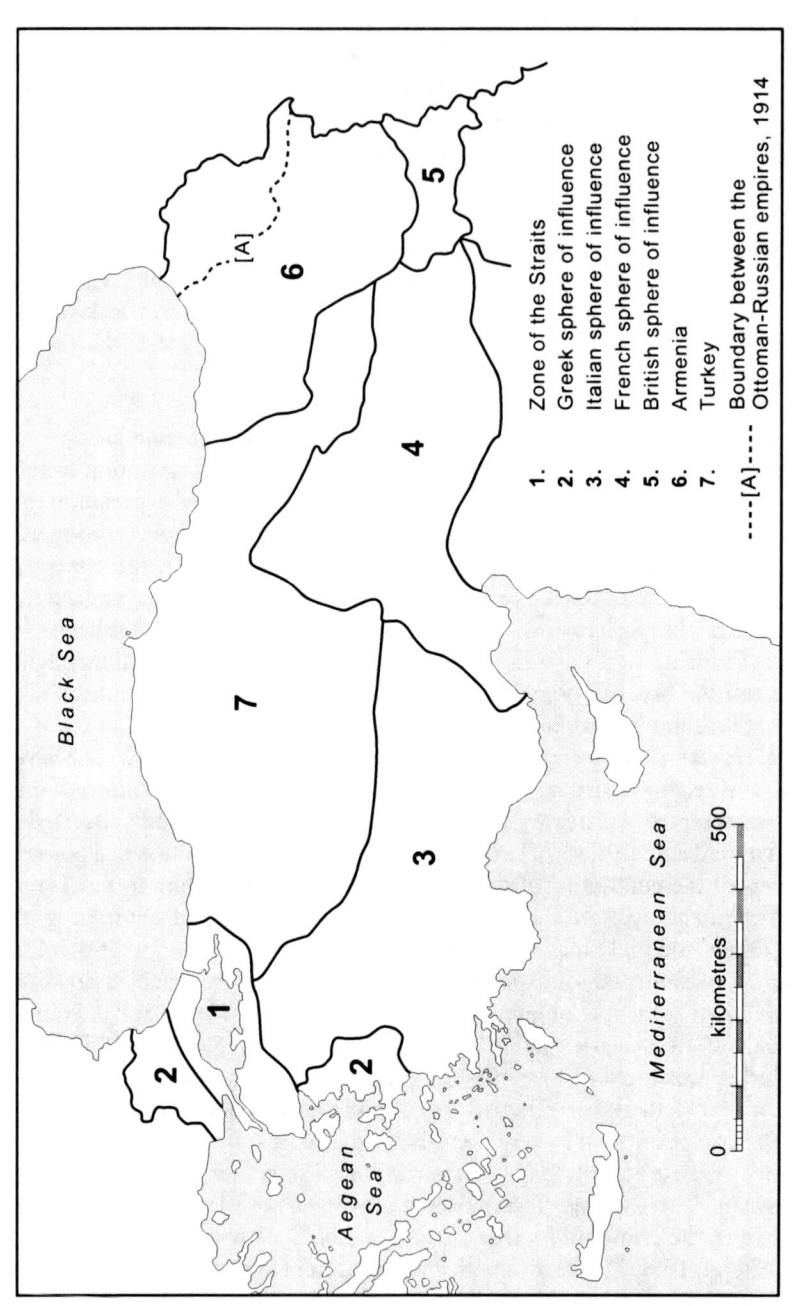

1.   Zone of the Straits
2.   Greek sphere of influence
3.   Italian sphere of influence
4.   French sphere of influence
5.   British sphere of influence
6.   Armenia
7.   Turkey

----[A]----   Boundary between the
            Ottoman-Russian empires, 1914

Map 3. Turkey's partition according to the Treaty of Sèvres, 1920

be very limited.'[75] In reality, Turkish sovereignty became an empty concept in practice. The Ottoman government would have a limited army, no more than 50,000 men, with restricted armaments as well as a restricted navy. The Ottoman army would also be subject to the advice of foreign officers. The Ottoman government would exercise little control over its own budget, taxes, customs duties, currency, and public loans. Not only were the Capitulations restored, but also a new Allied commission was established to supervise and regulate the public debt. In addition, the Ottomans agreed to make extensive concessions to non-Muslim subjects. Thus, the remaining Ottoman state was put under the military, political and financial control of the Allied powers. Neither the nationalist leaders nor the Turkish people could accept these limits on the national cause.

The Treaty of Sèvres was indeed a vindictive document which considered neither the needs of the Turks nor the political or demographic realities of the Ottoman Empire. It represented the demands of the Allies first and those of the Greeks and Armenians second. The harsh treatment of the Turks in the treaty was an indication of Allied prejudice and self-interest. Britain, France and Italy easily neglected ethical matters such as self-determination and Wilson's Fourteen Points,[76] since all wanted to gain the territories of the disappearing Ottoman Empire. It was a warning that the Allies had no intention of accepting the principle of national self-determination for the Turkish people of Anatolia. The Treaty of Sèvres, like the Treaty of Versailles with Germany, was the result of Allied concerns with post-war European order. 'Both were punitive treaties, imposed by victors who adopted a lofty moral tone to hide self-interest. Both treaties contained economic clauses intended to ensure that the vanquished would never rise again. Both limited the military strength and territory of the loser. However, the Sèvres treaty was the harsher.'[77] But the consequences of these treaties did not meet Allied expectations.

The first influence of the Treaty of Sèvres was seen in the nationalist foreign policy towards Armenia. In April 1920, the Turkish national movement consolidated its power in domestic politics with the opening of the GNA and was determined to save the country from 'foreigners – the British, the French, the Greeks and the Armenians'.[78] Although the Turkish nationalists did not adopt a xenophobic attitude towards the British and the French, they developed a strong feeling of 'otherness' towards the Greeks and the Armenians, with whom they lived together within the *millet* system for centuries. The Turks also anticipated the Greek and Armenian demands regarding Anatolian territories. As explained earlier, the diplomatic negotiations between Ankara and Moscow had already been initiated and the first Moscow meeting was halted as a result of the problems regarding Armenia.

More importantly, the indirect occupation of the eastern provinces by the Armenians through the articles of the Treaty of Sèvres would be the last straw: the establishment of an independent Armenian state in Anatolia was not acceptable to the national cause. Turkish foreign policy towards Armenia from that time on would be based on the rejection of giving up any Turkish soil to the Armenians. Moreover, the Armenians considered the stillborn Treaty of Sèvres, which in principle gave Armenia a large part of north-eastern Anatolia (the boundaries would be drawn by President Wilson), only a small consolation.[79] After this, the GNA designed a dual policy to solve the Armenian question. On the one hand, they would establish diplomatic relations with the Bolsheviks to decide the border between the two new regimes; on the other hand, they would pursue a military campaign against the Armenians in order to force them to reject the Treaty of Sèvres. Consequently, while Armenian territorial claims on Eastern Anatolia brought Lenin and Mustafa Kemal together, the treaty became a catalyst for the Turkish–Bolshevik rapprochement.[80]

The second influence of the treaty on Turkish foreign policy was on the decision of nationalist leaders in accepting the Bolsheviks as a natural ally against Allied plans. When the treaty was signed by the Istanbul government, the final disagreement between the Ankara and Istanbul governments occurred. The Ankara government rejected the Treaty of Sèvres on 19 August 1920 and denounced the Ottoman representatives who signed it, including the grand vizier, as traitors.[81] This reaction to the treaty in domestic politics consolidated the authority of the Ankara government against that of Istanbul, whose solution to the Turkish state question relied on the Allies. As explained in the previous chapter, the principles of the nationalist movement were defined by the National Pact, and its foreign policy had to serve the political, military and ideological independence of the state. The only support to this end could come from the Muslim countries of the East and from the newly emerged regime in Soviet Russia. At a GNA session, on 14 August 1920, Mustafa Kemal described the need to establish relations with the Bolsheviks and summarised the reasons for the Turkish offensive on the eastern front in June as the aim to regain the districts of Kars, Ardahan and Batum, since they had been given to Turkey according to the treaties of Brest–Litovsk and Batum.

However, Chicherin's letter of 16 June suggested mediation over the Turkish–Armenian and Turkish–Persian borders. Consequently, Mustafa Kemal ordered a halt to the Turkish offensive on 20 June. In order to explain the importance of Bolshevik co-operation, he emphasised that the two newly constituted governments were drawn together by mutual hostility against the Western powers and had joined hands to reach a settlement in the South Caucasus. In particular, the government in Ankara expected that the Bolsheviks would support Turkish demands on the Armenian question. The Bolshevik preparation for the Baku Congress was a sign of their new foreign policy towards the East. Although the Ankara government was not officially invited to the congress, a decision was taken to send some Turkish representatives. Kemal made it clear that the GNA had never considered accepting the principles of Bolshevism, but that it was determined to utilise any support which could help in bringing the national cause to a successful conclusion. Then, in answering a question from another member of the assembly, he stated that the official negotiations with the Bolsheviks had began but the Turkish delegation's reports on their progress had not yet reached Ankara.[82]

The third influence of the imposed Treaty of Sèvres, and maybe the most important in the long term, was the misperception of Western states' interests in relation to Turkey: the prejudice of the Allies against the Turkish people created a distrust towards the West. The Turkish leaders became very sensitive about sovereignty in the early years of the Turkish Republic. As a result, the protection of Turkey's territorial integrity has become an issue of concern in Turkish politics ever since.[83] The Turks have never forgotten that the Allies wanted to create independent Armenian and Kurdish states in Anatolia. As a result of this misperception, every time the West interfered in the Kurdish or Armenian questions, the Turks felt they were being haunted by the shadow of the Treaty of Sèvres. For example, in contemporary politics, every time the international media is preoccupied with the Kurdish question, because of the events in northern Iraq and Syria, Turkish leaders remind the nation that the West wants to divide up Turkey by implementing explicitly the Treaty of Sèvres.[84]

Rejection of the Treaty of Sèvres: military advance towards Armenia

The creation of an independent Armenia in the Eastern provinces of Anatolia was not acceptable to the Turkish nationalists. From the Turkish point of view, finding a solution to the Armenian question would not be possible unless Armenia abandoned its claims to the six eastern provinces of Anatolia.[85] As stated earlier, Kemal and Karabekir were deciding on the right time for an attack on Armenia in May and June.

Meanwhile, the Dashnak leaders underestimated the actual Turkish military strength in the area and occupied Olti and the Araxes Valley in June 1920.[86] It was a desperate attempt by the Armenians since the possibility of a mandate had faded with the withdrawal of the last Allied forces from the region.[87] 'In the anticipation of the boundaries that were to be drawn by President Wilson, the Armenian government tried to establish control over all land up to the pre-war frontier in order to be prepared to advance into whatever sector of Western Armenia would be awarded to the Republic'.[88] Ankara immediately required the Armenians to withdraw from Olti and retire behind the frontier drawn by the Treaty of Brest–Litovsk.[89] The Armenian Foreign Office Secretary, M. Ter-akopian, sent a telegram to Karabekir on 28 July 1920 expressing both his government's refusal to comply with Turkish demands and their desire to establish good neighbourly relations with Turkey. On the one hand, he criticised the foreign policy of the Turkish nationalists towards Armenia that had accepted the Brest-Litovsk and Batum treaties as a basis for negotiations. From the Armenian point of view, they were continuing to follow the aims of the Ottoman Empire by not recognising the existence of Armenia or the right of self-determination of Armenian nation. On the other hand, he emphasised that the Armenians would not renounce rights over the Armenian provinces in Anatolia, the boundaries of which would be settled by President Wilson.[90] The signature of the Treaty of Sèvres was the last straw which led the Turks to seek to solve the Armenian question on the basis of Turkish nationalism. On 10 August, the Armenians also signed an agreement with the Bolsheviks. According to Dennis, the new Soviet 'policy caught Armenia just at the time when Kemal was pushing his attack on the Turkish provinces. It seemed as though Armenia was to be overwhelmed on all sides.'[91]

As explained earlier, the first Moscow meetings were taking place at that time and the reports of Bekir Sami on the results of these negotiations reached Ankara on 29 August. The GNA held a session to evaluate the progress of relations with the Bolsheviks on 2 September.[92] Mustafa Kemal criticised the responses of Bolshevik leaders to the Turkish demands. This made them suspicious of Bolshevik aims towards the nationalist movement. It seemed that Moscow had the intention of using Turkey as a trump card against the West, while putting the nationalist movement off to gain time. While they established Soviet control in Azerbaijan, the Bolshevik leaders made it very clear that they would solve the Armenian question for the benefit of the Armenians. Consequently, the GNA took a decision to make the Bolsheviks sign an agreement in accordance with Turkish demands and make provision for financial aid. Based on this decision, the GNA issued a directive to the Turkish delegation in Moscow.[93]

Although the decisions on the conduct of foreign affairs were taken by the GNA, the Ankara government did not have a cohesive decision-making system at this time. Kazım Karabekir was a dissident voice who criticised Mustafa Kemal's conduct of Russian and Armenian affairs. As we saw earlier, differences between the two leaders began to develop when the decision was taken on the dispatch of the Turkish delegation to Moscow in May 1920.[94] Moreover, there were other competing actors – Enver Pasha and Mustafa Suphi – who challenged the authority of Mustafa Kemal in establishing relations with the Bolsheviks, a subject to which I shall return later. The fundamental differences between Kemal and Karabekir came to the surface on the means of solving the Armenian question. While Mustafa Kemal was exploring the possibility of a diplomatic solution to the Armenian question, Kazım Karabekir encouraged the Ankara government to take action by military means. At the beginning of September, the Armenians miscalculated the Turkish position following the Treaty of Sèvres and tried to establish control over the border districts of the pre-war frontier between Erivan and Kars.[95] From the Armenian point of view, the Turkish military offensive against Armenia was irrational at a time 'when the Greek armies had occupied the major cities of western Anatolia, the British navy patrolled the Black Sea, and Soviet Russia was still occupied with the Poles and General Wrangel'.[96] But contrary to these Armenian calculations, Kazım Karabekir made a surprise attack upon the Armenian forces that had been holding Olti since June.[97] The Armenians then applied to the Soviet government to protect the integrity of Armenia against the Turks. 'On 10 September 1920 the Armenian Social Democratic Party "GNCh.AK" sent a letter to Lenin accusing Karabekir and Kemal in person of pursuing a "policy of genocide", similar to that of the CUP in 1915, with the aim of the total extermination of the Armenian nation.'[98] According to Gökay, there is no evidence in the Soviet archives as to whether the Bolsheviks intended to intervene to stop the Turkish offensive. Yet they did not provide immediate protection for the Armenians.[99]

When the Armenian offensive began, although Karabekir was still expecting Ankara's permission to attack Armenia, he had decided independently to seize the Soğanlı passes between Sarıkamış and Kars on 13 September.[100] Meanwhile, Yusuf Kemal, a Turkish delegate at the Moscow meetings, arrived at Trabzon and sent a copy of the draft agreement with the Bolsheviks and Bekir Sami's report to Ankara by telegram on 18 September.[101] The GNA was not informed that Chicherin had proposed the return of Van and Bitlis to Armenia. Although there is no direct evidence in Turkish sources, this proposal probably influenced Kemal's decision to start his military offensive against the Armenians. It was far from being a coincidence when Kemal informed Karabekir in a cipher on 20 September 1920 that permission to attack Armenia had been granted in order to solve the Armenian question. Following Kemal's next order to start the military operation against Armenia, Karabekir occupied Sarıkamış on 29 September.[102] Clearly, the Turkish nationalists had chosen the Armenian theatre not only as a sign of their determination to reject the Treaty of Sèvres but also as a final warning to the Bolsheviks to solve the Armenian question by its own means.

Despite the Armenian request for Bolshevik protection against the Turks, the Bolsheviks did not go beyond diplomatic action. The Soviet government would provide Soviet military aid to Armenia if the Armenian government accepted Soviet arbitration to fix the frontiers between Armenia and Turkey. 'The offer was rejected; indeed according to Soviet sources, the Armenian government was at that very moment inviting the Georgian government to join in common action against the Bolsheviks.'[103] According to British documents, on 13 October 1920 the Soviet government officially demanded free transit for Russian troops across Armenia to Turkey and also the renunciation of the Treaty of Sèvres by the Armenian government.[104] Except for British sources, there is no evidence to prove these claims, but diplomatic relations between Ankara and Moscow were certainly progressing. For instance, the first official Soviet mission arrived in Ankara on 9 November 1920.[105] Meanwhile, Yusuf Kemal also arrived in Ankara and attended a secret session of the GNA on 16 November. He presented a copy of the initialled draft agreement and summarised the progress of the Moscow meetings. In a lengthy statement, he emphasised that the biggest debate between the two sides concerned the determination of the Turkish–Armenian border and the future of Kars, Ardahan and Batum.[106] On the same day, 16 November, Mustafa Kemal sent a telegram to Bekir Sami instructing him that the following decision had been taken by the GNA: the Ankara government would not give up Van and Bitlis, where the Armenians were not in a majority; and it accepted that the Ottoman Armenians could return to the provinces they had inhabited before the deportation. Kemal instructed Bekir Sami to arrange a meeting with Chicherin to announce this decision. Bekir Sami was authorised to sign the initial draft agreement on behalf of the GNA if Chicherin accepted the Ankara government's new decision.[107] Three days later, 22 October 1920, Mustafa Kemal addressed a telegram to Chicherin in which he to referred Chicherin's letter of 3 June and expressed the view that

> The high moral authority of the government of RSFSR among the toilers of Europe and the love of the Muslim world for the Turkish nation give us the assurance that our close alliance will suffice to unite against the imperialists of the west all those who have hitherto upheld their power through a subservience based on inertia and ignorance.[108]

This letter indicated that the relations between Ankara, as the representative of the 'oppressed Muslim peoples of Asia', and Moscow, as leader of 'the workers of Europe', could take a new direction on the basis of 'a bargain that neither ally would encroach on the preserve of the other'.[109] The new understanding between the two sides would reach its peak with the Sovietisation of Armenia in December 1920, as will be discussed in Chapter 6. Furthermore, the use of the Muslim world in finding a common ground with the Bolsheviks indicates the paradoxical relationship between Islam and secularism during the Turkish transition to modernity. This point will be further elaborated in the Conclusion.

Meanwhile, two important events between September and December directly influenced the further direction of relations: the participation of Turkey in the Baku Congress as the First Congress of the Peoples of the East, and the organisation of the first Turkish communists under the leadership of Mustafa Suphi in Russia. Both had the potential to provide the Bolsheviks with different options.

Concluding remarks

It was argued in Chapter 2 that there are two important implications of modernity for transitional states: the nation-state is the most prominent political form of modernity, and there is a direct relation between modernity and identity construction. The analysis in Chapter 3 focused on the former outcome by examining the emergence of Turkish nationalism as a modern ideology which aimed to transform the Ottoman imperial state into a nation-state. The National Pact declared the goals of the nationalist movement in terms of gaining the sovereignty of state and demarcating the national borders. These goals, theoretically, reflected the basic requirements of modern statehood: territory, government, sovereignty and nation. First, a provisional government was established with the opening of the GNA in Ankara, which filled the authority vacuum in domestic politics. Its first decision in foreign policy was to initiate relations with the Bolsheviks. The nationalist leaders recognised the importance of Russian co-operation in determining the Turkish–Armenian border, which had been problematic since the Ottoman–Russian war of 1878. The demarcation of national borders was given priority by the Ankara government since they aimed to construct a new territorial political unit.

Having stated that the goals of Turkish domestic policy were structured by the main principles of modern statehood, this chapter explained how the goals of foreign policy were modified accordingly. Hence, an explicit connection between domestic and foreign policies is examined as the fourth dimension of transitional foreign policy in this chapter. The acceptance of Soviet control in Azerbaijan by the Ankara government gave the first indication of a radical break between the nationalist policies and the CUP's imperial designs in the South Caucasus. The Ankara government pursued a pragmatic foreign policy by utilising the Sovietisation of Azerbaijan, since the stabilisation of regional security was important for both transitional regimes. The correspondence between Kemal and Lenin was examined to clarify the concerns of two regimes, which, although different, were both in transition. Ankara initiated the first diplomatic negotiations with Moscow regarding the future of the region but the disagreement on the determination of the Turkish–Armenian border brought these negotiations to a halt.

During the establishment of relations with Moscow, the differences between Karabekir and Kemal particularly indicated that there were competing voices in Turkish foreign policy-making. The examination of correspondence between the nationalist leaders – Kemal, Karabekir and Bekir Sami – showed that foreign policy decisions were not taken by one person, unlike Ottoman foreign policy-making under Enver Pasha's control. Furthermore, the influence of the Treaty of Sèvres on Turkish foreign policy was emphasised as a good example of the overlapping goals in both domestic and foreign policies. The creation of an independent Armenian state in Eastern Anatolia was not acceptable to the national cause. The rejection of this treaty by the Ankara government was interpreted as a sign of its determination to consolidate the authority of the GNA in foreign affairs and to solve the 'Armenian question' by its own means. The GNA gave permission to Karabekir to attack the Armenians. That is why Armenian territorial demands in the six Ottoman provinces paradoxically created the biggest obstacle for the emerging Turkish state within the determined borders of the National Pact while bringing the nationalists and the Bolsheviks together in the east. The determination of the border in Eastern Anatolia between the two governments in Ankara and Moscow became crucial, and this created the need to re-start the diplomatic negotiations. The result – the second Moscow meetings – will be examined in Chapter 7 and the Turkish question in the Baku Congress in the next one. This congress was the first international platform in which the Bolsheviks explicitly spelled out their support for the Turkish nationalists, in spite of their bourgeois character, instead of Islamists and communists.

Notes

1 The Azerbaijanis have been a people divided between the Iranian (southern) and the Russian (northern) Azerbaijans since the signing of the Treaty of Turkmanchay in 1828. The future of the two Azerbaijani peoples on both sides of the Araxes River would take different routes in history. David B. Nisman, *The Soviet Union and Iranian Azerbaijan: The Use of Nationalism for Political Penetration*, London, Westview Press, 1987, pp. 13–14.

2 Musa Qasimov, *Azerbaycan-Türkiye Diplomatik-Siyasi Münasebetleri (Aprel 1920-ci il – dekabr 1922-ci il)*, Baki, Mutercim Nesriyyati, 1998, p. 8. Qasimov argues that there were two main reasons for this period being neglected in the Soviet Union: Azerbaijani independence between 1918 and 1920 was intentionally not mentioned during the Soviet era and, as a result of this policy, the Soviet archives were closed to researchers until the collapse of the Soviet Union. Ibid., p. 12.

3 Tadeusz Swietochowski, *Russia and Azerbaijan: A Borderland in Transition*, New York, Columbia University Press, 1995, p. 85.

4 Qasimov, *Azerbaycan-Türkiye*, p. 7.

5 Despite the contradictory nature of the two pro-Turkish groups (the nationalist Musavat Party and the Islamist Ittihad Party), the Musavat Party saw the

Turkish presence as a way of protecting Azerbaijani independence against Russian domination.

6 There were some obstacles to the survival of independence. First of all, while the new Azerbaijani Republic was a good example of a colonial country having unexpectedly gained its independence, it lacked the experience of indigenous statehood. In order to create the institutional structure of statehood, the Azeri leaders had adopted the 'preindependence administrative machinery'. But the main difficulty was the shortage of human resources to staff these institutions. The independent Azerbaijani Republic also lacked the tradition of military service from which the Muslims had been exempt during the Russian rule. Swietochowski, *Russia and Azerbaijan*, pp. 78–79. After the withdrawal of the Ottoman troops with the Armistice of Mudros the Turkish 'military officers' stayed in Azerbaijan to stiffen the army. However, in 1919, the Turks were not in a position to do anything for Azerbaijan. Public Records Office, Kew, London, FO371/3664/152026, Report on the Situation in Transcaucasia, Admiral de Robeck, dated 4 November 1919.

7 Alfred L.P. Dennis, *The Foreign Policies of Soviet Russia*, London, J.M. Dent & Sons Ltd., 1924, p. 207.

8 Public Records Office, Kew, London, FO371/4931/E409/1/58, Telegram from Mr Wardrop, No. 23, dated 19 January 1921; FO371/4931/E410/1/58, Telegram from Mr Wardrop, No. 24, dated 20 January 1921; *Papers Relating to the Foreign Relations of the United States [PRFRUS], 1920, Vol. III*, Washington, US Government Printing Office 1920, p. 778; Firuz Kazemzadeh, *The Struggle for Transcaucasia (1917–1921)*, New York, 1951, p. 268.

9 Public Records Office, Kew, London, FO371/6269/E 8378/8378/58, outline of Events in Transcaucasia from the beginning of the Russian revolution in the summer of 1917 to April 1921.

10 Richard G. Hovannisian, *The Republic of Armenia: From London to Sèvres, February–August 1920, Vol. III*, Berkeley, CA, University of California Press, 1996, pp. 175–176.

11 Ibid., p. 176.

12 Swietochowski, *Russia and Azerbaijan*, p. 93.

13 Hovannisian, *The Republic of Armenia, Vol. III*, pp. 181–182; Swietochowski, *Russia and Azerbaijan*, p. 94; E.H. Carr, *The Bolshevik Revolution: 1917–1923, Vol. III*, London, Penguin Books, 1966, p. 350; D. Cameron Watt, ed., *British Documents on Foreign Affairs: Reports and Papers from the Foreign Office Confidential Print [BDFA], Vol. III*, University Publications of America, 1984, p. 99, Doc. 75.

14 Kazemzadeh, *The Struggle for Transcaucasia*, p. 285.

15 Public Records Office, Kew, London, FO371/3673/170790, Report on Political Situation in Azerbaijan, Mr. Wardrop, 20 December 1920. However, two days later, in the following despatch Colonel Stokes informs the Foreign Office that 'the "Volunteers" mentioned are Azerbaijanis and Turks but are officered by Turkish Officers … The Azerbaijan government is unaware that the "Volunteers" have any Bolshevik tendencies. Nuri Pasha is working in Daghestan in the interests of the Bolsheviks.' Public Records Office, Kew, London, FO371/3673/170794, Report on Turkish activities in Azerbaijan, Mr Wardrop, dated 23 December 1920.

16 Kazım Karabekir, *Nutuk ve Karabekir'den Cevaplar, Vol. 4*, Istanbul, Emre Yayınları, 1997, p. 1058.

17 İsmail Musayev, *Azerbaycan-Türkiye İlişkİleri (1917–1922 yillari)*, Baku, Baku Üniversitesi Yayınevi, 1998, p. 23.

18 Qasimov, *Azerbaycan-Türkiye*, p. 26.

19 Swietochowski, *Russia and Azerbaijan*, p. 87.
20 Public Records Office, Kew, London, FO371/4933/E2055/1/58, Report on understanding between Azerbaijan and Turkish nationalists, Admiral de Robeck, No. 233, dated 15 March 1920; FO371/4934/E2730/1/58, Report on Situation in Azerbaijan and Dagestan, Mr Wardrop, No. 87-Secret, dated 8 March 1920. Neither in British nor in Turkish documents is there evidence of an official agreement between the Ottoman and Azerbaijani governments. However, in the British documents there is a copy of the alleged Turkish–Azerbaijani Treaty which was published in a newspaper extract, *The Near East News*, FO371/4950/E4928/36/58.
21 Public Records Office, Kew, London, FO371/4933/E2157/1/58, Telegram from Mr Wardrop, Tiflis, No. 144 Cypher, 12 March 1920.
22 Karabekir, *Nutuk ve, Vol. 10*, p. 3160.
23 Karabekir, *Nutuk ve, Vol. 1*, pp. 79–80. See the original document in Ottoman Turkish, Karabekir, *Nutuk ve, Vol. 11*, p. 3360, Doc. 203; See also *Atatürk'un Tamim, Telgraf ve Beyannameleri* [*ATTB*], *Vol. IV*, Atatürk Kültür, Dil ve Tarih Yüksek Kurumu, Atatürk Araştırma Merkezi, Ankara, Türk Tarih Kurumu Basımevi, 1991, p. 318, Doc. 305.
24 Bülent Gökay, *A Clash of Empires: Turkey between Russian Bolshevism and British Imperialism, 1918–1923*, London, Tauris Academic Studies, 1997, p. 80.
25 Qasimov, *Azerbaycan-Türkiye*, p. 26.
26 Ibid., p. 27; Hovannisian, *The Republic of Armenia, Vol. III*, p. 177.
27 Osman Okyar, *Milli Mücadele Döneminde Türk-Sovyet İlişkİlerinde Mustafa Kemal (1920–1921)*, Ankara, Türkiye İş Bankası Kültür Yayınları, 1998, p. 71.
28 *PRFRUS, Vol. III*, pp. 780–782.
29 George A. Bournoutian, *A History of the Armenian People, Vol. II: 1500 A.D. to the Present*, Costa Mesa, CA, Mazda Publishers, 1994, p. 143.
30 Public Records Office, Kew, London, FO371/4937/E4814/1/58, Telegram from Commander Luke, No. 242-Very Urgent, dated 12 May 1920.
31 *PRFRUS, Vol. III*, p. 783.
32 Bournoutian, *A History of the Armenian People*, p. 145.
33 David Fromkin, *A Peace to End All Peace: Creating the Modern Middle East, 1914–1922*, London, Penguin Books, 1989, p. 533.
34 Public Records Office, Kew, London, FO371/4957/E6297/134/58, from Mr Aneurin Williams, British Armenian Committee, Frontiers of the Independent Armenia, dated 10 June 1920.
35 Mustafa Kemal Atatürk, Speech delivered at Angora, 15–20 October 1927, English Translation, Leipzig, 1929, p. 396; Ivar Spector, *The Soviet Union and the Muslim World, 1917–1958*, Seattle, University of Washington Press, 1959, p. 69.
36 Kazım Karabekir, *İstiklal Harbimiz, Vol. II*, Istanbul, Emre Yayınları, 1993, p. 50.
37 Ibid., pp. 10–14; Richard G. Hovannisian, *The Republic of Armenia: Between Crescent and Sickle, Partition and Sovietisation, Vol. IV*, Berkeley, CA, University of California Press, 1996, pp. 145–146.
38 Akdes N. Kurat, *Türkiye ve Rusya*, Ankara, Sevinç Matbaası, 1990, p. 588.
39 Karabekir, *İstiklal Harbimiz, Vol. II*, pp. 23–24; Hovannisian, *The Republic of Armenia, Vol. IV*, p. 147.
40 Karabekir, *İstiklal Harbimiz, Vol. II*, p. 25.
41 Ibid., p. 40.
42 G. R. Berridge, *International Politics: States, Power and Conflict since 1945*, New York, Prentice Hall/Harvester Wheatsheaf, 1997, p. 184.

43 Ibid., p.186.
44 Although the actual date of the establishment of diplomatic relations is not entirely
    clear, according to Spector 2 June 1920 'the date of Chicherin's reply to Kemal Pasha,
    is the date recorded in the Soviet *Diplomatitcheskii Slovar* (*Diplomatic Dictionary*)'.
    Spector, *The Soviet Union and the Muslim World*, p.69. However, according to
    Turkish sources the letter was written on 3 June 1920. There is a copy of this letter in
    French and its translation in Turkish. See *Atatürk'ün Milli Dış Politikası (Cumhuriyet
    Dönemine Ait 100 Belge: 1919–1923) [AMDP]*, Vol. I, Ankara, T.C. Kültür Bakanlığı
    Yayınları, 1994, pp.157–161, Doc. 24.
45 Public Records Office, Kew, London, FO371/5170/E10779/262//44, Director of
    Military Intelligence, M.I.2.B., Weekly Report from Constantinople, No. 81, 1/2
    September 1920; Karabekir, *İstiklal Harbimiz, Vol. II*, pp.77–78.
46 Okyar, *Milli Mücadele Döneminde*, p.85.
47 Mustafa Onar, ed., *Atatürk'un Kurtuluş Savaşı Yazışmaları [AKSY], Vol. II*, Ankara,
    G.Ü. Teknik Eğitim Fakültesi Matbaası, 1995, pp.157–158, Doc. 887; *AMDP, Vol. I*,
    pp.165–166, Doc. 25.
48 Public Records Office, Kew, London, FO371/5178/E14638/345/44, Minutes, Relations
    between Bolsheviks and Turkish nationalists, dated 20 November 1920.
49 Kazım Karabekir, *İstiklal Harbimiz, Vol. II*, p.100.
50 Başbakanlık Cumhuriyet Arşivi [BBCumA], Karar No. 273, Eski Defter, C. No. 2, S.
    No. 5.
51 Stefanos Yerasimos, *Türk-Sovyet İlişkİleri: Ekim Devriminden Milli Mücadele'ye*,
    Istanbul, Gözlem Yayınevi, 1979, pp.242–243, Doc. 44.
52 Ibid., p.244, Doc. 45.
53 *TBMM Zabıt Ceridesi*, I Dönem, Cilt 2, İçtima 30, 8.7.1920, p.209; Rasih N. İleri,
    Atatürk ve Komünizm, Istanbul, Sarmal Yayınevi, 1995, pp.123–124; Public Records
    Office, Kew, London, FO371/E 14638/345/44, Minutes, Relations between Bolsheviks
    and Turkish nationalists, dated 20 November 1920.
54 Okyar, *Milli Mücadele Döneminde*, p.81.
55 Ali Fuat Cebesoy, *Moskova Hatıraları (1920–1922)*, Istanbul, 1955, p.70.
56 Public Records Office, Kew, London, FO371/4959/E11703/134/58, Report on
    Situation in Armenia, From Commander Luke, No. 272, dated 24 August 1920.
57 Cebesoy, *Moskova Hatıraları*, p.72.
58 Ibid., p.73.
59 Ibid.
60 *TBMM Gizli Celse Zabıtlari*, İ.84, 16.10.1920, C.3, p.166.
61 See the First Draft of the Agreements initialled by the Turkish and Russian Delegates
    on 24 August 1920, Cebesoy, *Moskova Hatıraları*, pp.80–81; Yerasimos, *Türk-Sovyet
    İlişkİleri*, pp.247–248, Doc. 48.
62 Okyar, *Milli Mücadele Döneminde*, p.87.
63 *TBMM Gizli Celse Zabıtlari*, İ.84, 16.10.1920, C.4, p.171.
64 Cebesoy, *Moskova Hatıraları*, p.75; BBCumA, Karar No. 220, Eski Defter, C. No. 1, S.
    No. 133.
65 Eric Hobsbawm, *Age of Extremes: The Short Twentieth Century, 1914–1991*, London,
    Abacus, 1995, p.31.
66 A.J.P. Taylor, *The First World War: An Illustrated History*, London, Penguin Books,
    1966, p.271.
67 Ibid., p.272; *Parliamentary Papers*, Session 4 February 1919 – 23 December 1919;
    Vol. LIII, Cmd.53, pp.25–27.

68 Ahmet Hursit Tolon, *Birinci Dunya Savasi Sirasinda Taksim Anlasmalari ve Sevr'e Giden Yol*, Ankara, Turk Hava Kurumu Basimevi, 2004, pp. 119–21.
69 See Appendix 5: The Clauses of the Treaty of Sèvres.
70 See Emre Kongar, *21. Yüzyılda Türkiye: 2000'li Yillarda Türkiye'nin Toplumsal Yapısı*, Istanbul, Remzi Kitabevi, 1998, p. 89; Sina Akşin, *Ana Çizgileriyle Türkiye'nin Yakın Tarihi*, Ankara, İmaj Yayıncılık, 1996, p. 133; Erik J. Zurcher, *Turkey: A Modern History*, London, I.B. Tauris Publishers, 1995, p. 153; Stanford J. Shaw and Ezel Kural Shaw, *History of the Ottoman Empire and Modern Turkey, Vol. II – Reform, Revolution and Republic: The Rise of Modern Turkey, 1808–1975*, Cambridge University Press, 1995, p. 356.
71 According to Article 7 of the '1909 Modification to the 1876 Ottoman Constitution', in general it was the sultan's natural right to sign an international agreement but if the agreement was related to territorial secession or territorial gain, the *Meclis-i Mebusan* (Chamber of Deputies) had to ratify the agreement. Cevdet Atay, *Karşılastırmalı Türk Anayasaları (Değişme ve Gelişme)*, Istanbul, Ekin Kitabevi Yayınları, 1997, p. 127. The Istanbul government did not have the power to ratify the agreement since its parliament was closed in January 1920.
72 Public Records Office, Kew, London, FO371/6269/E 8378/8378/58, Outline of Events in Transcaucasia from the beginning of the Russian revolution in the summer of 1917 to April 1921.
73 Parliamentary Papers, Session 10 February – 23 December 1920, Vol. LI, Treaty Series No. 12, Cmd. 963, pp. 1–6.
74 Bülent Tanör, *Türkiye'de Kongre İktidarlari (1918–1920)*, Istanbul, Yapı Kredi Yayınları, 1998, pp. 24–26.
75 Shaw and Shaw, *History of the Ottoman Empire and Modern Turkey, Vol. II*, p. 356.
76 Erik J. Zürcher, *Turkey: A Modern History*, London, I.B. Tauris Publishers, 1995, p. 150.
77 Justin McCarthy, *The Ottoman Turks: An Introductory History to 1923*, London, Longman, 1997, p. 374.
78 Ronald G. Suny, *Looking Toward Ararat: Armenia in Modern History*, Bloomington, Indiana University Press, 1993, p. 129.
79 Ibid., p. 130.
80 Martin MacCauley, *The Russian Revolution and the Soviet State, 1917–1921: Documents*, London, Macmillan, 1980, p. 109.
81 *TBMM Zabıt Ceridesi*, I Devre, Cilt 3, İçtima 53, 19.8.2920, Celse 1, p. 299.
82 İleri, *Atatürk ve Komünizm*, pp. 129–138; *TBMM Zabıt Ceridesi*, I Donem, Cilt 3, İçtima 48, 14.8.1920, Celse 1, pp. 185–189.
83 Göcek, Fatma Muge, *The Transformation of Turkey: Redefining State and Society from the Ottoman Empire to the Modern Era*, London, I.B. Taurus, 2011, p. 98.
84 Doğu Perinçek, *Avrasya Seçenegi: Türkiye İçin Bağımsız Dış Politika*, Istanbul, Kaynak Yayınları, 1996, p. 69.
85 Richard G. Hovannisian, *The Republic of Armenia, The First Year, 1918–1919, Vol. 1*, Berkeley, CA, University of California Press, p. 417.
86 Suny, *Looking Toward Ararat*, p. 130; Hovannisian, *The Republic of Armenia, Vol. IV*, p. 184; Karabekir, *İstiklal Harbimiz, Vol. II*, p. 102.
87 Carr, *The Bolshevik Revolution, Vol. I*, p. 351.
88 Hovannisian, *The Republic of Armenia, Vol. IV*, p. 184.
89 Public Records Office, Kew, London, FO371/6269/E8378/8378/58, outline of Events in Transcaucasia from the beginning of the Russian revolution in the summer of 1917 to April 1921.

90 Public Records Office, Kew, London, FO371/4959/E11868/134/58, from Commander Luke, No. 282, dated 5 September 1920.

91 Dennis, *The Foreign Policies of Soviet Russia*, p. 211.

92 Cebesoy, *Moskova Hatıraları*, p. 75.

93 Ibid., p. 78.

94 Kazım Karabekir was one of the founding fathers of the Turkish national movement but his ideas and activities have attracted the least attention from both Turkish and Western scholars. When he published his memoir of the Turkish national struggle in 1960, it was banned in Turkey since he gave an unorthodox explanation of Turkish history. His ideas are important for two reasons. First of all, he was among the main ideologists of the Turkish national movement, which helps us to show that Mustafa Kemal was not the only decision-maker. Secondly, he was the commander of the Fifteenth Army Corps, which played a significant role in the determination of Turkey's eastern boundaries in 1921, as we will see in Chapter 6. His military achievements against the Armenians made him a 'father figure' in Eastern Anatolia, a legacy which has persisted to the present day.

95 Hovannisian, *The Republic of Armenia, Vol. IV*, p. 184.

96 Ibid., p. 185.

97 Public Records Office, Kew, London, FO371/6269/E8378/8378/58, Outline of Events in Transcaucasia from the beginning of the Russian revolution in the summer of 1917 to April 1921.

98 Gökay, *A Clash of Empires*, p. 85.

99 Ibid., p. 85.

100 Public Records Office, Kew, London, FO371/4960/E11896/134/58, Telegram from Commander Luke (Tiflis), No. 410, dated 22 September 1920.

101 Cebesoy, *Moskova Hatıraları*, p. 80.

102 Karabekir, *İstiklal Harbimiz, Vol. II*, pp. 173–175.

103 Carr, *The Bolshevik Revolution, Vol. III*, p. 295.

104 Public Records Office, Kew, London, FO371/4961/E13325/134/58, from Lord Derby (Paris), No. 3236, Military Situation in Armenia, dated 26 October 1920.

105 Carr, *The Bolshevik Revolution, Vol. III*, p. 296.

106 *TBMM Gizli Celse Zabıtlari*, Devre:1, Cilt:1, İçtima:1, Cilt:5, In'ikat:84, 16.10.1920, Celse: 4, p. 170.

107 Cebesoy, *Moskova Hatıraları*, p. 90.

108 Cited in Klyuchnikov i. Sabanin, *Mezhdunarodnaya Politika*, iii, i (1928), pp. 27–28 in Carr, *The Bolshevik Revolution, Vol. III*, pp. 296–297. See also in Turkish, Yerasimos, *Türk-Sovyet İlişkİleri*, pp. 259–260, Doc. 53. According to Carr, the date of this letter is given as 29 November 1920 in Russian sources. According to Turkish sources, Yerosimos argues that the letter was written on 22 October. It was held in Trabzon for various reasons until it was sent to Moscow by telegram on 29 November.

109 Carr, *The Bolshevik Revolution, Vol. III*, p. 297.

6

The Turkish question: Islamist, communist or nationalist?

In international politics, the period between 1918 and 1920 was a testing time in every sense for the two transitional states, administered from Ankara and Moscow. The peace treaties imposed on them at the end of the First World War, the Treaty of Brest-Litovsk and the Treaty of Sèvres, left no 'breathing space'. During the erosion of their imperial identities, neither the Turks nor the Russians could associate themselves with their imperial statehood and had to replace these old political structures with new political identities. With the loss of their empires, not only had Ottoman and Russian status in the international system diminished, but also their geostrategic location had made it difficult to decide their future as Islamist, nationalist or communist states. While the Bolsheviks were drawn into a revolution, the Turks favoured the Western European nation model in order to build new socio-political structures and modernise their country. Thus, they shared a commitment to the modernisation and socio-political transformation of their pre-modern empires.

Consequently, the Turkish nationalists found themselves in a position similar to that of the Bolsheviks. Both regimes were struggling against Western imperialism, but the struggle of the Turks was not the same as the ideological war of the Bolsheviks. This common ground was not solely that described by Mustafa Kemal and Lenin during their diplomatic correspondence. Both were renegades, trying to consolidate their power in domestic and foreign affairs, against the Istanbul government and foreign invaders in Turkish politics, and against the White Armies under Denikin in Russian politics. In this respect, they faced a common threat from the Caucasian region. They realised that control of the Turkish Straits and the South Caucasus by the Allies would be dangerous for the stability of new regimes in Ankara and Moscow. In terms of constructing their new political structures and identities, there was an overlap of security concerns and border problems in the South Caucasus. On the one hand, the Turkish nationalists wanted to finalise the Turkish–Soviet frontier through the resolution of the Armenian question; on the other, the Bolsheviks hoped that the Turks would help them gain control over the South Caucasus. Therefore, the overall theoretical concern of this chapter is explore the role of foreign policy in the construction of political identities, as one of the five dimensions of transitional foreign policy.

In the context of the Turkish political entity, the nationalists clearly defined the meaning of sovereignty, nation and territory in accordance with the main principles of a modern state but had difficulty in presenting themselves as the legal authority of the Anatolian people. In particular, the Ottoman government in Istanbul was still recognised as the only authority by the Allies. Moreover, the nationalist group was not the only potential ally of the Bolsheviks. Both Islamist Enver and communist Mustafa Suphi participated in the Baku Congress, which was the first international platform to discuss the Turkish question among the other issues of the Eastern peoples. Therefore, the next stage for the GNA would be to consolidate its authority in both domestic and foreign affairs. By exploring the existence of competing actors – Enver Pasha and Mustafa Suphi – in establishing relations with the Bolsheviks, this chapter in particular highlights how foreign policy plays an important role in consolidating the authority of a group in domestic and foreign affairs.

The Turkish question at the Baku Congress as the First Congress of the Peoples of the East

The Bolsheviks established the Communist International (or Comintern) in March 1919. The Second Congress gathered in Petrograd (St Petersburg) and Moscow in July 1920 and accepted a new policy for world-wide socialist revolution. However, on 29 June, the International's Executive Committee had issued a call to all peoples of Asia to participate in a congress at Baku three weeks before the Comintern Congress.[1] Afterwards, on 3 July, the Moscow *Izvestiia* published an appeal entitled to 'the Enslaved Masses of Persia, Armenia, and Turkey, signed by Zinoviev and Radek on behalf of the Executive Committee and by fourteen different communist parties and groups' when Chicherin had just agreed to exchange diplomatic missions with the Ankara government.[2]

The Baku Congress, described as the First Congress of the Peoples of the East, met between 1 and 7 September 1920.[3] The congress deserves close examination since it opened a new phase of Bolshevik policy towards the East and the Turkish nationalists. From the Soviet point of view, the Bolshevik Revolution in 1917 'was to be only the prelude to a series of revolutions in the West' that would lead to the emergence of world communism.[4] The idea of revolution in the East rather than the West did not find advocates among the top Bolshevik leadership in 1918–1919. Yet the defeat of the revolution in the West, especially in Poland, precipitated a more active Soviet interest in the East. The Second Congress of the Comintern in July 1920 debated a new policy on the possibility of an Asian revolution.[5] This new policy had a dual character: 'revolutionary agitation in the East combined with support for national liberation movements, even of a "bourgeois" nature, against Western imperialism. Whilst making peace with the British in the West, the Bolsheviks pursued an undeclared war against them in the East.'[6] The two main themes of the Baku Congress – a strong belief in an 'imminent world revolution' and a common hatred of 'English imperialism' – not only united the leaders of the Comintern and the peoples of the East but also represented the new Soviet policy.[7] Thus, the Baku Congress was the first Soviet attempt to spread the revolution to the East, although it would also be the last.[8]

The participation of pan-Islamist Enver Pasha in the Baku Congress

For the Turks, the Baku Congress was a turning point in establishing relations with the Bolsheviks. Three different Turkish representative groups participated in the congress.[9] First, Enver Pasha joined the congress with formal credentials from 'the Union of Revolutionary Organisations of Morocco, Algeria, Tunisia, Tripoli, Egypt, Arabia, and India'.[10] Second, Mustafa Suphi attended the conference on behalf of the Turkish Communist Party. Third, the representatives of the Ankara government – Ibrahim Tali, Hafız Mehmet, Aziz Bey and Arif Bey – participated in the congress to gain information.[11]

Among the seven sessions of the congress, the first and the fourth were directly related to the Turkish question.[12] In the first session, Zinoviev explained the aims and tasks of the Baku Congress.[13] In relation to the Turkish question, he explained that although the Soviet government supported Mustafa Kemal's movement they knew that it was not a communist movement. But, at the same time, he emphasised that they were ready to help any revolutionary struggle against the British government.[14] In the fourth session, the guest speakers from India and Turkey were allowed to express their ideas. Enver Pasha's declaration agitated some members of the congress, since he was seen as a bourgeois politician who had driven Turkish workers and peasants into the First World War.[15] In Enver Pasha's own defence, he emphasised that Turkey had entered the First World War in order to rescue the country from the claws of 'Imperialism' and 'Capitalism'.[16] Although he regretted that the Ottomans had joined the war on the side of German imperialism, he emphasised that their new trusted ally was the Third International. Enver did not regard the Ottoman Empire as having been defeated. Interestingly enough, he argued that the closure of the Turkish Straits had been one of the factors that had brought about the collapse of tsarist Russia.

Thus, Turkey had opened a new road for the salvation of the oppressed peoples of the East, which, in his opinion, was a victory. As the representative of 'the Union of Revolutionary Organisation of Morocco, Algeria, Tunisia, Tripoli, Egypt, Arabia, and India', he declared that they were in full solidarity with the Communists to break the teeth of the imperialists by using revolutionary means.[17]

After Enver's declaration, a statement in the same spirit was read by Ibrahim Tali, the representative of the Ankara government. In addition, he also enthusiastically explained the internal and external causes of the Turkish national movement to protect its national frontiers and to defend its productive forces from foreign exploitation. He also claimed that the Anatolian peasants and revolutionaries were opposed to both Western capitalism and Ottoman dictatorship. Therefore, the destiny of the Anatolian peasants was bound up with that of the Third International and friendship with the Soviet Union. Furthermore, the fifth session of the congress, on national and colonial questions, raised more interesting arguments in relation to the considerations of the Bolsheviks towards Turkey and the Caucasus.[18] The Congress emphasised that although it supported Mustafa Kemal's movement, knowing that it was a national liberation movement, it believed that this movement would develop into a social revolution as soon as the struggle against imperialism was concluded.[19] The Congress concluded, having accepted several resolutions and issuing two manifestos: the 'Manifesto to the peoples of the East' and an 'Appeal to the workers of Europe, America and Japan'.[20] The Baku Congress was a disappointment in general even though it was a great symbolic success from a propaganda point of view. Its general spirit had to be abandoned when the image of Soviet foreign policy, in the subsequent international events, changed radically in the months after the congress.[21] Although the congress was described as the first, it had no successor and its organ, the Council of Propaganda and Action, was dissolved within a year.[22]

In the final analysis, the outcomes of the Baku Congress had an impact on the future of the Turkish question in the following ways:

1. The Bolsheviks decided to help the Turks in their struggle against imperialism knowing that the Ankara government would not change to a communist regime. However, the decision of the congress did not differentiate between Kemal and Enver Pasha as the leader of the Turkish revolutionary national movement, even if it favoured the latter. The Soviet leaders preferred Enver probably for three main reasons: first, as a hero of the 1908 revolution in Turkey and a believer in pan-Islam, he could be utilised to influence the Muslims of the East; second, his hatred of Great Britain was sufficient to make him a potential ally for the eastern policy of the Baku Congress; and, finally, Enver was the best candidate for the leadership of the Anatolian movement in the event that Kemal should fail.[23] The congress emphasised that even if Kemal's movement was successful in rescuing the country from foreign occupation, the nationalists could not be trusted since they did not represent the interests of the Turkish peasants and workers.

This understanding of the congress encouraged Enver in relation to his role in the future of the national movement. After the CUP leaders fled from Turkey in 1918, they began a dialogue not only with Moscow but also with Ankara, and for two main reasons: on the one hand, Enver went to Moscow on 14 August 1920, four days after the signing of the Treaty of Sèvres, to gain Soviet support for an international Islamic revolutionary organisation to save the empire from an Allied invasion.[24] On the other hand, Enver Pasha planned to assume control of the Ankara government gradually and to lead the nationalist struggle to the end. Therefore, his attendance at the Baku Congress was a first sign of his plans. Before the congress, Enver wrote to Kemal on 26 August saying he planned to go to Baku to re-organise the Azerbaijani army and then to use these forces for the Anatolian movement.[25] Enver also explained in a letter to Karabekir on 7 September that he was satisfied with the result of the Baku Congress and hopeful for future developments. He also suggested to Karabekir that Turkish forces should attack Armenia before the winter.[26] From Enver's point of view, Bolshevik support for these plans was very strong, which explains the fact that he returned to Moscow with Zinoviev's delegation from Baku.[27] Thus, Enver challenged the authority of Kemal both in domestic and foreign policies.

2. The second influence of the Baku Congress was the emergence of the first Turkish communists, which will be discussed in detail in the next section, as the other group to rival Kemal's authority. Three days after the congress, on 10 September, the 'First and General Turkish Communists Congress' gathered in Baku and elected Mustafa Suphi chairman of the Turkish Communist Party (Türk Komünist Partisi, TKP).[28] At this meeting, a decision was taken to transfer the centre of the party to Anatolia in order to help the anti-imperialist nationalist movement in the short term and to establish a socialist order in the long term.[29] From an ideological point of view, this party could serve the Bolsheviks in spreading communism to Turkey. Consequently, the Ankara government had to be cautious about Bolshevik aims in that they would consider putting Turkey, like Turkestan and Azerbaijan, under Red Army control and had decided to control local communist movements in Anatolia.

3. The third influence was on Turkish–Armenian relations. As stated earlier, the Armenian forces attacked the Turkish frontier districts at the beginning of September 1920. I would like to argue that the Bolshevik support for Enver and Suphi at the Baku Congress was another weighty reason behind the GNA's decision to solve the Armenian question through its own capabilities. Interestingly enough, Richard Pipes draws our attention to the establishment of a 'Revolutionary Committee' of Armenia in Baku in the course of the congress.[30] It seems that this was the early sign of a Sovietised Armenia in December 1920. Thus, even if it was based on different considerations, the governments in Ankara and Moscow both realised that the Armenian question could serve the intended agreement between them.

4. The final influence of the Baku Congress was on the realisation of progressing diplomatic negotiations in Turkish–Soviet relations. The nationalists had to limit themselves to a political alignment with the Bolsheviks, but no more than this as the communist regime was incompatible with Turkish politics. The Bolsheviks were not powerful enough to give ammunition and arms to Turkey, but they could provide financial aid and diplomatic support for the national cause. The Ankara government decided to send official representatives to Baku and Moscow to re-initiate the negotiations which would lead to the second round of Moscow meetings between January and March 1921.

Thus, the Armenian question, the revolutionary character of the Anatolian movement and the foundation of the TKP all led the Bolsheviks to turn to Ankara. The relations between the Turkish communists and the nationalists, a subject to which I now turn, will illustrate the next stage in the consolidation of Kemal's authority in foreign affairs.

The first Turkish communists and Mustafa Suphi

We saw earlier that the Bolsheviks developed a new policy on revolution and the national question in the East in July 1920. After their defeat in Poland, Lenin admitted his mistake in not recognising that nationalism was a more powerful force than international communism.[31] Afterwards, the Bolsheviks targeted two main groups in relation to their national policy: the European peoples – the Balts and the Poles – living in Western Russia and the Eastern peoples – the Turks and the Persians – of their Asian neighbours.[32] Their policy was to appoint trusted commissars for these national groups who would organise the communist parties later. Mustafa Suphi's leadership of the TKP must be understood in relation to this new Bolshevik policy.

The first congress of the TKP gathered in Baku between 10 and 15 September 1920.[33] There the Turkish communists agreed to support the Ankara government, in accordance with the decision of the Baku Congress, for two reasons: first, to establish relations with Mustafa, Kemal's group would enable the TKP to gradually spread revolutionary ideas into Anatolia. Second, the Ankara government also had a pro-Soviet orientation. The Turkish communists probably thought that the time was ripe to transfer their activities to Anatolia. Given the fact that the new GNA government had requested Bolshevik financial and military aid, it would permit the establishment of communist organisations in Anatolia.[34] However, the TKP's criticism of the Ankara government did not cease after this decision. The TKP members believed that the national movement was based on the democratic bourgeoisie classes and that its policy towards the Bolsheviks was hypocritical: while they wanted to co-operate with the Bolsheviks against Western capitalism, they did not depart from nationalist policies.[35]

The way Kemal reacted to the role of Suphi in establishing relations with Moscow was an important sign of the developing nationalist authority in foreign affairs. During the correspondence between Suphi and Kemal before and after the Baku Congress, the main issue was Suphi's demand to continue his activities in Anatolia.[36] Kemal suggested that any communist movement or political activity in Turkey should be initiated by contacting the GNA. Therefore, if Suphi was determined to continue his activities in Anatolia, he had to co-operate with the Ankara government by sending a TKP representative to the GNA.[37] In fact, the official Turkish Communist Party was also established in Ankara through the initiative of Mustafa Kemal on 18 October 1920.[38] If Suphi insisted on continuing his activities in Anatolia, he could work within this official party. The official party's aim was, on the one hand, to control communist activities in Turkey, and, on the other, to gain the Bolsheviks' support through Kemal's own initiatives rather than Suphi's.[39] This tactical manoeuvre by Kemal indicated, in a way, that the government of Ankara had considered giving permission to the Turkish communists to enter Anatolia.[40] Although there is no document in Turkish sources to prove this claim, most Turkish scholars argue that permission was granted on 15 December 1920.[41]

It is likely that the GNA did not grant permission enthusiastically, but rather in the light of the need to establish relations with the Bolsheviks. In December

1920, the Ankara government was going through a critical period. On the one hand, as will be discussed in the next chapter, it forced the Armenians to sign an agreement that rejected the claims of the Treaty of Sèvres while negotiations with the Bolsheviks were cut off during the first Moscow meetings. On the other hand, Enver Pasha was still planning to obtain control of the nationalist movement when he returned to Moscow after the Baku Congress.[42] Mustafa Suphi, together with his new wife, some other comrades and the new Soviet ambassador, Mdiviani, with his diplomatic mission, arrived in Kars on 28 December 1920.[43] They stayed in Kars for three weeks, during which time Mustafa Suphi met Ali Fuat Pasha, the GNA's newly appointed ambassador to Moscow, and Dr Rıza Nur, both of whom were members of the Turkish delegation on their way to Moscow to re-start negotiations with the Bolsheviks.[44]

The GNA's concern was preventing Suphi's arrival in Ankara, a point which was left to Karabekir.[45] Mustafa Suphi and Ethem Nejad visited Karabekir on 11 January 1921. Interestingly enough, Suphi was suspicious of an assassination attempt and suggested that he and his comrades travel separately. He wanted to go to Ankara via Tiflis with a few friends, while the others continued their journey via Erzurum.[46] However, Karabekir told them there were only two options: they could either cancel their journey to Ankara altogether or the whole group would go to Ankara via Erzurum and Trabzon. Suphi accepted the second option and left for Erzurum and his final destination, Ankara.[47] However, the Turkish communists' entry to Erzurum was blocked by anti-communist demonstrations in the city.[48] On 16 January, Hamit Bey, the governor of Erzurum, sent a telegram to Mustafa Kemal to report on the decision that the group would be sent to Trabzon for deportation. After Kemal's confirmation, the group was sent to Trabzon on 22 January in order to return to Batum by sea en route to Baku.[49] At Trabzon they were also coldly received by the local people. Under these circumstances, Mustafa Suphi, his wife and between 14 and 17 comrades boarded a boat arranged by Captain Yahya during the night of 28/29 January 1921. As the boat containing Suphi and his party left Trabzon harbour, it was attacked by another vessel under the control of Captain Yahya, resulting in the deaths of Mustafa Suphi and his comrades.[50] The TKP's main aim of continuing their activities in Anatolia came to an end with this incident. Although Yahya was found guilty of murdering Suphi and the others, a dark shadow still remains over this incident in Turkish historiography.

Turkish historians have discussed the possibility of four different groups being behind the murder: Captain Yahya, the Ankara government, the former CUP leaders and the Russian Bolsheviks.[51] The first possibility is that Yahya decided to take this action himself in order to steal the Turkish communists' money (estimated at 8.000 golden tokens).[52] But the incident was probably far from being an ordinary robbery; Captain Yahya himself was mysteriously assassinated on 3 July 1922.[53]

The second possibility is that Kemal and/or Karabekir gave the order to murder Suphi.[54] However, this is mere speculation since there are no documents or conclusive evidence to prove the claim. More crucially, the counter argument would be the other way around: if Mustafa Kemal himself was aware of the importance of Bolshevik assistance for the national struggle, this incident would obstruct Russian help.[55] The Ankara government denied its involvement in the incident and insisted that it was a tragic maritime accident. Some Turkish historians argue that the order to kill Suphi was given by Karabekir. The TKP leaders at the time also blamed Karabekir and believed that Kemal was not involved.[56] In his memoirs, Kazım Karabekir did not admit any involvement but pointed a finger at the CUP leaders given the fact that Captain Yahya was working for them.[57]

Enver Pasha's involvement in murdering Suphi, as the third possibility, is the strongest hypothesis for two reasons: First, there was a deep distrust between Suphi and Enver, since Suphi had expelled the former CUP members from the TKP and reorganised the party in Baku.[58] After the Baku Congress, Enver Pasha continued to infiltrate the TKP in order to get it under CUP control.[59] Second, Enver wanted to remain the only channel for gaining Bolshevik support for the Turkish national movement. According to Kakınç, twelve lately discovered Russian documents shed new light on the incident, and showed that the CUP leaders had the strongest motives for murdering Suphi.[60] The participation of Enver in the Baku Congress was a sign of the Bolshevik leaning towards Enver as a result of his strong influential position in Egypt, Algeria and Morocco. From Enver's point of view, when the Ankara government decided to send the Turkish communists back to Russia, Suphi's increasing influence had the potential to upset the balance in CUP–Bolshevik relations.[61]

The fourth possibility, that the Soviet leaders were responsible for the murder of the first Turkish communists, is the least likely given the fact that the Bolsheviks trusted Suphi to carry the communist cause to Anatolia. More importantly, the Soviet regime could envisage the negative influence that any event of this kind would have on the image of the revolutionary communists in the East. Moreover, it is difficult to find any substantive motive for the Bolsheviks to murder Suphi except for one: Mustafa Suphi supported Sultan Galiev's ideas to unite the Muslim national communists among the oppressed eastern peoples.[62] However, Suphi made it clear that he did not share Galiev's belief in the possibility of creating a Soviet Muslim (or Turkic/Turan) state.[63]

An important question arises from this conflicting evidence and confusion about the death of the first Turkish communists: how in practice did it influence the relations between Ankara and Moscow? Interestingly enough, the Bolsheviks did not discover the fate of the first Turkish communists until the end of March, another two weeks after the signing of the Treaty of Moscow on 16 March 1921.[64] It is hardly convincing that the Soviet leaders did not discover what had happened for two months. When the Bolsheviks heard about the incident, Chicherin made inquiries to the Ankara government about the Suphi incident and received the explanation that it might have been a maritime accident.[65] The Bolsheviks were probably not convinced by this reply but they down played the incident at the time. Soviet historiography later accused both 'Kemalist gendarmes' of the murder and the Turkish government of 'not having taken the necessary steps to protect the lives of Suphi and his comrades'.[66] However, the Bolshevik leaders considered the case to be a matter of Turkish internal affairs and did not let the incident affect the common interests on which the growing rapprochement between the two newly emerging regimes was based. 'For the first, though not for the last, time, it was demonstrated that governments could deal drastically with their national communist parties without forfeiting the goodwill of the Soviet Government, if that were earned on other grounds.'[67] It is possible to argue that the Bolshevik reaction to the incident also indicated that their intention was not to interfere in the internal affairs of Ankara, whose authority was implicitly recognised.

The death of the Turkish communists had two important implications for the consolidation of Kemal's authority. First, the GNA consolidated its power against the opposition left-wing movements in domestic politics. While Suphi was organising the Turkish communists in Russia, the revolt of another bandit group under the leadership of Çerkes (the Circassian) Ethem threatened Kemal's authority.[68] It is far from being a coincidence that Ethem was also persuaded to join Kemal's official communist party when Mustafa Suphi decided to move activities to Anatolia in December 1920. According to a secret report among the British documents of November 1920, Mustafa Kemal was fearful of two developments: Enver's desire to dominate the nationalist movement and the spread of Bolshevism to Anatolia.[69] Kemal's decision to arrest Ethem in January 1920 in a way implies that the British report was not wrong. On 6 January 1921, when all his supporters were arrested, Ethem fled to the Greeks. The suppression of Ethem's movement was followed by the death of the first Turkish communists.[70] At this stage, I should like to submit that Enver Pasha was probably behind the final decision to murder Suphi. Nevertheless, Mustafa Kemal explicitly supported Enver's plan, thinking that it might thus kill two birds with one stone. In this way, Mustafa Suphi would not be a danger to the Ankara government and the CUP would be discredited with the Bolsheviks. Thus, the path to Kemal's consolidation of power would have been cleared in both domestic and foreign affairs.

The second implication is that, after the disappearance of Mustafa Suphi, the Bolsheviks had to decide between pan-Islamist Enver and nationalist Kemal if they wished to improve relations with the Turks. As stated earlier, despite the official contacts with Kemal, the Bolsheviks had supported Enver Pasha during the Baku Congress. There were two competing ideas among the Bolshevik leaders. On the one hand, Lenin and his group were in favour of supporting the leadership of Kemal; on the other, Radek and Ordzhonikidze suggested supporting Enver in order to use him as a springboard to control the Muslims in Anatolia and the east. Chicherin was also suspicious of Mustafa Kemal's movement.[71] Chicherin suggested helping Enver in order to organise those Turkish nationalists not supporting Kemal's group and also to influence the Muslims of Egypt, Algeria and Morocco. In Chicherin's opinion, despite his imperialist policies towards the Caucasus, Islamist Enver Pasha appreciated Bolshevik principles more realistically than did the nationalist Kemal.[72] However, the military success of the nationalists against the Armenians in December 1920 forced the Bolsheviks to reconsider their policies towards Kemal, as will be discussed next.

The importance of Bolshevik support for the Turkish nationalists

It was argued in Chapter 2 that the nation-state is the most prominent political form of modernity and that the demarcation of borders becomes crucial during the process of state-building. The construction of political identity, that is of statehood, and the demarcation of boundaries overlap during the transition to modernity. Hence, the Turkish–Bolshevik rapprochement that was facilitated by the aforementioned common causes has been emphasised in relation to the determination of the Turkish–Armenian border in the previous chapter. The Armenian question and the future of *Elviye-i Selase* (Kars, Ardahan and Batum) in Eastern Anatolia were closely related to the construction of the new Turkish political identity. When an independent Armenian state was created with the Treaty of Sèvres, it provoked the nationalist aspirations of the Ankara government, which declared that even a small piece of Turkish homeland could not be given to the Armenians. Resistance against the idea of a united independent Armenian state led the nationalist leaders to find a common ground with the Bolsheviks. Therefore, another factor which brought the governments based in Moscow and Ankara closer together was the territorial claim of Armenia in Eastern Anatolia. We saw earlier that although the first sign of the harmonised interests between Ankara and Moscow was noticeable during the establishment of Soviet control in Azerbaijan, the disharmony of interests appeared on two issues: the Bolshevik support for pan-Islamist Enver Pasha and communist Mustafa Suphi at the Baku Congress and the determination of the Turkish-Armenian border during the first Moscow meetings. Turkish foreign policy towards the Bolsheviks would focus on the solving of these two problems, which had crucial importance for Turkish state-building.

Having stated that the construction of identity and boundaries has always been closely related to interaction with an 'other', the rest of this chapter will analyse the importance of Turkish relations with the Bolsheviks and the Armenians in determining its national identity and borders. The role of Turkish–Bolshevik affairs in determining the Turkish-Armenian border will be examined in two stages: the establishment of Soviet control in Armenia and the signing of the Treaty of Alexandropol between the governments of Ankara and Erivan.

The quest for Soviet control in Armenia

The Ankara government chose the Armenian theatre to declare its determination to establish a nation-state within the proclaimed Anatolian territory of which the Allies had allocated the eastern part to the Armenians. From the Turkish point of view, the victory over Armenia would impress upon the world, especially the Allies, that the Turkish nationalists were determined to reject the Treaty of Sèvres.[73] The establishment of Soviet control in Armenia on 2 December 1920 thus had two important implications for the Turkish–Armenian border dispute: on the one hand, it invalidated President Wilson's decision on the Turkish–Armenian frontier; on the other, it indicated the 'new understanding' in Turkish and Soviet foreign policies towards the South Caucasus.

As has been stated in previous chapters, the Allies had asked President Wilson to decide on the Turkish–Armenian border. Wilson finally submitted his decision concerning this frontier to the President of the Supreme Council of the Allied powers on 22 November 1920.[74] It was fixed by giving the provinces of Erzurum, Bitlis and Van to the new Armenian state.[75] The most troubled issue was the province of Trabzon, which would provide access for Armenia to the sea. In the event of any disagreement between the detailed text of Wilson's decision and the map drawn, the text would be the final arbiter[76] (See Map 4: Wilsonian boundaries). Ironically, while Kars (30 October 1920) and Alexandropol – later Leninakan, and now Gümrü – (7 November 1920) was under Turkish occupation, Trabzon, Erzurum and practically all of Eastern Anatolia were given to Armenia.[77] Within ten days of the announcement of Wilson's decision, the independent Armenian Republic would in fact disappear from the scene.

According to Pipes, the Sovietisation of Armenia was a result of the Turkish–Armenian conflict.[78] The Bolsheviks indeed did not hesitate to take advantage of the Turkish–Armenian fighting over the eastern provinces of Anatolia. But the establishment of Soviet control in Armenia was also an integral part of general Bolshevik policy towards the Caucasus. For instance, Stalin emphasised the economic and strategic reasons for their interest in the region in November 1920:

> The importance of the Caucasus for the Revolution is determined not only by the fact that it is a source of raw materials, fuel, and food supplies, but also by its position between Europe and Asia, between Russia and Turkey in particular; and also by the presence of most important economic and strategic roads (Batum–Baku, Batum–Tabriz, Batum–Tabriz–Erzurum). All of this is taken into account by the Entente, which, possessing at present Constantinople, that key to the Black Sea, would like to keep a direct road to the Orient through Transcaucasia.
>
> Who shall finally firmly establish himself in the Caucasus? Who shall use the oil, the most important roads leading into the depth of Asia, the Revolution or the Entente – that is the whole question.[79]

The establishment of Soviet control in Armenia indicated that the 'new understanding' in Turkish and Soviet foreign policies was based on taking advantage of the weak positions of the small states of the South Caucasus: the Turks facilitated this new understanding to provide a solution to the Turkish–Armenian border dispute, and the Bolsheviks blocked possible threats from their borderlands.

The Allied powers, which had promised Armenia's freedom and protection, did not do anything when threatened by Turkish forces and the Red Army. When the Armenian government tried to gain the Allied powers' support once again by applying to the League of Nations, it was disappointed with the reply. On 3 December, the representatives of the British, French and Italian governments held a conference in London to discuss the question of the Treaty of Sèvres and a proposal that Armenia should forthwith be admitted to the League of Nations.[80] The French representative drew attention to the rapprochement between the nationalists and the Bolsheviks and proposed to prevent this alliance by offering an honourable peace to the Turks. Lloyd George pointed out the difference in points of view between himself and the French by arguing the possibility of

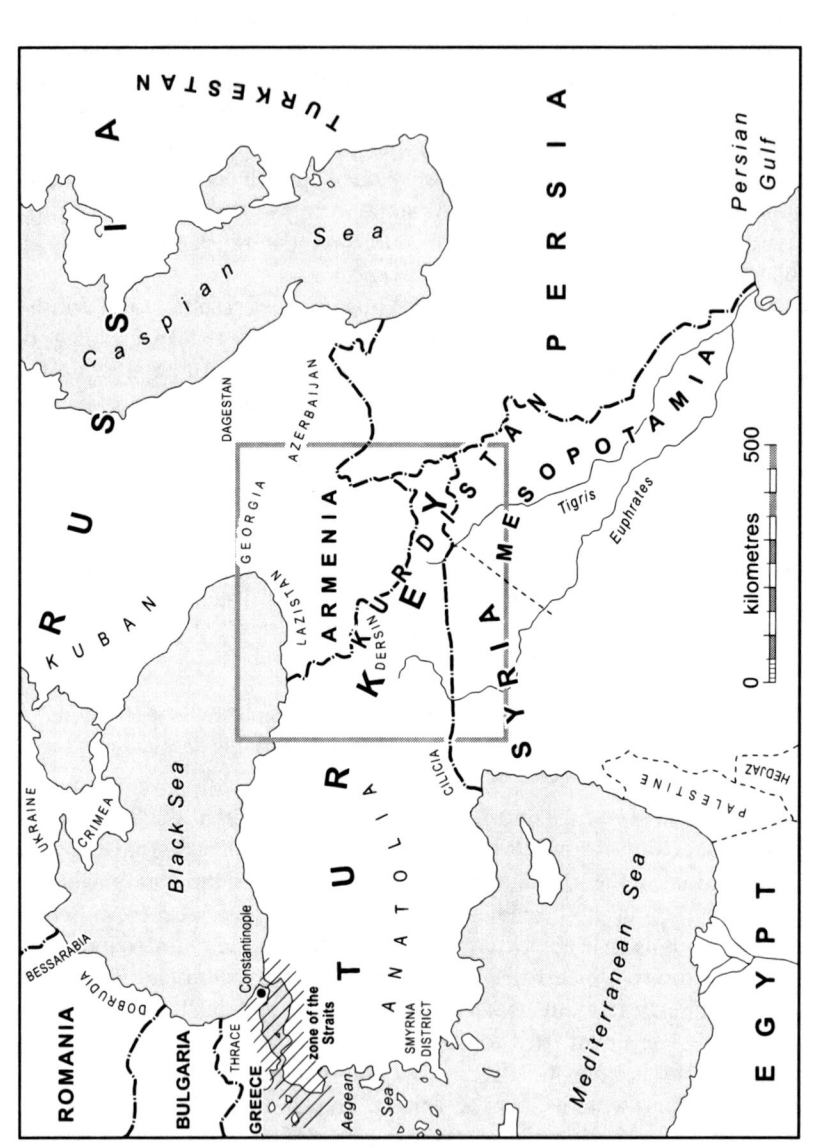

Map 4. Wilsonian boundaries, 1920

war breaking out between the Bolsheviks and the nationalists due to Mustafa Kemal's ambitions towards the east. The Turks had already taken Armenia, and the Bolsheviks and the nationalists were now rivals for an Armenian alliance. The Allies prepared a draft resolution to the effect that it was undesirable to arrive at a final decision as regards the steps, which ought to be taken to secure peace in Asia Minor until the Greek situation had developed further.[81]

In addition, the boundaries of Armenia as defined by President Wilson were so extended that the powers, which belonged to the League of Nations, could hardly accept the responsibility of guaranteeing or maintaining them.[82] When President Wilson informed the members of the Supreme Council of the League of Nations that his decision on the Armenian boundaries would be given to the press for publication on 18 December, the Allies asked him to delay making public his decision.[83] Then, three days later, when the Revolutionary Committee declared that all laws of the Soviet Russian government were in force in Armenia, there was no indication of wanting to regain the territories occupied by the Turks since October 1920.[84] On 26 December, the President of the Council of the League of Nations, Hymans, sent a telegram to President Wilson to inform him that there was nothing to be done since Armenia was now under the control of Soviet Russia.[85] With the loss of Western support, the change of government in Erivan did not essentially alter the Armenian question but placed the problem on the agenda of Turkish–Bolshevik relations.

The Turkish–Armenian Treaty of Alexandropol (Gümrü): the recognition of the 'other'

The Turkish nationalists caught the Armenians at a very critical time for imposing an agreement that aimed to determine their most controversial borders. The last act of Khatisian's Dashnak government in Armenia was to sign the Treaty of Alexandropol (Gümrü) with the Turks on 3 December 1920.[86] The new Bolshevik regime in Erivan indignantly refused to recognise the treaty.[87] Khatisian was denounced and branded a traitor by Soviet and other non-Dashnakist authorities, although he tried to justify his act later as a measure taken in the hope that the new Soviet Armenian government would repudiate this action and force the Turks to withdraw. However, the Soviet government did not support the efforts of the Soviet Armenian government to re-gain the lost territories and proceeded toward normalisation of relations with the Ankara government.[88]

Turkish scholars tend to neglect the role of the Treaty of Alexandropol in their analyses of Turkish politics.[89] The treaty ranks as the first official agreement of the Ankara government with a foreign state in the international arena, despite the fact that it was never ratified.[90] With the new border between Armenia and Turkey, the Ankara government literally regained all the eastern provinces which had been lost to Russia after the war of 1877–78. I would like to emphasise that the Treaty had very important consequences for both Turkish domestic and foreign policy.

In domestic politics, first, the nationalists' victory over the Armenians helped to consolidate the Ankara government's authority against the shadow government in İstanbul. This victory created ardent nationalist feelings among the Turks which arose from the view that the nationalists had the necessary military capabilities to fight against the foreign invaders. When the Armenian delegation agreed to denounce the provision of the Treaty of Sèvres concerning Armenia on 27 November, Karabekir celebrated this day as a turning point in Turkish history since the fight of the Turks against the Armenians was evidently a fight against the Treaty of Sèvres. The nationalist leaders used this opportunity to promote the nationalist morale of the Turkish people. For instance, Karabekir transferred the arms and ammunition which were requested from the Armenians during the signing of the Alexandropol Treaty to the western front against the Greeks as a first victory gift from the eastern front.[91] This symbolic transfer was an indication of the pragmatic nationalist strategy: first, to eliminate the Armenian threat on the eastern front, and then to concentrate on the Greek threat on the western front.[92] The nationalists were determined to eliminate the threat to their sovereignty from the others – the British, the French, the Greeks and the Armenians. Priority was given to the 'inside others', the Armenians and the Greeks, who had been part of the Ottoman *millet* system for centuries. After the defeat of the Armenians and the Greeks, the nationalists would be in a strong position to influence British and French policy in relation to the Turkish peace settlement.

The second, and probably more challenging, result is that the Armenians became the first 'other' during the construction of the Turkish national identity. According to orthodox Turkish historiography, the Turkish national movement was against the Western imperialist powers, especially Britain and France. However, the struggle against imperialism took an indirect form.[93] The Allied powers' desire to allocate the territories of the disintegrating Ottoman state to its non-Muslim subjects, the Armenians and the Greeks, laid the foundations of the Turkish national consciousness. Orthodox Turkish historiography emphasises the role of the Greeks and plays down that of the Armenians during the construction of the Turkish political identity. The reason is probably that Turkish historiography does not want to accept the counter arguments: it was the massacre and deportation of the Armenians which had persuaded the Allies to liberate the Armenians and to create an independent Armenian state.[94] From the Turkish point of view, the Armenians also had massacred the Turks, and the issue of massacres should not have been related to the creation of independent Armenian state in the eastern provinces of Anatolia. The possibility of an extended Armenian state was regarded as the major threat to the Turkish national borders.[95] This threat helped the Turks act as a national group and differentiate between 'us' (the Turks) and 'them' (the Armenians). Afterwards, the next crucial stage of identity construction was gaining the recognition of the Other, as explained in Chapter 3. Therefore, the Treaty of Alexandropol not only demarcated the Armenian–Turkish border in accordance with the principles of the Turkish National Pact of 1920, as stated in Chapter 4, but also indicated the willingness of both sides to recognise the political existence of the Other in international relations.

In foreign policy, first, the Turkish–Soviet rapprochement was to enter a new era after the Turkish victory over Armenia. With the Sovietisation of Armenia the two transitional states had a common frontier for the first time since the civil war.[96] On 4 December 1920, Karabekir sent a telegram to the GNA to inform it that the Moscow government had offered formally to sign a political and military agreement with the Turks.[97] From the Russian point of view, the Treaty of Alexandropol showed that the Turks did not have any intention of expanding their frontiers towards Russian Armenia. From the Turkish point of view, the Bolsheviks explicitly recognised the existing situation since they did not attempt to recapture the eastern provinces, which the Turks had gained by the Treaty of Alexandropol. This was, *de facto*, the implementation of a special Turkish–Soviet understanding in the region, which was based on partition. According to British documents, Lenin told an Armenian statesman at the end of December that he understood the importance of the Ankara government in establishing relations with the Eastern world and did not want to fight over Armenia with the Turkish nationalists.[98] As explained earlier, the Bolsheviks were also in contact with Enver and supported Mustafa Suphi after the Baku Congress. Despite the existence of competing actors in establishing relations between Ankara and Moscow, Lenin's policy was clearly leaning towards Kemal during the winter of 1920–21. It is worth emphasising that the weightiest reason behind Moscow's preference for Kemal was the Turkish nationalists' military success against Armenia. Even if the Treaty of Alexandropol had not been ratified by the Armenians and the Bolsheviks, its *de facto* frontier between Turkey and Armenia was to be approved by the Moscow Agreement in March 1921, to which I shall return in Chapter 7.[99]

Secondly, the Turkish victory over the Armenians also induced the Allies to reconsider their policies towards the nationalists. While the government of Ankara was determined to establish national unity and pursue the Allies to modify the Treaty of Sèvres, the Allies were suspicious of Turkish–Bolshevik co-operation in the East. Three important events occurred in regional politics: the defeat of Armenia by the Turks; the elimination of Wrangel in Russia; and the political overthrow of Venizelos in Greece. As a result of these events, the Allies realised that the settlement of the Turkish peace was no longer a matter of domestic policy, but one of foreign policy. The revision of the territorial terms of the Turkish treaty would spontaneously induce the nationalists to break with the Bolsheviks. In this way, Turkey could be recreated as a buffer state between a Europe exhausted by the First World War and a Russia in revolt. Under such circumstances, it would be possible to establish peace in the Near East and secure the British dominions of Egypt, Mesopotamia and India.[100]

According to Horace Rumbold, the British High Commissioner in Istanbul, the Bolsheviks had two main reasons for maintaining an alliance with the Turkish nationalists: to gain prestige and a theoretical right to declare themselves as the friends of Islam; and eventually to attain control of the Dardanelles.[101] If the British Foreign Office wanted to forestall Bolshevik policies in the East, friendship with the Turks was inevitable. Although this friendship would require the abandonment of the British policy of supporting Greek expansion in Turkey, it would bring the Islamic world to their side, which was vital to the continuance of its eastern empire.[102] In December 1920, the British Foreign Office reconsidered its policy towards the nationalists, as a result of the Turkish–Bolshevik rapprochement. It would be futile to wait on a 'hypothetical Greek defection' to formulate a policy towards the Turks, given the fact that the Nationalists were attacking the Greeks at Smyrna (Izmir). The British government agreed that the Treaty of Sèvres should be modified but it would be necessary to bring about a fusion of the Istanbul and Ankara governments into one body with which they could discuss modifications.[103] The change in the British policy indicated that the Ankara government was not considered an unlawful authority when deciding on the future of the Turkish state at that time.

Concluding remarks

This chapter argued that the Turkish–Armenian problem helped the Ankara government to consolidate its authority in domestic and foreign policies. The determination of the Turkish–Armenian border in accordance with the National Pact strengthened the legitimisation of the nationalist regime against the Istanbul government. In a meeting with the representatives of the Istanbul government on 5 December 1920, Mustafa Kemal made it very clear that the Turkish GNA was the only legal government of Turkey and that he did not recognise the Istanbul government.[104] In fact, the members of the last cabinet of the Istanbul government were dispersed and the government itself would cease claiming authority over the entire country by the end of January 1921.[105] While legitimising the nationalist regime against the pan-Islamist and communist rivals at home, the Armenians were chosen as the first 'other' state which had to recognise the authority of the Ankara government in foreign affairs.[106] It was not a coincidence that the Ankara government signed the Treaty of Alexandropol on behalf of the 'Turkish' Grand National Assembly. In this treaty, for the first time, the political identity of the Ankara government had been defined in terms of the territorial delineation of Turkey.[107] Consequently, the main findings of this chapter show how foreign relations played an important role in the construction of political identity, as the final dimension of transitional foreign policy.

Afterwards, the success of the transitional regime in Ankara would be dependent on securing national sovereignty within these proclaimed territorial borders and then gaining the recognition of its international existence by other states. Both the Bolsheviks and the Allies had already intended to reconsider their policies towards Ankara after its victory over the Armenians. Thus, the next stage of Turkish foreign policy would be to gain Moscow's recognition for the Turkish–Armenian border by eliminating the existing problems between the two transitory regimes, to which I turn next.

Notes

1 John Riddell, ed., *The Communist International in Lenin's Time: To See the Dawn (Baku, 1920 - First Congress of the Peoples of the East)*, New York, Pathfinder, 1993, p. 13.

2 Branko Lazitch and Milorad M. Drachkovitch, *Lenin and the Comintern*, Stanford, CA: Hoover Institution Press, 1972, pp. 396–397.

3 Riddell, ed., *The Communist International in Lenin's Time*, p. 20; According to the Turkish sources, the Congress was ended on 8 September see *Birinci Doğu Halkları Kurultayı: Baku 1920 (Belgeler)* [*BDHK*], Istanbul, Kaynak Yayınları, 1999, p. 9.

4 Walter Z. Laqueur, *The Soviet Union and the Middle East*, New York, Frederick A. Praeger, 1959, p. 7.

5 Ibid., p. 8.

6 Orlando Figes, *A People's Tragedy: The Russian Revolution, 1891–1924*, New York, Penguin Books, 1998, p. 703.

7 E.H. Carr, *The Bolshevik Revolution: 1917–1923, Vol. III*, London, Macmillan, 1961, p. 265.

8 Figes, *A People's Tragedy*, p. 703.

9 According to a list of delegates found among archival records of the congress there were 2,050 participants. Among these members, the Turks were the biggest group, followed by the Persians, Armenians, and Russians. *BDHK*, p. 13; Riddell, ed., *The Communist International in Lenin's Time*, p. 242.

10 Enver Pasha was not considered a delegate since he did not belong to the two main groups, the Communists and the non-party delegates, who were entitled to send representatives to the congress. Ali Fuat Cebesoy, *Moskova Hatıraları (1920-1922)*, Istanbul, 1955, p. 18; Mete Tunçay, *Türkiye'de Sol Akımlar (1908-1925)*, Ankara, Bilgi Yayınevi, 1967, p. 113.

11 Şevket S. Aydemir, *Makedonya'dan Ortaasya'ya Enver Paşşa, Vol. III*, Istanbul, Remzi Kitabevi, 1992, p. 543; Cebesoy, *Moskova Hatıraları*, p. 19.
Mustafa Kemal gave the following instructions to the Turkish representatives: (a) an administrative revolution must be achieved in Anatolia. Although a social revolution was also compatible with Turkish tradition and religion, the time was not right for this since the Ankara government was fighting against both the Allied powers and the Istanbul government. (b) The representatives must prove the revolutionary spirit of the Turkish national movement in order to gain the European delegates' confidence. (c) The Turkish representatives were not entitled to take any decision related to Turkey. Rasih N. İleri, *Atatürk ve Komünizm*, Istanbul, Sarmal Yayınevi, 1995, pp. 146–147.

12 The agenda of the Baku Congress included six main topics: 'tasks of the congress of the peoples of the East; the international situation and the tasks of the toiling masses of the East; the national and colonial question; the agrarian question; the question of the structure of the Soviets in the East; and organisational questions'. Lazitch and Drachkovitch, *Lenin and the Comintern*, p. 399.

13 Riddell, ed., *The Communist International in Lenin's Time*, p. 63; *BDHK*, p. 35.

14 Riddell, ed., *The Communist International in Lenin's Time*, pp. 73–74; Cebesoy, *Moskova Hatıraları*, pp. 22–23; *BDHK*, pp. 44–45.

15 *BDHK*, p. 94. According to British intelligence reports, Enver's activities in Baku were nevertheless a cause of some anxiety to the Bolshevik authorities. Public Records Office, Kew, London, FO371/5178/E13412/345/44, Secret Intelligence Report,

CX/5233/V, Proceedings of the Baku Congress, dated 30 October 1920. Because, as discussed in Chapter 4, the Ottoman Empire's policy in the Caucasus was mainly determined by Enver Pasha and Talat Pasha: establishing an 'Islamic state' in the region which was on the agenda until the Istanbul government's surrender in the Mudros Armistice on 30 October 1918.

16 Public Records Office, Kew, London, FO371/5178/E13412/345/44, Secret Intelligence Report, CX/5233/V, Proceedings of the Baku Congress, dated 30 October 1920.

17 Riddell, ed., *The Communist International in Lenin's Time*, pp.122–125; Aydemir, *Makedonya'dan Ortaasya'ya Enver Paşsa, Vol. III*, pp.545–546; Cebesoy, *Moskova Hatıraları*, pp.25–28.

18 Cebesoy, *Moskova Hatıraları*, pp.29–31; Riddell, ed., *The Communist International in Lenin's Time*, pp.126–129; *BDHK*, pp.98–101.

19 Riddell, ed., *The Communist International in Lenin's Time*, p.161.

20 *BDHK*, p.205; Riddell, ed., *The Communist International in Lenin's Time*, p.234.

21 Lazitch and Drachkovitch, *Lenin and the Comintern*, pp.406–407.

22 Carr, *The Bolshevik Revolution, Vol. III*, p.269.

23 Public Records Office, Kew, London, FO371/4946/E11431/1/58, Telegram from Commander Luke, No. 401, dated 12 September 1920.

24 Aydemir, *Makedonya'dan Ortaasya'ya Enver Paşsa, Vol. III*, p.538.

25 Kazım Karabekir, *İstiklal Harbimizde Enver Paşa ve Ittihat Terakki*, Ankara, Tekin Yayınevi, 1990, pp.26–30.

26 Ibid., pp.46–47.

27 Aydemir, *Makedonya'dan Ortaasya'ya Enver Paşsa, Vol. III*, p.549.

28 Mustafa Suphi fled to the Crimea as a political refugee in 1914 and worked with the Bolsheviks in Baku and Batum during the First World War. Yavuz Aslan, *Türkiye Komünist Fırkasının Kuruluşu ve Mustafa Suphi: Türkiye Komünistlerinin Rusya'da Teşkilatlanması (1918–1921)*, Ankara, Türk Tarih Kurumu Basimevi, 1997, pp.14–15.
After being influenced by Bolshevik revolutionary ideas Mustafa Suphi went to Moscow in 1918 and contacted Stalin, the Commissar of Nationalities, to make it known that he wanted to work for the revolution and establish a Turkish branch in the Commissariat of Islamic Bureau. Osman Okyar, *Milli Mücadele Döneminde Türk-Sovyet İlişkilerinde Mustafa Kemal (1920–1921)*, Ankara, Türkiye İş Bankası Kültür Yayınları, 1998, p.114; Aslan, *Türkiye Komünist Fırkasının Kuruluşu ve Mustafa Suphi*, p.24.

29 Tunçay, *Türkiye'de Sol Akımlar (1908–1925)*, pp.114–115, fn. 144.

30 Richard Pipes, *The Formation of the Soviet Union: Communism and Nationalism, 1917–1923*, Cambridge, MA, Harvard University Press, 1954, p.232.

31 Figes, *A People's Tragedy*, pp.702–703.

32 Lazitch and Drachkovitch, *Lenin and the Comintern*, p.368.

33 Aslan, *Türkiye Komünist Fırkasının Kuruluşu ve Mustafa Suphi*, p.207.

34 Okyar, *Milli Mücadele Döneminde*, p.116.

35 Tunçay, *Türkiye'de Sol Akımlar (1908–1925)*, p.106, fn.119.

36 The first letter from Suphi was sent to Kemal on 15 June 1920. See İleri, *Atatürk ve Komünizm*, pp.142–143; Okyar, *Milli Mücadele Döneminde*, p.117. In this letter, the Turkish communists sent their best wishes to the Turkish people in the War of Independence and explained the principles of the TKP. Additionally, they wanted to know what the GNA thought about Bolshevik relations and also whether it was possible to establish openly Bolshevik organisations in Anatolia. Mustafa Suphi and the

TKP's main aim was the success of the Bolshevik Revolution in Turkey and that the Bolsheviks' material aid would reach Turkey via this committee. Cebesoy, *Moskova Hatıraları*, p. 36; Tunçay, *Türkiye'de Sol Akımlar (1908-1925)*, p. 108; Okyar, *Milli Mücadele Döneminde*, p. 118; İleri, *Atatürk ve Komünizm*, p. 143. Kemal replied to this letter on 13 September 1920. İleri, *Atatürk ve Komünizm*, pp. 144-145; Okyar, *Milli Mücadele Döneminde*, pp. 119-120; According to Tunçay, Mustafa Suphi and Ethem Nejad together wrote to Mustafa Kemal in November 1920. Tunçay, *Türkiye'de Sol Akımlar (1908-1925)*, pp. 116-117, fn.145.

37 İleri, *Atatürk ve Komünizm*, pp. 144-145; Okyar, *Milli Mücadele Döneminde*, pp. 119-120.

38 *Atatürk'un Tamim, Telgraf ve Beyannameleri [ATTB], Vol. IV*, Atatürk Kültür, Dil ve Tarih Yüksek Kurumu, Atatürk Araştırma Merkezi, Ankara, Türk Tarih Kurumu Basımevi, 1991, p. 374, Doc. 355; İleri, *Atatürk ve Komünizm*, p. 170. The official party's leading names were also members of the GNA: Tevfik Rüştü (Aras), Mahmut Esat (Bozkurt), Yunus Nadi (Abalıoğlu), Eyup Sabri (Akgöl) ve Süreyya (Yiğit); Aslan, *Türkiye Komünist Fırkasının Kuruluşu ve Mustafa Suphi*, p. 295, fn. 78.

39 Aslan, *Türkiye Komünist Fırkasının Kuruluşu ve Mustafa Suphi*, p. 295.

40 İleri, *Atatürk ve Komünizm*, p. 128.

41 Aslan, *Türkiye Komünist Fırkasının Kuruluşu ve Mustafa Suphi*, pp. 288-289.

42 Public Records Office, Kew, London, FO371/5178/E14638/345/44, FO Minutes, Relations between Bolsheviks and Turkish nationalists, dated 20 November 1920.

43 Ergün Aybars, 'Mustafa Suphi'nin Anadoluya Gelişi Öldürülüşüyle İlgili Görüşler ve Erzurum'dan Trabzon'a Gidişiyle İlgili Belgeler', *Tarih Araştırmaları Dergisi*, 13:24 (1979-1980), p. 89; Tunçay, *Türkiye'de Sol Akımlar (1908-1925)*, p. 118.

44 Aslan, *Türkiye Komünist Fırkasının Kuruluşu ve Mustafa Suphi*, p. 302.

45 Aybars, 'Mustafa Suphi'nin Anadoluya, pp. 92-93, Doc. 1-2; Aslan, *Türkiye Komünist Fırkasının Kuruluşu ve Mustafa Suphi*, p. 300.

46 Karabekir, *İstiklal Harbimiz, Vol. II*, p. 194.

47 Ibid., p. 195.

48 Okyar, *Milli Mücadele Döneminde*, 125.

49 Aslan, *Türkiye Komünist Fırkasının Kuruluşu ve Mustafa Suphi*, p. 318.

50 Tunçay, *Türkiye'de Sol Akımlar (1908-1925)*, p. 120; Carr, *The Bolshevik Revolution, Vol. III*, p. 301; Lazitch and Drachkovitch, *Lenin and the Comintern*, pp. 412-413; Bülent Gökay, 'The Turkish Communist Party: The Fate of the Founders', *Middle Eastern Societies*, 29:2 (April 1993), p. 229.

51 Aslan, *Türkiye Komünist Fırkasının Kuruluşu ve Mustafa Suphi*, p. 348.

52 Ibid., p. 342.

53 Yahya was arrested later by Kazım Karabekir on grounds of helping Enver Pasha attempt a coup against Mustafa Kemal. During his trial, he did not confess as to who had given the order but implied that he was not alone in taking the action. Aybars, 'Mustafa Suphi'nin Anadoluya', p. 91. Interestingly enough, in his memoirs published in 1977, Mustafa Kemal's private escort, İsmail Hakkı (Tekçe), confessed that he had killed Captain Yahya. Aslan, *Türkiye Komünist Fırkasının Kuruluşu ve Mustafa Suphi*, p. 353.

54 Ibid., p. 350.

55 Aybars, 'Mustafa Suphi'nin Anadoluya', p. 92.

56 Tunçay, *Türkiye'de Sol Akımlar (1908-1925)*, pp. 121-122, fn.153.

57 Karabekir, *İstiklal Harbimiz, Vol. II*, p. 416, fn.1.

58 Aslan, *Türkiye Komünist Fırkasının Kuruluşu ve Mustafa Suphi*, p. 86.

59 Public Records Office, Kew, London, FO371/5178/E14638/345/44, FO Minutes, Relations between Bolsheviks and Turkish nationalists, dated 20 November 1920; Gökay, 'The Turkish Communist Party', p. 225.

60 S. Halit Kakınç, 'Gün Işığına Çıkartılan 12 Yeni Belge Tartışmalara Soru İşareti Getiriyor: Mustafa Suphi ve Yoldaşlarını İttihatçılar mı Öldürttü?', *Toplumsal Tarih*, 61:11 (January 1999), pp. 30–35.

61 Aslan, *Türkiye Komünist Fırkasının Kuruluşu ve Mustafa Suphi*, pp. 358–359.

62 Sultan Galiyev was a Tatar communist whose nationalist-communist opposition to Bolshevik policies caused a discussion of the national question in the Soviet Union between 1921–1923.
Alexandre A. Benningsen, and S. Enders Wimbush, *Sultan Galiyev ve Sovyetler Birliği'nde Milli Komünizm*, Istanbul, Anahtar Kitaplar, 1995, p. 97; See also M. Sultan-Galiev, 'The Social Revolution in the East', *Review*, 4:1 (Summer 1982), pp. 3–11.

63 Masayuki Yamauchi, *Sultan Galiyev: İslam Dünyası ve Rusya*, Istanbul, Bağlam Yayıncılık, 1998, p. 241.

64 Laqueur, *The Soviet Union and the Middle East*, pp. 28.

65 Tunçay, *Türkiye'de Sol Akımlar (1908–1925)*, pp. 120–121, fn.153; Carr, *The Bolshevik Revolution, Vol. III*, p. 301.

66 Laqueur, *The Soviet Union and the Middle East*, pp. 28.

67 Carr, *The Bolshevik Revolution, Vol. III*, p. 301.

68 Tunçay, *Türkiye'de Sol Akımlar (1908–1925)*, p. 123. Ethem was the most successful leader of the Green Army, which, recruited from the small and landless peasants, formed a major part of the national forces. Carr, *The Bolshevik Revolution, Vol. III*, p. 300.

69 Public Records Office, Kew, London, FO371/4948/E14786/1/58, from Mr. G.H.Q Constantinople, To War Office, No. 9578, dated 26 November 1920.

70 Carr, *The Bolshevik Revolution, Vol. III*, p. 301.

71 S. Halit Kakınç, 'Gün Işığına Çıkartılan 12 Yeni Belge Tartışmalara Soru İşareti Getiriyor: Mustafa Suphi ve Yoldaşlarını İttihatçılar mı Öldürttü?', *Toplumsal Tarih*, 61:11 (January 1999), p. 30.

72 Ibid., p. 31, Doc. 2.

73 Richard G. Hovannisian, 'Caucasian Armenia between Imperial and Soviet Rule: The Interlude of National Independence', in Ronald G. Suny, ed., *Transcaucasia: Nationalism and Social Change*, Michigan, The University of Michigan, 1983, p. 285.

74 *Papers Relating to the Foreign Relations of the United States [PRFRUS], Russia, 1920, Vol. III*, Washington, US Government Printing Office, 1937, pp. 789–790.

75 *PRFRUS, Vol. III*, p. 792, Enclosure 1.

76 Ibid., pp. 796–803, Enclosure 2.

77 Kazım Karabekir, *İstiklal Harbimiz, Vol. II*, İstanbul, Emre Yayınları, 1993, p. 182, p. 185.

78 Pipes, *The Formation of the Soviet Union*, p. 231.

79 Cited Stalin, *Sochneniia, Vol. IV*, p. 408 in Firuz Kazemzadeh, *The Struggle for Transcaucasia (1917–1921)*, New York, 1951, p. 294.

80 Bilal N. Şimşir, ed., *İngiliz Belgelerinde Atatürk (1919–1938) [British Documents on Atatürk] (1919–1938) [BDA], Vol. II*, Ankara, 1973, p. 433, Doc. 189.

81 *BDA, Vol. II*, pp. 435–441.

82 Public Records Office, Kew, London, FO371/4964/E15025/134/58, from Mr. Fisher (Geneva), No. 46, Admission of Armenia to League of Nations, dated 1 January 1920.

83 Public Records Office, Kew, London, FO371/4966/E15616/134/58, from Lord
    Hardinge, No. 1391, Boundaries of Armenia, dated 14 December 1920; *PRFRUS, Vol.
    III*, pp. 807–808.
84 Pipes, *The Formation of the Soviet Union*, p. 233.
85 *PRFRUS, Vol. III*, p. 809.
86 There is a disagreement about the day on which the Turkish–Armenian treaty was
    signed. Allen and Muratoff, Carr, and Suny argue that it was signed on 2 December,
    while Hovannisian, Onar, and Karabekir give the date as 3 December. Probably
    the confusion is due to the signing of the treaty after midnight on 2 December.
    Ronald G. Suny, *Looking Toward Ararat: Armenia in Modern History*, Bloomington,
    Indiana University Press, 1993, p. 130; Hovannisian, 'Caucasian Armenia between
    Imperial and Soviet Rule', p. 289; E. H. Carr, *The Bolshevik Revolution: 1917–1923*,
    Vol. I, London, Macmillan, 1961, p. 352; W.E.D. Allen and Paul Muratoff, *Caucasian
    Battlefields: A History of the Wars on the Turco-Caucasian Border, 1828–1921*,
    Cambridge, The University Press, 1953, pp. 499–500.
87 Salahi R. Sonyel, *Turkish Diplomacy:1918–1923; Mustafa Kemal and the Turkish
    National Movement*, London, Sage, 1975, p. 54.
88 Hovannisian, 'Caucasian Armenia between Imperial and Soviet Rule, p. 289.
89 Kamuran Gürün, *Türk–Sovyet İlişkileri*, Ankara, Türk Tarih Kurumu Basımevi, 1991,
    p. 39. Gürün argues that the treaty has only an historical value and is not worth ana-
    lysing while Gökay and Özsoy have not mentioned it at all in their recent books since
    it was never ratified. See Bülent Gökay, *A Clash of Empires: Turkey between Russian
    Bolshevism and British Imperialism, 1918–1923*, London, Tauris Academic Studies,
    1997; Osman Özsoy, *Saltanat'tan Cumhuriyet'e Giden Yolda Kurtuluş Savaşı'nın
    Perde Arkası*, İstanbul, Aksoy Yayıncılık, 1999; Bulent Gökay, *Soviet Eastern Policy
    and Turkey, 1920–1991*, London, Routledge, 2006.
90 The Treaty of Alexandropol (Gümrü) had 18 articles. The most important articles
    were the following: the Turks and Armenians agreed to a cease-fire (Article 1); the
    fixing of the Turkish–Armenian frontier (along the Araxes River and Arpaçay and
    then the Karasu stream) by the two commissions (Article 2); the disarmament and
    demilitarisation of Armenia (Article 4); the rejection of the provisions of the Treaty
    of Sèvres, concerning Armenia, by the Erivan government, in addition to which,
    Armenia would not appeal to European states and the United States of America to
    prove its goodwill to establish friendly relations with Turkey (Article 10); the GNA
    pledged of military assistance to the new Armenian state should if require it (Article
    13); the repudiation by the Erivan Republic, of all the treaties between Armenia and
    other powers, whenever such treaties contained clauses in any way detrimental to the
    Turks (Article 14); the establishment of commercial and diplomatic relations between
    the two sides (Article 15). *Atatürk'un Milli Dış Politikası (Cumhuriyet Dönemine Ait
    100 Belge: 1919–1923) [AMDP]*, Vol. 1, Ankara, T.C. Kültür Bakanlığı Yayınları, 1994,
    pp. 523–528, Doc. 94; *TBMM Zabıt Ceridesi*, 1.Devre, Cilt 6, İçtima 108, 4.12.1920,
    pp. 199–202.
    I have abbreviated the text of the treaty from Turkish sources. The text does not
    coincide accurately with the text quoted from Armenian sources in Kazemzadeh,
    The Struggle for Transcaucasia, p. 289. Carr also mentions that Kazemzadeh's quota-
    tion does not correspond with the text in Russian sources. See Carr, *The Bolshevik
    Revolution, Vol. III*, p. 297, fn. 2.
    The copy in the British documents also corresponds with the Turkish sources, Public
    Records Office, Kew, London, FO371/6265/E115/23/56, from Colonel Stokes (Tiflis),

No. 586(R), Treaty between Armenian Government and Turkish Nationalists, dated 31 December 1920; FO371/6265/E1118/23/58, from Colonel Stokes (Tiflis), No. 2/2(136), Treaty between Armenia and Turkish Nationalists, dated 31 December 1920.

91 Karabekir, *İstiklal Harbimiz*, Vol. II, pp.187–188.
92 Ibid., p.111.
93 Taner Akçam, *İnsan Hakları ve Ermeni Sorunu: İttihat ve Terakki'den Kurtuluş Savaşi'na*, Ankara, İmge Kitabevi, 1999, p.501; Taner Akcam, *From Empire to Republic: Turkish Nationalism and the Armenian Genocide*, London, Zed Books, 2004.
94 *BDA, Vol. III*, p.190, Doc. 72.
95 Akçam, *Insan Haklari ve Ermeni Sorunu*, p.517.
96 Ivar Spector, *The Soviet Union and the Muslim World, 1917–1958*, Seattle, University of Washington Press, 1959, p.70.
97 *TBMM Gizli Celse Zabıtları*, Devre 1, Cilt 1, İçtima 1, 12 Aralık 1920, p.352.
98 FO371/6266/E2303/23/58, From Colonel Stokes, No. 95/2(5), Attitude of Bolsheviks towards Armenia, dated 2 February 1921.
99 Okyar, *Milli Mücadele Döneminde*, p.106; *AMDP, Vol.1*, p.528.
100 R. Butler, J.P.T. Bury and M.E. Lambert, eds, *Documents on British Foreign Policy:1919–1939* [*DBFP*], *Vol. XIII*, London, Her Majesty's Stationery Office, 1963, p.189, Doc. 181.
101 *BDA, Vol. II*, p.505, Doc. 212.
102 *DBFP, Vol. XIII*, p.170, Doc. 171.
103 *BDA, Vol. II*, pp.456–457, Doc. 193.
104 Ünsal Yavuz, *Atatürk: İmparatorluktan Milli Devlete*, Ankara, Türk Tarih Kurumu Basımevi, 1990, p.70.
105 See Appendix 4.
106 D. Cameron Watt, ed., *British Documents on Foreign Affairs: Reports and Papers from the Foreign Office Confidential Print* [*BDFA*], *Vol. IV*, University Publications of America, 1984, pp.190–191, Doc. 147.
107 Ihsan Güneş, *Birinci TBMM'nin Düşünce Yapısı (1920–1923)*, Türkiye İş Bankası Kültür Yayınları, 1997, p.74.

7

The recognition of the modern Turkish state

Although Mustafa Kemal asserted himself as the only leader of the Turkish national movement, he was under threat from Islamist Enver Pasha in terms of dominating the national movement. Moreover, the Allies did not acknowledge Kemal's leadership until the first serious defeat of the Armenians in December 1920. For instance, the CUP was still regarded as the major political power in Turkey in the British Secret Intelligence Services' report of December 1920. A British policy based on increasing the rivalry between Mustafa Kemal and Enver Pasha was suggested to the Foreign Office.[1] At that time, the Bolsheviks also had a similar attitude towards the two leaders. When the nationalists decided to implement the military offensive against Armenia, they knew that Enver Pasha was planning to return to Moscow. In his letter to Karabekir on 14 December 1920, Enver applauded the Turkish success against the Armenians. He suggested that if Armenia were put under Soviet control, it would be better for the nationalist movement to, have co-operation with the Bolsheviks rather than the British.[2]

After the Baku Congress, Enver's ambitions to lead the movement in Anatolia increased. The Russian documents confirm that his expectations of financial aid from the Bolsheviks had indeed materialised in 1920–21.[3] Therefore, Kemal was right to be suspicious of an Enver–Bolshevik conspiracy against his leadership. As a result of this distrust, Kemal continued to communicate with Enver, but only to control his activities and to keep him away from Anatolia. During this correspondence between the two leaders, Kemal clearly emphasised that the Turkish nationalists did not support any pan-Islamic policy, other than the national movements in the East. Kemal's main intention was to discredit the Islamist policies of Enver in order to bring the Bolsheviks to the side of the Ankara government. Therefore, this chapter first highlights the leadership rivalry between Enver and Kemal Pashas to gain Bolshevik support. Its main theoretical concern is to explain the crucial stages of the construction of new Turkish political identity through external relations in the form of bilateral relations. The chapter concludes by emphasising the importance of the recognition of the Turkish state by the international society.

A rivalry for leadership between pan-Islamist Enver Pasha and nationalist Mustafa Kemal

Despite the establishment of a new Turkish–Bolshevik understanding, the existing distrust between the two sides lay along their path. While the Ankara government could not trust the Bolsheviks due to their support of pan-Islamist Enver Pasha, there were also signs of disagreement among the Soviet leaders on the Turkish question. For instance, on the one hand, one day after Mustafa Kemal's telegram of 29 November, an article appeared in *Pravda* in which Stalin expressed his suspicion about the 'serious attempt of the [Allies] to play with the Kemalists and perhaps a certain shift of the Kemalists to the Right' in November 1920.[4] On the other hand, in December 1920 *Narkomnats* – the official journal – argued that

> friendly relations with nationalist Turkey would make a good impression on the Muslims of the Caucasus. At the eighth All-Russian Congress of the Soviets in the same month Lenin, dwelling once more on 'the coincidence of fundamental interests among all peoples suffering from the oppression of imperialism', spoke of the impending treaty with Persia and the strengthening of relations with Afghanistan and 'still more' with Turkey.[5]

More importantly, the Bolshevik leaders had decided to send a certain quantity of money and ammunition to the Turkish nationalists.[6] If we remember, Mustafa Suphi was on his way to Ankara at that time and the Bolshevik leaders probably thought that the situation in Turkey was inclined towards communism. However, the Bolshevik expectations were not realised after the death of the first Turkish communists, and Enver's policies continued to be an obstacle for the Ankara government in legitimising its regime in domestic and foreign affairs. After examining how Enver Pasha became a threat to the nationalist regime, the following sections will focus on the consolidation of the Ankara government's authority during the second Moscow meetings and the London Conference.

From the Turkish point of view, further good relations with the Bolsheviks were important, not only in consolidating the authority of the Ankara government against Enver Pasha but also in securing its eastern frontier with the Armenians. In a telegram to Karabekir, dated 1 December 1920, Mustafa Kemal explained that the *reason d'être* of the Ankara government was to gain the political and economic independence of the Turks within the national boundaries, as defined in the National Pact, in such a way to not leave the eastern provinces to the Armenians. Any shift from this goal would bring the Ankara government to an end and transfer national sovereignty to the British-backed government in Istanbul. Under such circumstances, Britain would be free to utilise the power of the Caliphate to manipulate the Muslims of the East in Caucasus and Central Asia for its imperialist aims and its opposition to the spread of Bolshevism.[7] In this case, the nationalists had only one option. They had to continue to gain the support of the Bolsheviks in order to further the cause of an independent Turkey by emphasising the importance of Turkish–Bolshevik co-operation in the East against the spectre of British imperialism. Mustafa Kemal sent another letter to

Lenin on 5 January 1921 to express his pleasure on hearing that the Soviet government had recognised Dagestan's independence. He was convinced that this decision would positively influence relations between the Soviet government and the
Muslim world and would also unite the Turkish nationalists and the Bolsheviks.[8]
Lenin replied in a letter of 7 January 1921 in which he explained the Soviet government's new national policy. It supported the establishment of autonomous
regional republics, in accordance with the self-determination rights of all the
peoples living in Soviet territory. The Soviet government was also pleased to know
that the Ankara government understood Soviet policy towards the small nations
correctly and was ready to support these policies.[9] This letter clearly indicated that
Soviet foreign policy was moving towards Ankara, in addition to the on-going
official relations between the two governments, which I now examine.

The second Moscow meetings: a critical point in Turkish-Bolshevik relations

The Turkish–Bolshevik rapprochement entered a new stage at the beginning
of 1921 despite the Bolsheviks' support for Enver Pasha. The first ambassador
of the Ankara government, Ali Fuat Cebesoy, was appointed to Moscow on 21
November 1920.[10] According to Karabekir and Cebesoy, the Soviet Georgian
ambassador to Ankara, Budu Mdivani, arrived at Kars in December 1920.[11]
Mdivani informed Karabekir that a Turkish delegation was expected by Moscow
to recommence negotiations. The Ankara government did not lose any time in
electing and sending a new delegation, consisting of Yusuf Kemal Tengirşek, Ali
Fuat Cebesoy and Dr Rıza Nur, to Moscow.[12]

When the Turkish delegation arrived in Kars, they had a meeting with Mdivani
before they left for Moscow. Cebesoy's delegation asked Mdivani four important
questions which had been the cornerstones of further Turkish–Bolshevik relations. First, following the eastern military operation, would the eastern borders
with the Armenians, defined in the National Pact, be recognised? Second, if a
military agreement was not signed, would the Bolsheviks sign a friendship treaty
with the Turkish nationalists? Third, would the Bolsheviks provide sufficient
financial aid? Finally, would the Russian Commissariat for Foreign Affairs be
willing to negotiate and resolve the aforementioned issues? Mdivani told them
that the political atmosphere in Moscow was very different from that of August
1920 and that the Soviet leaders were in favour of establishing close relations with
Turkey. On 14 January 1921, Mdivani gave them a letter which confirmed that the
Soviet leaders were ready to negotiate with the Turkish delegation. Mdivani also
emphasised that neither in his meeting with Stalin nor in the instructions of the
Soviet government was there any word of giving the Turkish eastern provinces to
the Armenians?[13] As a result of their satisfaction, the following day the Turkish
delegation left Kars and arrived in Moscow on 19 February 1921.[14]

The Turkish delegates first met with Chicherin on 21 February and then with
Stalin on the night of 22/23 February. During these meetings, the Turks expressed
the Ankara government's willingness to sign the political and military agreement
which had been suggested by the Soviet government, showing the Soviet leaders
Mdivani's letter of 14 January 1921. The Soviet leaders emphasised that they

could not sign a military agreement but only a friendship treaty. Both Chicherin and Stalin drew the Turkish delegation's attention to the following issues. The Soviet government was negotiating a trade agreement with the British government, and a Turkish–Soviet political and military agreement could be hazardous to the Anglo-Soviet trade agreement. Also, the Soviets considered the Treaty of Alexandropol as not being in their own interest and expressed concern that the Turks had not accepted Soviet mediation, but had preferred to solve the Armenian question in their own way. The Turkish forces still had not evacuated Alexandropol. In particular, Stalin said that the Turks had solved the Armenian question themselves. If there was anything left to be solved, the Turks could solve it by informing the Bolsheviks when they decided to act.[15] As far as the Turkish delegates, Ali Fuat and Rıza Nur, were concerned, the major decision-maker in Turkish–Soviet negotiations was Stalin, having become the second most important leader after Lenin in Soviet politics at that time.[16] Stalin's last statement on the Armenian question indicated a change in the Soviet policy towards the nationalists. Meanwhile, the Turkish delegation's request to meet Lenin was refused because he was unwell at the time.[17] In the end, the two sides decided to convene a conference on 26 February to discuss the details of the Turkish–Bolshevik treaty. For the Turkish delegation, it was not easy to understand what lay behind the shift in Soviet policy.[18]

There were, however, two important reasons behind this shift, which help us to understand the close relation between domestic and foreign policy. The first reason was related to the question of Batum. In this respect, when the Turkish delegation arrived in Moscow the Georgian question was on the Soviet agenda. After the Sovietisation of Azerbaijan and Armenia, Georgia was left with its independence. As has been discussed earlier, the Turkish National Pact claimed Kars, Ardahan and Batum to be within the borders of the new Turkish state (see Appendix 3). The delegates from these three provinces had sent a memorandum to the British government, putting forward arguments in favour of the restoration of the above districts from Russia to Turkey. They argued that the overwhelming majority of this region was Muslim (90 per cent of the population) with close religious, national language and historic connections with Turkey. Therefore, these provinces were geographically and historically a natural part of Turkey, but had been incorporated into Russia in spite of the clearly expressed wishes of the people.[19]

As was pointed out earlier, the Turkish forces occupied Kars, leaving Ardahan and Batum, which had been an important part of the Ottoman Empire until it was ceded to Russia following the war of 1877–78. However, during the power struggle in the Caucasus neither the British nor the Turks and Bolsheviks wanted to leave Batum, which was the crucial port for exporting Azeri petroleum through the Baku-Batum pipeline.[20] While the Turkish delegates were having meetings with Chicherin and Stalin, the Soviet politics towards Georgia entered a new phase. The Soviet military operations against the Georgian Republic had been in progress since 16 February 1921.[21] Meanwhile, Karabekir invaded Ardahan on 23 February after the retreat and acceptance of Georgia.[22] In response, on 25 February, one day before the commencement of the Moscow Conference, the Red

Army entered Tiflis, the capital of Georgia and proclaimed the Georgian Soviet Socialist Republic.[23] With these new developments, Turkish–Soviet negotiations had now reached an extremely critical point.

The second reason behind the change of Soviet policy towards the nationalists was due to the fact that, as stated earlier, Stalin had been suspicious of a possible shift in Turkish policy in the direction of the Allies.[24] Stalin was correct in questioning the policy of the nationalists towards the Allies since the Ankara government was negotiating both with London and Moscow at the same time. Although the new Soviet policy was aimed at preventing Turkish–Allies co-operation, the Ankara government was determined to take advantage of every international event to assert its authority in foreign affairs.

The London Conference: the first signs of Turkish–Allied compromise

From the very start of the nationalist movement, the Allies did not recognise the authority of the Ankara government, preferring to deal with the Istanbul government. However, the Turkish victory over the Armenians and the Turkish–Soviet co-operation in the South Caucasus helped the Ankara government to consolidate its authority in foreign affairs. After securing the eastern borders with the Armenians, the nationalists decided to undertake an offensive against the Greeks on the western front. The Greek advance into Anatolia had been in progress since June 1920. When the Turks made their stand at the first Battle of İnönü on 9 January 1921 the Greeks began their retreat from western Anatolia.[25]

While the nationalists were establishing their military power on both fronts, their attempts to consolidate the authority of the GNA in domestic politics came to fruition with the acceptance of the first Turkish Constitution on 20 January 1921. It clearly declared that 'sovereignty belonged to the nation' and 'the government of Turkey was the Turkish Grand National Assembly' (Articles 1 and 3).[26] This was the *de jure* end of the Istanbul government in internal politics. Subsequently, nationalist foreign policy began a new stage in order to secure the recognition of the GNA government by the Allies. As a result of the recent developments in Turkish politics, the Allies decided to hold a conference in London to discuss the modifications to the Treaty of Sèvres.[27] Although the Istanbul government was seen as the representative of Turkey, the Allies for the first time accepted the need to approach the nationalists. The Istanbul government informed Mustafa Kemal that the Ankara government was also invited to participate at the London Conference. In his reply, Kemal was very explicit that the GNA was the only legitimate government of Turkey and that the Istanbul government did not have any right to send representatives to the conference.[28]

This unexpected invitation of the Ankara government to the London Conference was the first indication of its *de facto* recognition by the Allies. The Turkish victory over the Armenians in December 1920 and then the Greeks in January 1921 coupled with the existing Turkish–Soviet relations were the main reasons behind the Allies' decision. In relation to the South Caucasus, after the defeat of the Armenians the Allies realised that the considerable danger existed of Georgia, including Batum, sharing a similar fate. Therefore, before the nationalists reached an agreement with the Bolsheviks, it was necessary to get the Ankara government to agree with the Istanbul government with a view to the acceptance of the Treaty of Sèvres.[29] The London Conference was held amongst the representatives of Britain, France, Greece, Italy, Japan and Armenia, and those of the governments in Ankara and Istanbul between 21 February and 12 March 1921. The Allies proposed making small modifications to the Treaty of Sèvres and did not accept the retreat of the Greek forces from western Anatolia. At the meeting on 26 February, Lord Curzon's statement was very explicit and placed the Armenian question at the centre of negotiations:[30]

> He wished the Turkish delegation to understand clearly that Europe – that is, the Powers who had been victorious in the war – were solemnly pledged to create an independent State of Armenia. It was therefore quite impossible to conceive of any peace which did not provide for this independence and which did not give Armenia definite frontiers. Although he did not desire to discuss the details of such frontiers, yet it must be laid down at once that the Powers would not contemplate the creation of any Armenia which did not include the towns of Kars, Ardahan, and Alexandropol.

In his reply, Bekir Sami, the president of the Ankara government delegation and Minister for Foreign Affairs, stated that the Ankara government did not object to the creation of an independent Armenia where the Armenians were in the majority. The Turkish claims to the disputed districts were based on the principle of nationality. For instance, the Turks were in the majority at Kars and Ardahan and the Turks made no claim to Alexandropol, which was an entirely Armenian town. In the end, little or nothing was accomplished at the London Conference, except its two indirect, but important, consequences: first, the authority of the GNA government was *de facto* recognised by the Allies; second, the Turkish–French contact was established, which 'ultimately led France to be the first of the Allies to break the solid front and recognise the Ankara government' in October 1921.[31]

Whilst Bekir Sami was negotiating with the Allies in London, the second Moscow meetings with the Bolsheviks began on 26 February 1921.[32] At these meetings, the Turkish delegation's main aim was to sign an agreement with the Soviet government which would result in the recognition of the Turkish territorial borders as defined in the National Pact. The nationalists argued that the Soviet government would not recognise any international treaty that was not recognised by the GNA government, that the Turkish Straits should be open to other states for trade and that the Soviet government should abolish the Russo-Ottoman agreements, the Ottoman debts to Russia and that all Turkish prisoners of war being held in Russia should be returned to Turkey. More importantly, as Ali Fuat writes in his memoirs, the Turkish delegation did not raise the question of Batum until the last minute of the discussions. They kept this issue as a trump card to force the Soviet side to accept the Turkish proposals.[33] On 9 March, Karabekir received the Turkish General Army Commander's order to occupy Ahılkalak, Ahıska and Batum.[34] At the Turkish delegation's meeting with Stalin on the same day, Stalin declared that the Soviet government was ready to accept the Turkish demands, including financial and military aid, but in return Batum should be left to Russia.[35] Meanwhile, Turkish forces occupied Batum on 11 March 1921.[36] However, as Rıza Nur argues in his memoirs, the Turks knew that the Russians would not agree to leaving Batum, and they did not want to seriously put the Turkish–Soviet Treaty in danger.[37]

Consequently, the Turkish negotiators accepted Stalin's condition to give Batum up. Between 10 and 14 March the Turkish delegation and Chicherin drafted the details of the Treaty of Moscow, which would be signed on 16 March 1921, five days after Karabekir had occupied Batum.[38] According to Rıza Nur, when the negotiations to decide the details of the treaty were concluded on 14 March, the Soviet side suggested that the treaty should be signed two days later, being the anniversary of the occupation of Istanbul by the British forces.[39] The treaty was declared on 18 March.[40] It is likely that while on the one hand the Bolsheviks did not want to make the British suspicious and decided to wait until the Anglo-Soviet trade agreement was signed on 16 March, on the other they wanted to give the impression to the Ankara government, at least symbolically, that they still supported the Turkish national movement against Britain. With the signing of the Moscow Treaty, Kars and Ardahan were ceded to the Turks, and, in return, Batum was left to the Russians. When the Turkish delegation sent a telegram to Karabekir on 20 March that the Moscow Treaty had been signed with the Bolsheviks, he ordered the Turkish troops to withdraw from Batum.[41] Not surprisingly, the independent state of Georgia capitulated to the Russians and became a Soviet Socialist Republic on 18 March 1921.[42] Indeed, the fate of Georgia was very similar to that of Azerbaijan and Armenia, and it became the final step in the Turkish–Soviet settlement in the South Caucasus.

First steps towards the construction of new Turkish political identity

The character of the international system after the First World War, within which the Turkish nationalists had to operate, brought the process of nation-state building and the implementation of new foreign relations together. The establishment of a modern nation-state in Anatolia was regarded as being the best solution to the disintegration of the Ottoman Empire. The first foreign policy decision of the Turkish nationalists was to approach the Bolsheviks in their struggle against the imposed Allied solutions. In this respect, the signing of the Turkish–Soviet Treaty of Friendship indicated the first radical break with the old state structures and the foreign relations of the Ottoman Empire. For the first time, the historic Ottoman–Russian enmity was changed to 'good neighbourly' relations through the establishment of regional co-operation in the South Caucasus, in spite of the existence of ideological differences. Ironically, the protectors of the Ottoman Empire – France and Britain – against Russian expansionism turned out to be the common enemies of the two newly emerging states in Ankara and Moscow. The main area of antagonism between the Ottoman and Russian Empires – the South Caucasus – became the subject of co-operation between the two new regimes. The treaty had not only been a turning point in the history of Turco-Soviet relations, but it also established the foundations of a new policy which is still valid in current affairs.

Thus, the next section will aim to demonstrate that the treaty meant more than a mere 'friendship' agreement for both sides, and it was not based only on their common struggle against Western imperialism. In particular, the conclusion of the Moscow Treaty had crucial importance for the political transition of the Turkish state in terms of reasserting its sovereignty within the proclaimed national borders.

The first recognition of modern Turkish statehood: the Treaty of Moscow

The most important articles of the treaty's sixteen articles will be analysed in accordance with the main principles of modern statehood in order to understand its significance in the construction of Turkish political identity.[43] First, the Moscow government recognised the Ankara government, represented by the GNA, as the only legal authority in Turkey. Both sides agreed not to 'recognise any peace treaty or other international agreement imposed upon the other against its will'. In particular, the Moscow government agreed not to recognise any international agreement relating to Turkey which was not recognised by the Ankara government (Article 1). This implied rejection of the Treaty of Sèvres by the Soviet government.

Second, the expression 'Turkey' was understood to mean the territory proclaimed by the Turkish National Pact. The north-eastern border of Turkey was recognised in accordance with the settlement of the Treaty of Alexandropol (Article 1). Whilst the Soviet Union left Kars and Ardahan to Turkey, the Turks agreed to cede the right of suzerainty over the town and the port of Batum to Georgia (Article 2), and therefore, de facto, to the Soviet Union. Although in principle Turkish sovereignty over the Turkish Straits was recognised, the final elaboration of an international agreement concerning their status would be decided in the future by a conference composed of delegates of the Black Sea littoral states (Article 5). Therefore, with the exception of Batum and the Turkish Straits, the Turkish national claims over the territory of the new Turkish state were recognised.

Third, each side agreed not to interfere in the affairs of the other. They agreed not to tolerate the existence of organisations or associations in their territories which would aim to wage warfare against the other state. More importantly, they mutually accepted the same obligations with regard to the Soviet Republics of the Transcaucasus. 'Turkish territory', within the meaning of this article, was once more understood to be territory under the direct civil and military administration of the Ankara government (Article 8). Thus, the sovereignty of the Ankara government over Turkish territory was not only recognised by the Soviet Union, but would also be recognised by the South Caucasian states.

Fourth, Turkish nationalism was implicitly restrained within the new territorial borders. By agreeing to refrain from supporting secessionist activities on the other's territory in Article 8, both parties reached an unwritten agreement. The Moscow government pledged, at least officially, to abandon its support for communist activities in Turkey, and the Ankara government promised to cut its ties with pan-Turkish movements and to ignore the existence of the Turkic peoples in the Soviet Union.[44] In this respect, one can argue, 'state-sponsored nationalism has sought to anchor the Turkish identity in Anatolia, rather than in the Turkic regions to the east'.[45] During the diplomatic correspondence between the two governments, the Turkish leaders had used the word '*millet*' (nation) and avoided the word '*halk*' (people), although the Soviet leaders preferred the word 'people'. The Turkish emphasis was reflected in the treaty: the contracting parties recognised the national liberation movements of 'Eastern nations' and the struggle of the workers of Russia for a new social regime (Article 4); and the previous treaties between the two 'nations' would be considered null and void if they did not correspond with their mutual interests (Article 6).

Fifth, both parties recognised each other's new status in terms of international relations. In particular, Article 6 not only considered the previous treaties between the two sides as nullified but also liberated Turkey 'from all financial and other liabilities based on agreements concluded between Turkey and the tsarist government'. By following this decision, the Soviet government declared the Capitulations regime 'and any rights connected therewith to be null and void' (Article 7). By recognising each other's sovereignty in internal affairs at the highest level (Article 8), they aimed to strengthen each other's position in international affairs. Both sides agreed to conclude a consular agreement and other arrangements regulating all economic and financial issues (Article 14). In this respect, the previous relationship between the two empires was replaced with the new sets of regulations to secure each other's new status in international relations.

Finally, with regard to South Caucasian affairs, both parties were determined to establish their power in the region and gain the recognition of new status by the regional states. The Moscow government agreed to take the necessary steps to secure the endorsement of this treaty by the regional republics and ensure the signature of separate treaties between them and Turkey (Article 15). Article 3 determined the boundaries of the Nakhichevan district which 'form an autonomous territory under the protection of Azerbaijan, on condition that the latter cannot transfer this protectorate to any third state'. Thus, the new Turkish state secured its overland contact with Azerbaijan through the enclave of Nakhichevan.

The Treaty of Moscow had been a turning point in the construction of the new Turkish political identity, that is of modern statehood. For the first time, the existence of a new Turkish state was *de jure* recognised by the Soviet government in their international affairs. More importantly, the major obstacle during the construction of the Turkish nation-state, the determination of the Turkish–Armenian border, was resolved in accordance with Turkish demands. Moreover, the Turkish nationalists gained the moral and material support of the Soviet government. Although there was no direct article relating to Soviet aid in the Treaty of Moscow, the two sides later exchanged letters in which the Soviet government undertook to send financial aid and arms to the Ankara government.[46] When the Turkish nationalists decided to establish relations with the Bolsheviks on 26 April 1920, their main motivation was to obtain money and ammunition from Moscow.

Given the fact that the amount of Turkish resources was very scarce after the First World War, Soviet financial and military aid would automatically take on special importance during the process of Turkish state-building. Although there is no clear evidence on the definite amount of Soviet financial aid, both Soviet and Turkish sources argue that the Soviet government promised to give a sum of 10 million gold roubles.[47] A list of rifles, artillery and bullets which were sent from Moscow to the Turkish nationalists can be found in Turkish sources.[48] In particular, after solving the Armenian question on the eastern front, the Soviet weapons and ammunition would be used by the Turkish forces against the Greeks in the western front. The Ankara government received a large amount of Soviet military aid during the winter of 1921–2.[49]

In the final analysis, the Turks gained financial and military aid from Moscow and the main principles of the modern Turkish statehood were recognised by the Soviet government. But what was the real thinking behind the Soviet policy? The first motivation was that, as Spector argues, the Soviet leaders probably considered using Turkey 'as the vanguard of the Bolshevik Revolution in the Muslim world, especially in the Near and the Middle East'.[50] Conceivably, it was not a coincidence that both the Turkish and Soviet governments signed treaties separately with Afghanistan.[51] The Soviet–Afghan treaty was signed on 28 February and the Turkish–Afghan treaty on 1 March 1921.[52] With treaties with Turkey, Iran and Afghanistan, the Bolshevik regime secured its borderlands and gained prestige among the Muslim peoples of the East. The second motive was the need for an alliance during their attempts to participate in the European international system. The Moscow Treaty and the Anglo-Soviet Trade Agreement were the first official treaties of the Soviet government. In particular, the trade agreement signalled the Soviet 'search for a new basis of East–West diplomacy'.[53]

Therefore, the generally assumed main motive of the two sides, namely their common struggle against Western imperialism, as emphasised during the Kemal–Lenin correspondence and in the preamble of the Moscow Treaty, must be approached with caution since this was not in essence representative of their policies at that time.[54] If their special relations were based mainly on this rhetoric, why did both sides try to establish relations with Britain at the same time, especially given the fact that the Ankara government did not refuse to participate at the London Conference on 21 February 1921, and the Anglo-Soviet Trade Agreement was signed on 16 March 1921?[55] Did this sudden shift in Soviet foreign policy mean a retreat from the principles of communism and world revolution? It could be seen as the interesting beginning of a 'normal' foreign policy, that is having to deal with undesirable realities and an acceptance that the world could not be immediately remade in the Bolshevik image. Carr's analysis of this change is powerful:

> The change of front carried out by Moscow in March 1921 affected the climate in which Soviet foreign policy henceforth operated rather than the substance of that policy. It did not mean, in domestic affairs, the abandonment of the goal of socialism and communism, or, in foreign affairs, of the goal of world revolution. But it meant a recognition of the necessity of a certain postponement in reaching these goals, and in

the meanwhile of building up the economic and diplomatic strength of Soviet Russia by all practicable means, even if these means were in appearance a retreat from the direct path to socialism and world revolution.[56]

The beginning of 1921 was also a turning point for the Bolsheviks: on the one hand, civil war in Russia was coming to an end and, on the other, the failure of war communism's economic system urged the exigency of new methods to deal with Russian internal problems. The Soviet government's decision to introduce the 'New Economic Policy' (NEP) in March 1921 was an attempt to resolve the conflict between industry and agriculture by rapid industrialisation.[57] According to Margot Light, '[p]eaceful coexistence was an essential ingredient of NEP, since economic development would depend on foreign capital, or, as Lenin phrased it, concessions would be a way of "directing the development of capitalism into the channels of state capitalism". But the concessions were not enough – Russia had to be reintegrated into the international economic system.'[58]

The Soviet motive behind the signing of the Anglo-Soviet Trade Agreement in London did not, therefore, contradict that of the Moscow Treaty. The outcome of the NEP had been the implementation of a new Soviet foreign policy, and these two treaties were its first practical manoeuvres. On the one hand, the trade agreement provided a temporary co-operation with Western imperialism and, on the other, the Treaty of Moscow eliminated the interference of foreign powers from the South Caucasus and the Turkish Straits. After the Turks left Batum to the Russians, a Soviet republic in Georgia was proclaimed in March 1921. With the Sovietisation of Georgia not only did the region cease to be a power vacuum, but the Bolsheviks also completed the process of reconquering the separated borderlands and initiating 'the last phase in the formation of the Soviet Union: the integration of the conquered territories into a single state'.[59] Therefore, the main motivation behind the signature of the Moscow Treaty was not solely their common struggle against Western imperialism, or more correctly against Great Britain, but their need to recognise each other's new status in regional and international affairs.

The consolidation of the new Turkish statehood in the East: the Kars agreements
It was argued earlier that both the Armenians and the Greeks became the 'other' during the construction of new Turkish nation-state. The rapprochement between the governments of Ankara and Moscow had played a crucial role in the consolidation of Turkish power against the Armenians. This rapprochement also strengthened the Turkish position against the Greeks. It was therefore not a coincidence that the Turks engaged in the Second Battle of İnönü against the Greeks on 31 March 1921, having already secured the Turkish–Armenian frontier.[60] The Turkish forces would never have been transferred from the eastern front towards the west if they had not entrusted Soviet co-operation in the east. By the Treaty of Moscow (Article 15), the Ankara government's implicit recognition of a Russian tutelage in the South Caucasus and the Soviet government's agreement to pursue the three Transcaucasian republics to sign agreements with Turkey constituted a

clear indication of this trust on both sides. When the last Turkish forces evacuated Alexandropol on 23 April 1921, Turkish and Soviet relations seemed promising. But it would have been naive to expect that the relations could continue without any problems at all.

For the nationalists, the main problem was still the support of the Bolsheviks for Enver, in spite of their recognition of the Ankara government as the legal representative of Turkey. It is interesting to note that Enver was also in Moscow during the negotiation of the Turkish–Soviet treaty.[61] When Enver returned to Moscow in February 1921, his plan was to establish an *Islam İhtilal Cemiyetleri İttihadı* (Union for Revolutionary Islam Organisations) in Moscow, which would consist of all the exiled former CUP members. He even thought that the Moscow government would provide financial aid to this organisation.[62] After convening a congress of the Islamic revolutionary movements in Moscow, Enver's final plan was to transfer his activities to Anatolia. Rıza Nur argues that during the negotiations of the Moscow Treaty, Trotsky asked the Turkish delegation whether Enver Pasha was leading the Turkish national movement from Russia. Rıza Nur replied that Enver had no relations with the nationalists.[63] However, this question aroused the suspicions of the Turkish nationalists with regard to the relations between Enver Pasha and the Bolshevik leaders. Further developments strengthened the Ankara government's distrust of Enver's plans. The Soviet authorities welcomed his arrival at Batum in July 1921. The Turkish nationalists knew that Enver was planning to go to Anatolia in order to organise the '*Türkiye Halk Şuralar Fırkası Kongresi*' (Congress of the Turkish People's Council) at that time.[64] On 12 March 1921, the Ankara government issued a warrant for the arrest of Enver Pasha when he crossed the Turkish border.[65] The Soviet leaders probably considered using Enver as a trump card for their plans in the Muslim world, in the event of Kemal's failure, since the nationalist movement had been going through its most difficult stages, both in domestic and foreign affairs, during the summer of 1921.

On the one hand, the political opposition to Kemal's leadership and nationalist policies arose within domestic politics. The advocates of Enver – composed of the ex-CUP members, the *ulema* (religious conservatives), a few civil servants and businessmen – considered the Ankara government a temporary group that would dissolve once victory was won.[66] While the difference between the supporters of Enver and those of Kemal had become a threat to the existence of the Ankara government, the Greeks were preparing a new offensive in mid-June of 1921. The new Soviet ambassador to Ankara, S. P. Natsarenus, wrote to Chicherin that there were indications of a *coup d'état* in Ankara by Enver's supporters.[67]

On the other hand, at the same time, the South Caucasian states still had expectations of repudiating the existing power structure in the region. The republics of Armenia, Azerbaijan, North Caucasia and Georgia signed the Transcaucasian Alliance Declaration on 10 June 1921 and appealed to the League of Nations on 6 July 1921. The contracting parties emphasised how the failure to solve 'the Armenian question in Turkey [had] been one of the chief obstacles in the way of establishing a Union of Caucasian States'.[68] However, the attempts of the republics to gain the support of the Allied powers for the new proposed Transcaucasian confederation paradoxically brought about the speedy Sovietisation of the region and the solidification of Turkish demands.[69]

Simultaneously, the Turkish victory at the Battle of Sakarya, less than fifty miles west of Ankara, against the Greeks on 13 September 1921, had played a crucial role in the consolidation of Kemal's authority in domestic and foreign policy. It was evident that the Ankara government was the only power to ensure the sovereignty of the Turkish nation. The opposition groups in the GNA were reunited under the leadership of Kemal, who was awarded the rank of 'Mareşal' (Field Marshal) and the title 'Gazi' (fighter for the faith against the infidel) by the GNA.[70] After the Sakarya victory no one was able to challenge the authority of Mustafa Kemal and the Ankara government in domestic politics. As a result, Enver had to reverse his decision to go to Anatolia.[71] In foreign policy, the GNA now considered itself in a stronger position to implement active diplomatic relations. The governments of Ankara and Moscow had exchanged the Treaty of Moscow's ratification letters on 22 September and decided to organise a conference with Armenia, Azerbaijan and Georgia.[72]

The Kars Conference was held between 26 September and 10 October.[73] The Treaty of Kars between Turkey and the Transcaucasian Soviet republics under the supervision of Moscow was signed on 13 October 1921.[74] The treaty had twenty articles, of which the following played an important role during the construction of the new Turkish state.[75] The term 'Turkey' was interpreted as the territories included in the National Pact (Article 2). The Transcaucasian republics also declared null and void the system of Capitulations (Article 3). The northeastern frontier of Turkey was defined on a similar basis to that of the Treaty of Moscow (Article 4). The detailed demarcation of the frontier on the site would be carried out by a mixed Boundary Commission, consisting of an equal number of members with the participation of representatives of the Soviet Union, Turkey, Azerbaijan and Armenia. The Nakhichevan district within the frontiers, which were indicated in Appendix 3 of the present agreement would form an autonomous territory under the protection of Azerbaijan (Article 5). Turkey agreed to cede sovereign rights over the port and the town of Batum to Georgia (Article 6). Turkey and Georgia agreed to leave the final drafting of an international agreement for the Black Sea and the Turkish Straits to a special conference of the delegates of those powers which bordered the Black Sea (Article 9).

In general terms, the Treaty of Kars generally tied up the loose articles of the Treaty of Moscow related to the South Caucasus. Once more, the authority of the Ankara government over the Turkish territories as defined by the National Pact was recognised by the three regional states. Hence, the most difficult issue for the new Turkish nation-state, the determination of the eastern borders, was solved by implementing the Treaty of Moscow and repealing the Treaty of Alexandropol. The Treaty of Kars was not only 'the charter of diplomatic agreements' in Eastern Anatolia and the South Caucasus, but it also created its current existing borders.[76] After securing the mutual recognition of the new *status quo* in the region, the Turkish nationalists would be free to deal with the Greeks on the western front and to normalise their relations with the West. The issuing of a general protest against alleged Greek atrocities in Asia Minor by the Soviet government on the signature of the Treaty of Kars on 13 October 1921 was an indication of Soviet support for the Turkish nationalists' policy. The Turks were ready to utilise their relations with Moscow in their struggle against the Greeks.[77]

Not surprisingly, neither the Georgians nor the Armenians were satisfied with the settlement of the Treaty of Kars. Aharonian, the President of the Delegation of the Armenian Republic, informed the British government that the treaty had been imposed by the Bolshevik administration and did not represent the Armenian national will. The Georgian government made a similar statement.[78] According to Hovannisian, the Soviet government had sacrificed the Armenian question to cement the Turkish alliance on the international front. In return for Turkey abandoning its claims to Batum, not only were the borders fixed in favour of Turkey but Nakhichevan was not attached to Soviet Armenia.[79] These settlements formed the basis of regional affairs, even after the disintegration of the Soviet Union. For instance, the Armenian attack on Nakhichevan in May 1992 brought the settlements of the Moscow and Kars treaties to the attention of Ankara. The Turkish leaders claimed that Turkey had the right under Article 3 of Treaty of Moscow to send troops into Nakhichevan in the eventuality that all or part of it was occupied by Armenia.[80]

However, when the new regimes in Ankara and Moscow defined a new friendship policy in 1921, based on the mutual concessions in the South Caucasus, it was too late for the Allied powers to change the fate of these republics. The power vacuum in the region was filled by *de facto* and *de jure* Soviet control. For the nationalists, the new Turkish–Soviet friendship helped the Ankara government to consolidate its power, not only in regional affairs, but also in domestic politics. Chicherin's letter to Lenin on 20 October 1921 suggested that the Soviet leaders had to carefully consider the pros and cons of supporting Enver. Chicherin argued that the Soviet government's friendly relations with Kemal had influenced the Afghans to sign the Soviet–Afghan Treaty in March 1921. The continued Soviet support for Enver could harm the new *status quo* in the East.[81]

Enver was himself dissatisfied with the new Turkish–Soviet *status quo* when he arrived in Bukhara at the beginning of November 1921. He decided to work for the liberation of Turkestan by uniting the local dissidents, rather than by continuing his uncertain role as a communist agent.[82] It was believed at the time that the British government was providing him with ammunition, arms and money.[83] When he joined the Basmachi movement against the Bolsheviks, it was clear that he could not adapt himself to the new Soviet foreign policy, and as a consequence he lost Soviet support.[84] Thus, Enver ceased to be a potential threat to the authority of the Ankara government and he was killed by the Red Army in Tashkent, Central Asia, on 4 August 1922.[85] Having consolidated its power and gained the recognition of the regional states, the Ankara government's next aim was to impose the National Pact on the Allied powers. As a future result, the Turkish–Soviet co-operation in the South Caucasus would pave the way for the newly emerging Turkish state to take its place as a new member of international society – a subject to which I now turn.

The recognition of the Turkish statehood by the international society

The *de jure* recognition of the Ankara government by the Soviet and the Transcaucasian states confirmed its international status. In addition to this political success, the Ankara government's military success against the Greeks at Sakarya influenced the Allied powers' perception of the nationalist movement. For the first time, the Allies understood the inevitability of Turkish victory and had to make necessary adjustments in their policies towards Ankara. As was explained earlier, the first contact between Turkish and French representatives had already been made at the London Conference. Later, France became the first Allied power to sign an agreement with the Ankara government on 20 October 1921.[86] With the Ankara Accord, France agreed to retreat from Cilicia, where French control had been established in accordance with the Treaty of Sèvres and the Three Party Agreements. Thus, France not only undermined the Sèvres settlement, but also accepted the National Pact, moving the boundary between Turkey and its Syrian mandate to its present line, with the exception of Hatay (Alexandretta).[87] As a result, for the first time the Ankara government was *de jure* recognised by an Allied power, as the new official face of the Turkish government. From this point on, the differences amongst the Allies concerning the Turkish settlement would start to come to the fore. Italy was the next state to realise that any hope of imposing a settlement on Turkey and holding land in Anatolia was impossible. An Italian delegation was sent to Ankara to negotiate with Mustafa Kemal in October and November 1921.[88] Although they could not reach an agreement, these developments persuaded the British government to adjust its policies towards the Turkish nationalists.

On 22 March 1922, the foreign ministers of Britain, France and Italy offered an armistice to the governments of Istanbul, Ankara and Greece that reinforced the settlement of Sèvres. The GNA not only rejected this proposal but also demanded the complete evacuation of all foreign armies from Turkey.[89] In particular, Greek forces remained in Anatolia, despite the Turkish victories at the battles of Inönü and Sakarya. The Ankara government preferred to find a solution through diplomatic channels since neither their military strength nor their finances were strong enough to drive the Greeks out. It was also assumed that the Allied powers could not have an united policy towards the Turks after the Turkish–French agreement. Turkish politics then passed through a critical period of decision-making during the summer of 1922.

After eliminating the Armenian and the Greek threat, it seemed that the Ankara government's need to gain Soviet aid and recognition had diminished. The Soviet government was itself searching for Western aid and *de jure* recognition by stressing 'its readiness to rejoin the international community, "not as a supplicant, but as an equal"' at the beginning of 1922.[90] The Turks experienced diplomatic isolation when the Allies decided to invite the Soviet government to an international conference at Genoa, but not the Turkish government. The Genoa Conference and the Treaty of Rapallo in April 1922 represented an attempt at 'appeasement' and 'peaceful co-existence' in Soviet–Western relations.[91] In addition to this general attempt, both the British and the Soviet governments tried to use the conference as an opportunity to strengthen their position on control of the Turkish Straits and to establish a peace settlement in the Near East. After the failure of the conference, the Bolsheviks informed Mustafa Kemal that they had not accepted the Allies' demands for a neutral Soviet position in a Near Eastern settlement and for an end to support for the Ankara government. They asserted their belief in continuing Turkish–Soviet relations.[92] Thus Ankara, once more, avoided isolation in international relations, and decided to use the Soviet factor in its relations with the Allies.

In addition to the Soviet factor, two important events influenced Turkish–Allied relations: the final Turkish attack against the Greeks and the decision of the Allied powers to sign an armistice with the Turks. In relation to the Greek issue, the Ankara government first tried to find a solution through diplomatic negotiations. The Minister for Foreign Affairs, Yusuf Kemal (Tengirşek), travelled to Paris for a meeting with his French, British and Italian counterparts on 18 March 1922. He put the Turkish argument forward that the evacuation of Anatolia by Greek forces was the pre-condition for any settlement. The Allied proposal for a Turkish–Greek armistice was accepted by the Greeks, subject to minor reservations. Mustafa Kemal also accepted the proposal in principle and proposed a meeting in İzmit. His suggestion led to an unnecessary discussion on the possibility of other venues, such as Beykoz in Istanbul or Venice.[93] While the Foreign Minister, Yusuf Kemal, was still trying to arrange a meeting in İzmit in June,[94] the Turkish Interior Minister, Ali Fethi (Okyar), went to Paris and London. On 23 July of 1922, he met the French prime minister, Raymond Poincaré, and declared that the Turks were capable of winning a military victory but did not want bloodshed. But in London, neither Lord Curzon nor his deputy A. J. Balfour agreed to have a meeting with him. On 4 August, Ali Fethi managed to see a Foreign Office delegate who told him that the British government did not want to sign a peace treaty with the Turks at that time. In his report to the GNA, Fethi suggested that the Turkish national aims could be achieved only through military means, as the only method to drive the Greeks out of Anatolia.[95]

The situation turned out to be to the advantage of the Turks when the Greeks suggested to the Allies that the only way to bring about peace was for the Greeks to occupy Istanbul. 'This was too much even for the British government, which warned Greece on 29 July that any violation of the neutral zone of Istanbul and the straits would be resisted by the Allies.'[96] These developments influenced Mustafa Kemal's decision to drag out the negotiations and prepare for the attack against the Greeks at the beginning of August. 'Finally, on 26 August the Turkish army began to move forward in what has come to be known to the Turks as the Great Offensive (Büyük Taaruz)'.[97] The Greek army was defeated by the end of the month. On 13 September, Mustafa Kemal issued a declaration to the Turkish nation that the Greek occupation of Anatolia was over and the Turkish War of Independence had been won.[98] The liberation of Anatolia from the Armenians and the Greeks was part of the national plan to unite the Turkish nation under the sovereignty of the Ankara government. The next stage in the establishment of the Turkish nation-state was to gain the Allies' recognition of the new territorial arrangements.

This precipitated the famous Chanak (Çanakkale) crisis, which was a triumph for the new Turkish state and a serious humiliation for the British government of Lloyd George. In order to take common military action against the Turkish nationalists on 15 September 1922, the British government decided to defend the Neutral Zone of the Turkish Straits and Istanbul by securing support from France, Italy and the Dominions. Having failed to obtain the support they needed, the British forces were left alone to confront the Turkish forces at Chanak on the shore of the Dardanelles. The first advance of Turkish forces towards the British line was on 23 September, but both sides refrained from being the first to fire. It was a strange confrontation which could only be solved through diplomatic bargaining. On 23 September 1922, Lord Curzon finally agreed with the French and Italian proposal to ask Kemal to stop the Turkish military offensive and to negotiate a peace settlement.[99]

This decision triggered the Bolsheviks to send an ultimatum to the Allies, Yugoslavia, Greece and Bulgaria on the following day. It stated that the Turks had the right to control the straits and that the agreements between tsarist Russia and the Allies were nullified. As a result, if the Allies decided the future status of the Turkish Straits without involving the Soviet Union, fighting would ensue.[100] The Soviet government maintained that the future status of the Turkish Straits and Istanbul should be decided in accordance with the of treaties of Moscow (Article 5) and Kars (Article 9). However, the Soviet ultimatum should not be interpreted as a sign that the Bolshevik leaders were determined to intervene in the British–Turkish crisis at Chanak. As S.I. Aralov, the Soviet Ambassador in Ankara, writes in his memoirs, the Bolsheviks expected that the Turkish forces would enter Istanbul and regain control of the straits.[101] The Soviet factor doubt-less strengthened the Ankara government's position against the Allies. When the Turkish forces crossed the neutral zone on 28 September, the Allies sent Henri Franklin-Bouillon, the pro-Turk French Senator, to İzmir to negotiate a way out with Kemal. He accepted the Allies' proposal to sign an armistice on 29 September on the condition that the Allies prevailed upon the Greeks to evacuate eastern Thrace.[102]

Armistice negotiations between the British and the Turks began on 3 October and the Armistice of Mudanya was concluded on 11 October, to come into effect at midnight on 14/15 October.[103] From the Turkish point of view, the armistice was a true success for the national cause. Mustafa Kemal secured the terms he had outlined in the National Pact without deviation: 'an independent Turkish nation-state to be established in Anatolia and eastern Thrace'.[104] It was not long before the Ankara government took control of Istanbul, the Dardanelles, and eastern Thrace from the departing Allied powers. The Allies not only recognised the Ankara government, but also yielded to its demands for the determination of its western borders.

The creation of a new Turkish state was then to move on to its final diplomatic stage, when the Allies invited the Ankara government to the peace conference at

Lausanne on 27 October.[105] However, the Istanbul government was also invited to the conference. The response of the nationalists to this invitation demonstrated the influence of foreign affairs on Turkish domestic politics. On 1 November 1922, the GNA decreed new legislation separating the Sultanate and the Caliphate, and abolishing the former. From this time on, the Ankara government was the only representative of the new Turkish state. The Istanbul government resigned, since it had lost its legal foundation and the last Ottoman sultan, Vahdettin, had fled Istanbul into exile on a British destroyer on 17 November. When the peace talks between the Allies and the Ankara government at Lausanne began on 20 November, the six-hundred-year-old Ottoman Empire came to an end and the new Turkish nation-state sought to take its place in the European system.[106] Thus, the Turkish state question was finally resolved in 1922.

Concluding Remarks

The First World War brought to the fore the Turkish and the Russian settlements as the two major issues of the post-war arrangements in the Middle East. The first issue, the disintegration of the Ottoman Empire, was settled by the termination of the Ottoman Sultanate, the establishment of a Turkish nation-state and the partition of its Middle Eastern domains between Britain and France. The second issue at stake was the question of where Russia's political frontier in the East would be drawn. 'Russia's territorial frontier in the Middle East was established by the draft constitution of the USSR promulgated at the end of 1922, while [its] political frontiers emerged from the treaties [it] signed with Turkey, Persia, and Afghanistan, and, to some extent, from the trade agreement [it] signed with Britain in 1921.'[107] The Middle Eastern settlement of 1922, as Fromkin states, was based on the outcome of the disintegration of the Ottoman and Russian Empires at the beginning of the twentieth century.

Following the disintegration of the two empires, it is clear that the Turkish and Soviet state-building processes did not take place in a vacuum but rather within an international context, which forced these transitional states to redefine their identities and roles within international society. On the theoretical level, the rapprochement between the two newly emerging regimes between the years 1918 and 1921 draws attention to the relations between foreign affairs and the process of state-building. These relations can be verified through the empirical findings of Chapters 6 and 7, with respect to four important issues.

First, foreign policy became the means of determining territorial borders. It has been argued that during the establishment of Turkey's territorial unity, the most controversial dispute was over the Turkish–Armenian border. The special Turkish–Bolshevik understanding enabled the Turks to impose an agreement on the Armenians to determine the borders in accordance with Turkish demands. This in turn brought about the Sovietisation of Armenia. Stalin's statement during the second round of Moscow meetings gave the Turks a 'blank cheque' to solve the Armenian question through their own resources.

Second, foreign policy became an important 'tool' in the construction of the

Turkish nation. The analysis of the Treaty of Alexandropol demonstrated that the Armenians were regarded as the Other. The Armenian claims over the eastern provinces of Anatolia strengthened Turkish consciousness by differentiating between 'us' and 'them'. There was no place for the Armenians in a Turkish nation, defined in territorial and religious terms.

Third, foreign policy became a means of consolidating a group's authority in domestic and foreign affairs, thereby reducing foreign interference in domestic politics. In specific terms, Mustafa Kemal's relations with the Bolsheviks disqualified Enver from the leadership race to lead the Turkish national movement. The Ankara government also used its participation in the London Conference to consolidate its authority against the Istanbul government.

Fourth, foreign policy played a crucial role during the construction of the new political identity in terms of mutual recognition. The Moscow government was the first international actor which recognised the 'reason of the Turkish state' by the Treaty of Moscow. The ambiguous status of the Ankara government gained its first legitimate basis in foreign affairs through this recognition, with the Transcaucasian states following in terms of the recognition of a distinct Turkish political identity. In particular, during the post-First World War arrangements, some international treaties confirmed the attainment of independence, identity, integrity, security and sovereignty of nations.[108] More importantly, international treaties may serve as a means of recognition. The examination of the treaties of Moscow and Kars indicated that the sovereignty, political identity and territorial integrity of the Turkish state were recognised for the first time by the Soviet Union. Their dubious and weak positions in international society led to the need to recognise each other's new status in a regional context, which strengthened their positions in the international arena by influencing the Allied powers' decisions concerning the need to recognise the two newly emerging states at that time. However, it must be emphasised that recognition and international law are necessary but have their limitations in providing legitimacy for a newcomer in international society. They must be supported by other internal elements, such as a successful nation-building process and the establishment of an effective government.

Thus, I conclude that the process of foreign policy goal-formulation and the achievement of statehood are reciprocally influential. One the one hand, the rationalist dimension of the Turkish nationalists' first decision to establish relations with the Bolsheviks certainly contributed the most to reinforcing the Turkish state-building process. On the other hand, the aforementioned linkages of Turkish foreign policy with the main principles of modern statehood – territory, nation, authority and recognition – confirm the influence of state-building on the formulation of foreign policy goals.

On the empirical level of the analysis, the formal establishment of the new Turkish and Soviet states began in October 1922 and was completed in 1923. This was the result of a complex historical process that was brought to a conclusion between the years 1918 and 1921. For the Bolsheviks, '[t]he integration into a single state of the borderlands conquered in the course of civil war began in 1918 and terminated in 1923 with the establishment of the Union of Soviet Socialist Republics'.[109] For the Turkish nationalists, the tough diplomatic bargaining with regard to the consolidation of the Anatolian territories into a single state commenced at the Lausanne Conference on 21 November 1922 and was completed within a nine-month time frame. During the negotiations, the Anglo-Russian rivalry over the control of the Turkish Straits reached its peak. Although the Soviet government had not been invited as an official participant at the conference, it succeeded in being represented during the negotiations on the question of the straits and insinuated itself as an essential actor in terms of international relations.[110] The Turkish nationalists, pragmatically and strategically, played the Soviet factor in an attempt to gain British support for their territorial demands. Curzon, the head of the British delegation, accepted the Turkish demands so as to reach a satisfactory settlement which might dissolve the Turkish–Soviet co-operation. Hence, the new Turkish state could be utilised to isolate the Bolsheviks and create 'an effective buffer next to the Soviet-controlled lands'.[111] Consequently, the Soviet factor continued to play a determining role in the creation of the new Turkish state.

Turkey was *de jure* recognised by the British, French, Italian, Japanese, Greek, Romanian and Serbo-Croat Slovene governments, with the signing of the Treaty of Lausanne on 24 July 1923.[112] The Ankara government gained full sovereignty for the Turkish nation-state within the agreed territorial boundaries. The treaty legalised Turkey's borders as specified in the National Pact, with the exception of Mosul, as follows: the Turkish–Bulgarian border (Article 2/1); the Turkish–Greek border (Article 2/2) in Western Thrace; and confirmation of the Turkish–Syrian border as demarcated in the Ankara Accord with France (Article 3/1). Iraq's mandatory acceptance of its borders with Turkey, as determined between Britain and Turkey, would come into effect within nine months. The proviso was that if the contracting parties did not reach an agreement within this time limit the issue would be referred to the League of Nations (Article 3/2) (See Map 5: The boundaries of the modern Turkish state).[113] The Lausanne settlement was a real success for the national cause since there was no word of an independent Armenia or Kurdistan as designated in the Treaty of Sèvres. But the result could not have been achieved without the establishment of a Turkish–Bolshevik rapprochement between 1918 and 1921. The exchange of Greek and Turkish minorities was agreed in a separate agreement at Lausanne, which can be interpreted as the homogenisation of the Turkish nation within the new modern state. With the achievement of these ends, the specific conditions of the Turkish–Bolshevik alignment disappeared. There was no particular, pressing need to rely on each other's support in international relations. They could now pursue their own ends.

In accordance with the terms of the Treaty of Lausanne, the last British troops began to leave Istanbul on 2 October and the first Turkish nationalist army entered the city on 6 October. The Turkish national movement had succeeded in securing its national boundaries. On 13 October, the GNA accepted Ankara as the official capital of the Turkish state. On 29 October 1923, the new Constitution declared the Turkish state a 'republic' with sovereignty coming

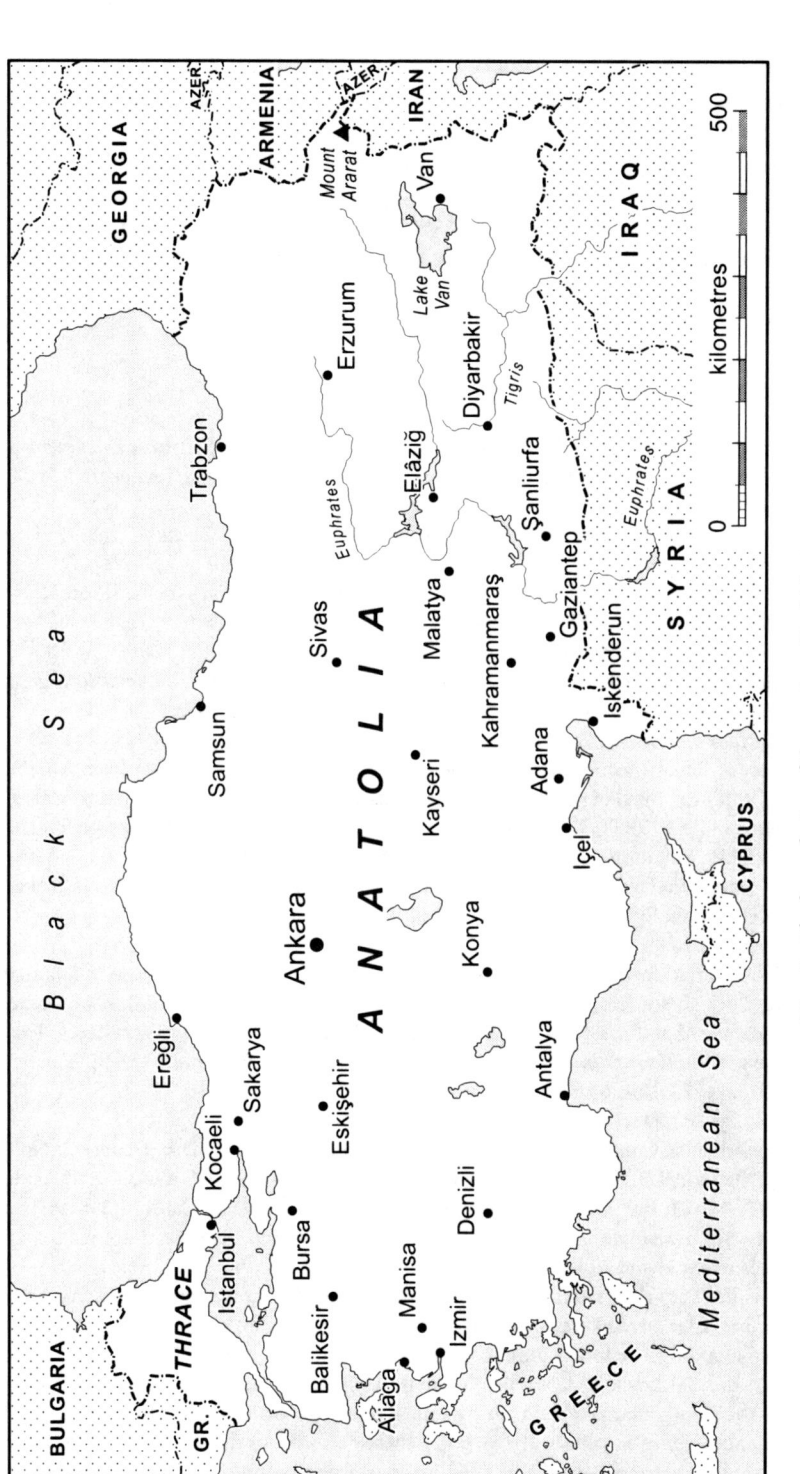

Map 5. The boundaries of the modern Turkish state

from the nation.[114] The creation of the modern Turkish state was a crucial factor in enabling Turkish participation in the world of nation-states. Having achieved socio-political modernity, the Turkish state solved its 'identity crisis' on an international level, but not on an societal level. The transition to modernity is a very long and complex process, the initial stages of which Turkey passed through, beginning in 1923. The political consequences of the Turkish transition, which opened up state-society gaps, indicate that Turkey has a long way to go in order to complete the transition to modernity. This factor will be examined further in the concluding chapter.

Notes

1 Bilal N. Şimşir, ed., İngiliz Belgelerinde Atatürk (1919–1938) [British Documents on Atatürk] (1919–1938) [BDA], Vol. II, Ankara, 1973, pp. 454–456, Enclosure 2 in Doc. 193.

2 Kazım Karabekir, İstiklal Harbimizde Enver Paşa ve İttihat Terakki, Ankara, Tekin Yayınevi, 1990, pp. 91–92.

3 S. Halit Kakınç, 'Gün Işığına Çıkartılan 12 Yeni Belge Tartışmalara Soru İşareti Getiriyor: Mustafa Suphi ve Yoldaşlarını İttihatçılar mı Öldürttü?', Toplumsal Tarih, 61:11 (January 1999), pp. 30–31, Doc. 1–2.

4 Cited in Stalin, Sochineniya, Vol. IV, pp. 411–12 in E.H. Carr, The Bolshevik Revolution: 1917–1923, Vol. III, London, Macmillan, 1961, pp. 301–302, fn. 3.

5 Carr, The Bolshevik Revolution, Vol. III, p. 302.

6 Public Record Office, Kew, London, FO371/5171/E13552/262/44, from Director of Military Intelligence, No.M.I.2.B., Situation in Turkey and Caucasus, dated 1 November 1920; FO371/5171/E12882/262/44, from Director of Military Intelligence, M.I.2.B., Situation in Turkey and Caucasus, dated 19 October 1920.

7 Mustafa Onar, ed., Atatürk'ün Kurtuluş Savaşı Yazışmaları [AKSY], Vol. II, Ankara, G.Ü. Teknik Eğitim Fakültesi Matbaası, 1995, pp. 211–212, Doc. 965.

8 AKSY, p. 230, Doc. 992.
However, Yerasimos argues that although the date of this letter is given as 5 January in Turkish sources, a document of Lenin's reply of 7 January in Russian sources indicates that it must have been written on 18 December. Stefanos Yerasimos, Türk-Sovyet İlişkileri: Ekim Devriminden 'Milli Mücadele'ye, Istanbul, Gözlem Yayınevi, 1979, p. 273, Doc. 63, fn.2.

9 Ibid., p. 282, Doc. 68.

10 Başbakanlık Cumhuriyet Arşivi [BBCumA], Karar No. 335, Eski Defter, C. No. 2, S. No.38; Ali F. Cebesoy, Moskova Hatıraları (1920–1922), Istanbul, İsmail Akgün, 1955, p. 101; Public Record Office, Kew, London, FO371/5179/E16173/345/44, from General Harrington to War Office, L9678, Relations between Nationalists and Bolsheviks, dated 20 December 1920.

11 It is not very clear from Turkish sources whether Budu Mdivani was the first Soviet ambassador to Ankara, or whether it was the Georgian ambassador. There is an explanation to be found only in Karabekir's memoirs, viz. that they were two brothers: the Bolshevik Mdivani as the Soviet ambassador and the Menshevik Mdivani as the Georgian ambassador to Ankara. Kazım Karabekir, İstiklal Harbimiz, Vol. II, Istanbul, Emre Yayınları, 199, p. 194. Cebesoy also writes that the Soviet government first decided to appoint Shalva Z. Eliava as an ambassador to Ankara, but the decision

was changed to appoint Budu Mdivani. Cebesoy, *Moskova Hatıraları*, p. 117. Budu Mdivani was a Georgian Communist who had been a member of a special Caucasian Bureau, formed in February 1920, their aim being to establish Soviet rule throughout the entire Caucasus. Richard Pipes, *The Formation of the Soviet Union: Communism and Nationalism, 1917–1923*, Cambridge, MA, Harvard University Press, 1954, p. 224.

During his stay at Kars, Mdivani helped to organise Mustafa Suphi's activities in Anatolia. The Turkish nationalist did not understand this change in Soviet policy since Eliava was more familiar with Turkish politics than Mdivani. Eliava had been sent to Istanbul by the Bolsheviks to investigate the situation of the Ottoman Empire and contacted the nationalists in September 1919. Cebesoy, *Moskova Hatıraları*, p. 60.

12 Osman Okyar, *Milli Mücadele Döneminde Türk-Sovyet İlişkilerinde Mustafa Kemal (1920–1921)*, Ankara, Türkiye İş Bankası Kültür Yayınları, 1998, p. 129.
13 Cebesoy, *Moskova Hatıraları*, pp. 118–119.
14 Okyar, *Milli Mücadele Döneminde*, p. 134.
15 Cebesoy, *Moskova Hatıraları*, pp. 138–140.
16 Rıza Nur, *Hayat ve Hatıratım, Vol. III*, Istanbul, İşaret Yayınları, 1992, p. 151; Cebesoy, *Moskova Hatıraları*, p. 146.
17 Nur, *Hayat ve Hatıratım, Vol. III*, p. 147.
18 Cebesoy, *Moskova Hatıraları*, pp. 119–120.
19 Public Record Office, Kew, London, FO371/4974/E3225/3225/58, from Admiral de Robeck, No. 413/M/2747, Restoration of Districts of Batum, Kars, Ardahan from Russia to Turkey, dated 26 March 1920.
20 Louis Fischer, *The Soviets in World Affairs: A History of the Relations Between the Soviet Union and the Rest of the World 1917–1929, Vol. I*, Princeton, NJ: Princeton University Press, 1951, p. 392.
21 Pipes, *The Formation of the Soviet Union*, p. 237.
22 Karabekir, *İstiklal Harbimiz, Vol. II*, p. 207.
23 Pipes, *The Formation of the Soviet Union*, p. 238.
24 Carr, *The Bolshevik Revolution, Vol. III*, pp. 301–302, fn.3; Ivar Spector, *The Soviet Union and the Muslim World, 1917–1958*, Seattle, University of Washington Press, 1959, p. 73.
25 Osman Özsoy, *Saltanat'tan Cumhuriyet'e Giden Yolda Kurtuluş Savaşı'nın Perde Arkası*, Istanbul, Aksoy Yayıncılık, 1999, p. 367.
26 Ünsal Yavuz, *Atatürk: İmparatorluktan Milli Devlete*, Ankara, Türk Tarih Kurumu Basımevi, 1990, p. 71.
27 Taner Akcam, 'Sevr and Lozan'in Baska Tarihi', in *İmparatorluktan Cumhuriyete Turkiye'de Etnik Catisma*, Erik J. Zurcher, ed., Istanbul, Iletisim, 2005, p. 51.
28 *TBMM Zabıt Ceridesi*, D.1, I.1, C.7, I.139, 29.1.1921, pp. 410–415.
29 R. Butler, J.P.T. Bury and M.E. Lambert, eds, *Documents on British Foreign Policy:1919–1939* [DBFP], *Vol. XIII*, p. 174, Doc. 174.
30 *BDA, Vol. III*, pp. 188–199, Doc. 72.
31 Stanford J. Shaw and Ezel Kural Shaw, *History of the Ottoman Empire and Modern Turkey, Vol. II – Reform, Revolution and Republic: The Rise of Modern Turkey, 1808–1975*, Cambridge University Press, 1995, p. 358. During the London Conference, the delegates of the Allied powers predicted that some compromise would be reached with Bekir Sami to modify the Treaty of Sèvres. Bekir Sami signed an agreement with Britain for the exchange of Turkish–British war prisoners. He also signed agreements with the representatives from France and Italy. But, the GNA did not ratify these

agreements since they were not in accordance with the principles of the National Pact. Y. Hikmet Bayur, *Türkiye Devletinin Dış Siyasası*, Ankara, Türk Tarih Kurumu Basımevi, 1973, pp. 86–87.

32 Özsoy, *Saltanat'tan Cumhuriyet'e Giden Yolda*, p. 389.

33 Cebesoy, *Moskova Hatıraları*, p. 147.

34 Karabekir, *İstiklal Harbimiz, Vol. II*, p. 209.

35 Okyar, *Milli Mücadele Döneminde*, p. 143.

36 Karabekir, *İstiklal Harbimiz, Vol. II*, p. 210.

37 Nur, *Hayat ve Hatıratım, Vol. III*, pp. 164–165.

38 Kamuran Gürün, *Türk-Sovyet İlişkileri*, Ankara, Türk Tarih Kurumu Basımevi, 1991, p. 68.

39 Nur, *Hayat ve Hatıratım, Vol. III*, p. 166.

40 Cebesoy, *Moskova Hatıraları*, p. 150.

41 Karabekir, *İstiklal Harbimiz, Vol. II*, p. 214.

42 Pipes, *The Formation of the Soviet Union*, p. 239.

43 *Atatürk'un Milli Dış Politikası (Cumhuriyet Dönemine Ait 100 Belge: 1919–1923)* [*AMDP*], *Vol. 1*, Ankara, T.C. Kültür Bakanlığı Yayınları, 1994, pp. 547–554, Doc. 96; Karabekir, *İstiklal Harbimiz, Vol. II*, pp. 226–230 and the copy of the treaty in English sources: Public Record Office, Kew, London, FO371/6272/E5810/116/58, from Director of Military Intelligence, Secret, Bolshevik–Turkish Treaty, dated 19 May 1921; J.C. Hurewitz, *Diplomacy in the Near and Middle East: A Documentary Record: 1914–1956, Vol. II*, Princeton, 1956, New York, Van Nostrand, pp. 95–97.

44 Patricia M. Carley, 'Turkey and Central Asia: reality comes calling', in Alvin Z. Rubinstein and Oles M. Smolansky, eds, *Regional Power Rivalries in the New Eurasia: Russia, Turkey and Iran*, London, M.E. Sharpe, 1995, p. 179.

45 William Hale, 'Turkey, Black Sea and Transcaucasia', in John F. R. Wright, Suzanne Goldenberg and Richard Schofield, eds, *Transcaucasian Boundaries*, London, UCL Press, 1996, p. 61.

46 Okyar, *Milli Mücadele Döneminde*, p. 144.

47 Alptekin Müderrisoğlu, *Kurtuluş Savaşının Mali Kaynakları*, Ankara, Atatürk Kültür, Dil ve Tarih Yüksek Kurulu, 1990, p. 546; B. Gökay, *A Clash of Empires: Turkey between Russian Bolshevism and British Imperialism, 1918–1923*, London, Tauris Academic Studies, 1997, p. 111.

48 Müderrisoğlu, *Kurtuluş Savaşının Mali Kaynakları*, pp. 548–549.

49 Hamit Aliyef, 'Kemal Atatürk'ün Türkiye ile Sovyetler Birliği Arasında Dostluğun Kurulması ve Sağlamlaştırılmasındaki Rölü', *Siyasal Bilgiler Fakültesi Dergisi*, C.36, No.1–4, Ocak-Aralik 1981, p. 75.

50 Spector, *The Soviet Union and the Muslim World*, p. 64.

51 The Soviet government also signed a treaty with Iran on 26 February 1921, which reaffirmed the border protocol of 1883 and reasserted the control of the two new regimes over the territory they had inherited. Fred Halliday, 'Condemned to react, unable to influence: Iran and Transcaucasia', in Wright, Goldenberg and Schofield, eds., *Transcaucasian Boundaries*, p. 76.

52 Branko Lazitch and Milorad M. Drachkovitch, *Lenin and the Comintern*, Stanford, CA, Hoover Institution Press, 1972, p. 411; *AMDP, Vol. I*, pp. 533–535, Doc. 95; Karabekir, *İstiklal Harbimiz, Vol. II*, p. 239, p. 243.

53 Carole Fink, 'The NEP in foreign policy: the Genoa Conference and the Treaty of Rapallo', in Gabriel Gorodetsky, ed., *Soviet Foreign Policy, 1917–1991: A Retrospective*, London, Franc Cass, 1994, p. 12.

54 In the preamble of the Treaty, the government of the USSR and the government of the GNA of Turkey emphasised their belief in 'the principles of the liberty of nations and the right of each nation to determine its own fate' and moreover 'the common struggle undertaken against imperialism'. In the Turkish source, 'imperialism' is described as the policy of expansion and occupation. *AMDP, Vol. I*, p.547, Doc. 96. However, in Kazım Karabekir's memoirs it is referred to as 'imperialism'. Karabekir, *İstiklal Harbimiz, Vol. II*, p.226.

55 Public Record Office, Kew, London, FO371/6275/E5998/235/58, from Mr. Norman (Tehran), No. 304(R), Supplies for Caucasus, dated 21 May 1921.

56 Carr, *The Bolshevik Revolution, Vol. III*, p.304.

57 Tony Cliff, *State Capitalism in Russia*, London, Bookmarks, 1988, pp.151–152; see further in Carr, *The Bolshevik Revolution, Vol. II*, chapters 18 and 19, pp.269–357.

58 Margot Light, *The Soviet Theory of International Relations*, Sussex, Wheatsheaf Books, 1988, p.30.

59 Pipes, *The Formation of the Soviet Union*, p.240.

60 Özsoy, *Saltanat'tan Cumhuriyet'e Giden Yolda*, p.394.

61 Cebesoy, *Moskova Hatıraları*, p.157; Nur, *Hayat ve Hatıratım, Vol. III*, pp.157–161.

62 Şevket S. Aydemir, *Makedonya'dan Ortaasya'ya Enver Paşa, Vol. III*, Istanbul, Remzi Kitabevi, 1992, p.551.

63 Nur, *Hayat ve Hatıratım, Vol. III*, p.160.

64 Aydemir, *Makedonya'dan Ortaasya'ya Enver Paşa, Vol. III*, p.573.

65 BBCumA, Karar No. 34, Eski Defter, C.No. 2, S.No. 385.

66 Shaw and Shaw, *History of the Ottoman Empire and Modern Turkey, Vol. II*, pp.359–360.

67 Gökay, *A Clash of Empires*, p.116.

68 Public Record Office, Kew, London, FO371/6273/E8664/116/58, from the Cabinet Secretariat, Alliance of the Caucasian States, dated 27 July 1921.

69 Public Record Office, Kew, London, FO371/6272/E7295/116/58, from General Bagratouni (Conversation), Transcaucasian Federation, dated 27 June 1921.

70 Arnold J. Toynbee, *Turkey*, London, Ernest Benn Limited, 1926, p.101.

71 Aydemir, *Makedonya'dan Ortaasya'ya Enver Paşa, Vol. III*, p.582.

72 Karabekir, *İstiklal Harbimiz, Vol. II*, p.280.

73 Karabekir, *İstiklal Harbimiz, Vol. II*, p.288; BBCumA, Karar No. 1078, Eski Defter, C. No. 3, S. No. 38.

74 Karabekir, *İstiklal Harbimiz, Vol. II*, pp.296–299; Public Record Office, Kew, London, FO371/6273/E12675/116/58, from General Bagratonui, No. 469, dated 16 November 1921.

75 *AMDP, Vol. I*, pp.571–579, Doc. 97. The Turkish document corresponds with the copy in the British documents. Public Record Office, Kew, London, FO371/6269/E8378/8378/58, Outline of Events in Transcaucasia from the beginning of the Russian revolution in the summer of 1917 to April 1921; FO371/6274/E13062/116/58, from Sir H. Rumbold (Constantinople), No.1061, Agreement between Angora and Caucasian Republics of 13 October 1921, dated 22 November 1921.

76 Sulejman Alijarly, 'The Republic of Azerbaijan: notes on the state borders in the past and the present', in Wright, Goldenberg and Schofield, eds., *Transcaucasian Boundaries*, p.113.

77 Alfred L.P. Dennis, *The Foreign Policies of Soviet Russia*, London, J.M. Dent & Sons Ltd., 1924, p.221.

78 Public Record Office, Kew, London, FO371/6273/E12675/116/58, from General Bagratonui, No. 469, dated 14 November 1921.

79 Richard G. Hovannisian, 'Caucasian Armenia between Imperial and Soviet Rule: The Interlude of National Independence', in Ronald G. Suny, ed., *Transcaucasia: Nationalism and Social Change*, Michigan, The University of Michigan, 1983, p. 291.

80 Hale, 'Turkey, Black Sea and Transcaucasia', pp. 63–64.

81 Kakınç, 'Gün Işığına Çıkartılan', p. 33, Doc. 8.

82 Pipes, *The Formation of the Soviet Union*, p. 257.

83 D. Cameron Watt, ed., *British Documents on Foreign Affairs: Reports and Papers from the Foreign Office Confidential Print [BDFA]*, *Vol. VI*, University Publications of America, 1984, p. 268, Doc. 170.

84 'The dissatisfaction of the native population with Soviet rule found expression in partisan warfare, which had its origin the Ferghana valley, spread to the neighbouring provinces and finally embraced nearly all of Turkestan, including the principalities of Khiva and Bukhara. This popular resistance movement, perhaps the most persistent and successful in the entire history of Soviet Russia, became known as Basmachestvo and its participants as Basmachis.

The Basmachis were originally ordinary bandits who had preyed on the countryside even before the outbreak of the Revolution. The tsarist regime had never been quite successful in suppressing them'. They never achieved their major aim, to overthrow Russian rule in Turkestan. Pipes, *The Formation of the Soviet Union*, p. 178.

85 Of other CUP leaders, Talat Pasha was assassinated in Berlin by an Armenian on 16 March 1921 and Cemal Pasha was killed in Tiflis, again by an Armenian, on 22 July 1922. Gürün, *Türk-Sovyet İlişkileri*, p. 44; Fahrettin Çiloğlu, *Kurtuluş Savaşı Sözlüğü*, Istanbul, Doğan Kitap, 1999, p. 65; Lazitch and Drachkovitch, *Lenin and the Comintern*, p. 413.

86 *AMDP*, *Vol. I*, pp. 587–590, Doc. 98.

87 Yavuz, *Atatürk*, p. 76. The issue of Hatay would remain a problem during the determination of Turkish border with Syria until the city joined the Turkish Republic in 1939, as we will see in the Conclusion.

88 Özsoy, *Saltanat'tan Cumhuriyet'e Giden Yolda*, p. 431.

89 Bayur, *Türkiye Devletinin Dış Siyasası*, pp. 109–110.

90 Fink, 'The NEP in foreign policy', p. 13.

91 Ibid., p. 18.

92 Gökay, *A Clash of Empires*, p. 119.

93 Andrew Mango, *Atatürk*, London, John Murray, 1999, pp. 336–337.

94 *AKYS*, *Vol. II*, p. 344, Doc. 1164.

95 Mango, *Atatürk*, pp. 337–338; Özsoy, *Saltanat'tan Cumhuriyet'e Giden Yolda*, pp. 463–464.

96 Mango, *Atatürk*, p. 337.

97 Shaw and Shaw, *History of the Ottoman Empire and Modern Turkey*, *Vol. II*, p. 362.

98 *AKYS*, *Vol. II*, pp. 373–74, Doc. 1216.

99 David Fromkin, *A Peace to End All Peace: Creating the Modern Middle East, 1914-1922*, London, Penguin Books, 1991, pp. 549–551. There was a possibility that the confrontation could develop into a British–Soviet conflict: on the one hand, Chicherin declared at the Genoa Conference that the Soviets would not be neutral in the event of war with Turkey; on the other, Karakhan sent a note to Curzon stating that the question of the Turkish Straits had to be solved in accordance with the Treaty of Moscow. Moreover, the Ankara government officially demanded Soviet

intervention in the event of the Balkan states participating on the side of Britain in the Chanak confrontation. Gökay, *A Clash of Empires*, p. 140.

100 Özsoy, *Saltanat'tan Cumhuriyet'e Giden Yolda*, p. 484.

101 S. I. Aralov, *Bir Sovyet Diplomatının Türkiye Hatıraları* – 2, Cumhuriyet Gazetesi Yayınları, 1997, p. 185.

102 Özsoy, *Saltanat'tan Cumhuriyet'e Giden Yolda*, p. 486.

103 *AMDP, Vol. I*, pp. 607–610, Doc. 100.

104 Fromkin, *A Peace to End All Peace*, p. 551.

105 Shaw and Shaw, *History of the Ottoman Empire and Modern Turkey, Vol. II*, p. 365.

106 Yavuz, *Atatürk*, p. 81.

107 Fromkin, *A Peace to End All Peace*, p. 559.

108 Louis Henkin, 'The role of law and its limitations', in Marc Williams, ed., *International Relations in the Twentieth Century: A Reader*, London, Macmillan, 1989, p. 190.

109 Pipes, *The Formation of the Soviet Union*, p. 245.

110 Dennis, *The Foreign Policies of Soviet Russia*, p. 228.

111 Gökay, *A Clash of Empires*, p. 153.

112 Eighteen separate documents were signed between the contracting parties at Lausanne. Like the Treaty of Sèvres, it was a detailed settlement, but was unlikely to be legalised in the creation of a new Turkish state.
Reha Parla, ed., *Belgelerle Türkiye Cumhuriyeti'nin Uluslararası Temelleri: Lozan, Montrö ve Türkiye'nin Komşularıyla İmzaladığı Başlıca Belgeler (Suriye, İrak, İran, SSCB, Bulgaristan, Yunanistan)*, Lefkoşa, Tezel Ofset ve Matbaacılık, 1985, pp. 1–103.

113 Ibid., pp. 1–3. Accordingly, Turkey and Britain held a conference (Haliç Konferansı) between 19 May and 5 June 1924 in Istanbul and decided to refer the Turkish–Iraqi border to the League. After long diplomatic negotiations, the Turkish–Iraqi border was determined by a treaty between Turkey, Britain and Iraq in 1926 in accordance with the Council of the League's recommendation and the decision of the Permanent Court of International Justice of 1925. The Turkish–Iranian border was the last and the least problematic to demarcate, which was settled by a treaty between the two states in 1932 and modified in 1937. Hüseyin Pazarcı, *Uluslararası Hukuk Dersleri*, II. Kitap, Ankara, Turhan Kitabevi, 1993, pp. 231–232. 'In fact the Turkish–Iranian border is one of the oldest borders between the two countries in the world. Significantly, it was the only boundary of the Ottoman Empire not to change with the emergence of the modern Turkish state'. Philip Robins, *Turkey and the Middle East*, New York, Council on Foreign Relations Press, 1991, p. 21.

114 Shaw and Shaw, *History of the Ottoman Empire and Modern Turkey, Vol. II*, p. 368.

8
Conclusion

This book critically analysed Turkey's historical engagement with European modernity as the transformation of an Islamic, Ottoman state structure into a modern nation-state, in particular in order to understand the role of its foreign policy towards the East during this process. It is unlikely that we will come across a closely similar historical transformation, but it is also true that some 'stateless' nations, such as the Palestinians and Kurds in the Middle East, are driven towards becoming nation-states via the driving force of nationalism as part of modernity, and that new states are still joining international society. In the modern international system, all modern states and nations are territorial since they claim particular geographical space and collective identities. In this context, the territoriality and national identity aspects of the modern state continue to provide the corseting, so to speak, of contemporary international politics.

Historically, the emergence of new states and regimes usually takes place during international turmoil such as the end of empires, wars and revolutions. At the beginning of the twenty-first century, an alternative history making is taking place and social revolution is sweeping across the Arab world. Since the fall of Hosni Mubarak in Egypt on 11 February 2011, unfolding pre-democracy protests and uprisings shook the Middle East and North Africa. At the time of writing this book, the shock waves of people power and protests continue rocking authoritarian regimes from Bahrain via Libya to Syria. As the theoretically informed historical analysis of the Turkish case in this book indicates, the relationship between Islam, modernity and nation-state building in a Muslim context is a complex and long process. Hence, it is too early to make any sound judgments how the unintended outcomes of the Arab Spring of 2011 will unfold in the MENA in the following decades, if not centuries.

In this concluding chapter, I will first point out the specific findings of each chapter in order to support the above-stated general finding of the book. I will also attempt to draw some theoretical and empirical conclusions from this case-study about Islam, foreign policy, nationalism and state transformation. These self-reflections might be useful for understanding some of the problems other Islamic societies, such as post-Taliban Afghanistan, post-Saddam Iraq, post-Mubarak Egypt and post-Gaddafi Libya currently face in overcoming the challenges of regime change and nation-building while also engaging in new foreign and regional policies in the regions since 9/11 and the Arab Spring of 2011.

I argued that the main characteristics of the period 1918–21 in Turkish politics were the transition of an Islamic imperial state structure to a modern state as an integral part of modernity and a rapprochement between the two new regimes in Ankara and Moscow, which altered the historical animosity between the Ottoman and Russian empires and their rivalry in the South Caucasus. The main concern of the theoretically informed historical analysis, therefore, was to investigate the causes of the unique Turkish–Bolshevik rapprochement in the East in accordance with the requirements of state transformation.

The theoretical framework – the first three chapters – was based on a new interdisciplinary approach to foreign policy of transitional states by bringing foreign policy, modernity and nationalism together in order to provide a better analysis of the relationship between Turkish state transformation and foreign policy-making. The ultimate aim of the new approach was to understand the complexity of state transformation and foreign policy making when understanding a Muslim country's engagement with European modernity.

It was stated in Chapter 1, orthodox foreign policy analysis has a general tendency to focus on either domestic politics and/or the level of leadership of newly emerging states. Having accepted the importance of studying these two levels, while pointing out the insufficiency thereof, the new approach aimed to provide a multi-causal analysis within a wider historical context from an interdisciplinary perspective. This chapter identified the five main dimensions of foreign policy in relation to the transition to modernity as follows: the elements of continuity and change in policy-making, the impact of structure on decision-making, the domestic-foreign inter-relation, the role of charismatic leader, and the role of foreign policy during the construction of national identity.

Chapter 2 explored the causal link between nation-state building and the transition to modernity. It was stated that the concept of modernity went beyond the model of modernisation theory in providing a theory of historical and sociological causation to identify the internal and external causes of Turkish socio-political change, as a non-European society. The concept of alterative modernity not only highlighted the possibility of change in non-European, Islamic societies but also contributed to bridging the gap between FPA and historical sociology. The direct relation between modernity and identity construction was emphasised in order to trace the implications of modernity for the Turkish state transformation. On the one hand, Ottoman modernisation was related to the expansion of capitalism; on the other, the Turkish 'identity crisis' at the margins of Europe was regarded as a consequence of its partial incorporation into the capitalist international system since 1856.

Chapter 3 explained why the study of nationalism, is the third pillar of the interdisciplinary approach to understanding the foreign policy of a transitional state. The relationship between nationalism and modernity was specifically scrutinised in order to understand the emergence of Turkish nationalism not only as an unintended consequence of the Ottoman Empire's attempts at modernisation from the time of the *Tanzimat* era but also as a phenomenon inseparable from the creation of the modern state. This chapter also highlighted the historical continuity and change between the Ottoman and Turkish regional affairs, as the first dimension of transitional foreign policy.

Hence, in parallel with the theoretical premises of the new framework, the last four empirical chapters of the book offered a detailed analysis of Turkish foreign policy towards the South Caucasus between 1918 and 1921 in order to evaluate the main dimensions of its transitional foreign policy. The main concern of the empirical work was to provide a critical analysis of the importance of Eastern affairs during Turkey's transition from an Islamic empire to a modern nation-state. By examining Turkey's foreign policies *vis-à-vis* its Eastern neighbours – Armenia, Azerbaijan and the Soviet Union – it offered a novel interpretation of orthodox Turkish historiography, which departs from conventional works that tend to focus almost exclusively on Turkey's engagement with the West in the process of its transition to a modern state.

Chapter 4 explored the challenges of nationalist foreign policy in order to understand the causes of the initiation of relations with the Bolsheviks in the South Caucasus. While the first dimension was discussed in Chapter 3, the other three dimensions of Turkey's transitional foreign policy were identified in the next chapter as follows:

The second dimension – the impact of structure on decision-making – was found in examining the influence of the determining structure of Ottoman socio-political change on policy-making in relation to the creation of a nation-state. The possibilities of an American mandate and the Anatolian solution of local congresses were explored to identify the historical structure behind Turkey's state transformation. The rise of the Turkish nationalist movement under the leadership of Mustafa Kemal was thus located within a broad historical and social context, which shaped and constrained the choices of decision-makers.

The third dimension – the role of the charismatic leader – was related to the rise of Mustafa Kemal's charismatic leadership as a revolutionary force in introducing a new order based on the European model and in establishing relations with the Bolsheviks that changed the traditional Ottoman–Russian animosity. The unique rapprochement between the two strong leaders, Kemal and Lenin, was analysed through the study of diplomatic correspondence and conferences that indicated rational decision-making in their foreign policy behaviours. It was argued that the role of the charismatic leader cannot be separated either from domestic structural change itself or the international systemic constraints within which foreign policy goals are determined under specific conditions, such as the state transformation.

The fourth theoretical dimension of transitional foreign policies – the inter-relation between the domestic and foreign spheres – was the subject of Chapter 5. After the nationalist leaders decided on the primary goals of Turkish domestic policy in accordance with the main principles of modern statehood in the Turkish National Pact, they modified the goals of foreign policy towards the South

Caucasus accordingly. The first major test of nationalist foreign policy appeared during the Sovietisation of Azerbaijan. When Bolshevik control was established in Azerbaijan, it became clear that the Turkish nationalists were determined to restrict their policies to within national borders and that they recognised the importance of the stabilisation of regional security and the determination of the Turkish–Armenian border with the co-operation of the Bolsheviks. The influence of the Treaty of Sèvres on Turkish foreign policy was interpreted as a sign of the close interplay between domestic and foreign policies. Furthermore, Bolshevik support for Enver Pasha and Mustafa Suphi after the Baku Congress induced Mustafa Kemal to consolidate the national movement and his authority in domestic and foreign affairs.

Chapters 6 and 7 analysed the final dimension of transitional Turkish foreign policy – national identity construction. Turkish–Armenian relations were related to the question of borders and identity construction. It was argued that the Armenians played a crucial role in the creation of the Turkish national identity in two ways: Armenian claims on the eastern part of Anatolia helped Turkish leaders to invoke national feeling regarding the Turkish homeland, and the Armenians became the first 'other' with the signing of the Treaty of Alexandropol, by which they had to recognise the existence of a separate Turkish nation within the borders of Turkey that had been decided upon. This interpretation challenged orthodox Turkish historiography, which claimed that Turkish identity was the product of Turkey's struggle with the Greeks. Mustafa Kemal skilfully manipulated the channel of foreign policy to emphasise the importance of the Ankara government to the Bolsheviks, not only in securing the South Caucasian borderlands but also in approaching the Islamic world. With the signing of the Treaty of Moscow, the existence of modern Turkish statehood was recognised by another state for the first time. This act of recognition was described as an essential stage of political identity construction in the international arena.

In short, the Turkish–Bolshevik rapprochement played an important role in determining both Turkey's problematic border with the Armenians and the country's political identity through the international relations of the South Caucasus at the beginning of the twentieth century. As a result of the establishment of the *de facto* nationalist government, there was a 'dual administration' within the Ottoman state between 1918 and 1921: the Istanbul government and the Ankara government. The Turkish nationalists determined a foreign policy which highlighted the new state's *raison d'être*. As the findings of this book indicate, the foreign policy of the Ankara government served the nationalist movement by helping political integration through first establishing its authority in opposition to that of the Istanbul government and the other competing actors – Enver Pasha and Mustafa Suphi – in domestic and foreign affairs. One can establish similarities between the Ankara government and the new governments in Kabul in Afghanistan, Baghdad in Iraq and Cairo in Egypt at the beginning of the twenty-first century.

In particular, achieving political integration and national sovereignty is crucial and partly based on creating channels of interaction with the other states to establish a government's legitimacy in the regional and international arenas. The consolidation of the nationalist regime in domestic politics and its sense of identity were founded essentially in Turkish foreign affairs with the Bolsheviks and the South Caucasian states. More importantly, the Turkish–Bolshevik rapprochement was a sign of the recognition of each other's new political identity in the international arena as the two newly emerging states of the region, rather than just being a sign of their common struggle against Western imperialism. This rapprochement not only influenced the policies of the Allied powers in planning the Turkish and Russian settlements at the end of the Great War but also played an important role in solving the Turkish identity crisis by facilitating the newly constructed Turkish state's participation in international society. Both the Turkish nationalists and the Bolsheviks were now subjects in the post-war international order rather than the objects of violent struggles during the partitioning of the collapsed Ottoman and Russian empires. After they had completed the process of transformation in 1923, the Turkish Republic and the Soviet Union pursued their own ends.

Key theoretical findings of the book

The following further suggestions of wider relevance from this book's interdisciplinary approach to foreign policy can be drawn about the relationship between foreign policy, nationalism and modernity. First, foreign policy serves to facilitate the political integration of a newly emerging regime and/or state. If a new political entity aims to participate in an international society, it has to follow the norms of this society in that the main actors are nation-states. Most of the modern nation-states underwent the legitimation of authority within a territorial political unit at some time between the seventeenth and twentieth centuries. In this case, authority legitimation has been a constitutive element of the transition of society from traditional social relations to the presence of a *political* society' which develops a capacity for collective action and decision-making along with a common sense of political identity.[1] While the political legitimacy of a state in internal politics requires national integration, its external relations contribute to this integration process through the representation of national interests and counter-identification with the other states.

Second, foreign policy becomes an efficient tool of constructing a national identity of a state. By definition, states operate in internal and external spheres within which identity construction and foreign policy-making are interlinked through the territorial aspect. Foreign policy operates in the spheres of inside and outside by differentiating between 'us' and 'them', which strengthens the national integration process. In specific terms, the manipulation of foreign policy issues reflects historical claims on a particular territory and effectively creates a national consciousness, so as to possess the land against the claims of others. In this event, the foreign policy of a newly emerging state becomes an integral part of its search for national and political identity unification.

Third, the role of a strong leadership is a very important factor, although not the only one, to understand the relationship between foreign policy and state-building. As argued in this book, leadership can become a revolutionary force in relation to the construction of a political identity as an integral part of socio-political change. Thus, foreign policy-making and national identity construction inevitably overlapped on the level of leadership. Foreign policy became central to the self-appointed goals of the national leadership in order to construct a new identity during the erosion of traditional identities. During this process, as was specified earlier, the role of charismatic leadership in nation-building and in foreign policy has to be situated within the historical and social structure to highlight the complexity of state transformation. Consequently, an analysis of transitional foreign policy must focus on the combination of historical circumstances and charismatic leaders as an efficient instrument for pursuing the goals of political integration, nation-building and authority legitimation in newly emerging states.

Fourth, foreign policy becomes a salient means of locating a new political identity in the international arena through its recognition by other actors. In general terms, the identity construction of a new actor takes place in two spheres in international relations. On the one hand, the legitimacy of a newly emerging state in domestic politics revolves around the creation of the nation and the territorial integrity to exercise its sovereignty within the boundaries of the nation-state. On the other hand, as well as gaining internal legitimacy, 'the state has to be legitimised externally. This requires that its sovereignty has to be recognised by other states'.[2] In this respect, international law, of which the most important legal mechanism is international agreement, becomes essential to set the relationship between recognition and foreign policy.[3] However, as stated in this book, recognition and international law are necessary but not sufficient to an understanding of the role of foreign policy during the transition to modernity. They must be supported by other factors, such as the processes of nation-building and state consolidation.

These general conclusions can be helpful, in one way or another, in analysing the relationship between foreign policy and state-building when, for example, relatively new states, such as Armenia, Azerbaijan, Georgia, Kazakhstan, Kyrgyzstan, Tajikistan, Turkmenistan and Uzbekistan of the former the Soviet Union joined the international system at the end of the twentieth century. All these ex-Soviet republics lacked some of the main features of sovereign nation-statehood and were aiming to create effective political-administrative units. They also acquired diplomatic recognition from the international society of states.[4] In general terms, each republic's separate relations with the three regional powers – Russia, Turkey and Iran – made contributions toward either strengthening or weakening their state-building processes.

Historical lessons of the Turkey's engagement with modernity

Having suggested these general theoretical outcomes of this book, some specific lessons can be drawn from Turkey's engagement with European modernity as a Muslim country.

In the process of nation-building, the relationship between foreign policy and the construction of a modern nation has not been analysed directly but through an indirect analysis of their relationship with the state-building process. This was a consequence of accepting the arguments of modern theories of nationalism in nation construction and also of the empirical evidence of Turkish nation construction, namely that the state had to be formed first in order to construct a separate Turkish nation. As mentioned earlier, the use of 'state-nation' would make better sense in understanding nation-building in a Muslim context.[5]

The role of foreign policy was emphasised during the initial stages of political identity construction, that of statehood – differentiation between 'us' and 'them' and recognition by other actors on the international level – but not during its final stages on the societal level. The nationalist elites focused on state formation until 1923. Thereafter, some practical measures and socio-political reforms were carried out between 1923 and 1935 to consolidate the modern national state.[6] These reforms introduced radical institutional changes at the executive and legislative levels:[7]

- the abolition of the Caliphate in 1924;
- the forcible dissolution of the pious foundations and the religious orders in 1925;
- the substitution of a secular civil code of law from Switzerland for the religious law (Şeriat) in 1926;
- the establishment of the national education system under the authority of the Ministry of Education in 1926;
- the replacement of the Arabic alphabet with the Latin in 1928;
- a constitutional amendment in 1937 which deleted the clause, 'the religion of the Turkish state is Islam', and declared that the Turkish Republic was a 'secular state'.

During the construction of the Turkish nation, not only were education and language reformed in accordance with secular norms by de-legitimising religious education and the Ottoman language, but also there was a rewriting of a national history within the context of re-interpretation of the past. After the establishment of the modern Turkish state, the establishment of national unity and the secularisation of society progressed reciprocally.

These developments in Turkish external affairs were supported by the implementation of rational Turkish foreign policy in order to secure its new borders and to assert its sovereign rights in international society between 1923 and 1938, which was aimed at solving Turkey's four important problems with its neighbours created by the Treaty of Lausanne.[8]

The first problem was the exchange of minorities between Turkey and Greece under the provisions of the Treaty of Lausanne in 1923. The Greek minorities of Anatolia were exchanged for the Muslims of Greece by the Turkish–Greek agreement of 1923, which did not include the Greek inhabitants of İstanbul and the Muslim inhabitants of western Thrace. This exchange was a clear indication of making the new Turkish nation homogenous within the boundaries of the new state. Although the exchange of minorities caused some new problems between the two countries, a rapprochement between Venizelos and Atatürk developed and a new Turkish–Greek agreement was signed on 10 June 1930, which dealt with the questions arising from the application of the Treaty of Lausanne and with the agreement on the exchange of minorities.

The second problem was that, as stated earlier, the Treaty of Lausanne left the Turkish–Iraqi frontier undetermined and to be settled with Britain, which was ruling Iraq under a mandate from the League of Nations. The question of Mosul brought the Turkish–British negotiations to a stalemate but the two sides reached an agreement concerning the status of Mosul and the Turkish–Iraqi border in 1926.[9] Interestingly enough, the Mosul question served as the motivation for Turkey to sign a Pact of Non-Aggression and Security with the Soviet Union on 17 December 1925 – one day after the League's decision on Mosul.

The third problem in Turkish foreign policy during the consolidation of state was related to the status of the Turkish Straits. The Turkish government asked the signatories of the Treaty of Lausanne for a revision to the demilitarisation of the Turkish Straits. At the Montreux Conference in 1936, Turkey re-established its full sovereignty over the straits, as a result of British support for Turkish claims as well as that of the Soviet Union. At this point, the deterioration of Turkish–Soviet relations was caused by the Turkish–British rapprochement. The real reversal in Turkish–Soviet relations was to come after Atatürk's death in 1938.[10]

The final territorial problem in Turkish foreign policy, which still has contemporary implications, was the status of Hatay (Alexandretta), which concerned Turkey and Syria. The Turkish–French agreement of 1921 and the Treaty of Lausanne left Hatay outside Turkey's borders. When France announced in 1936 that it had decided to include Hatay in the new independent Syrian state, the Turkish government reacted negatively. The issue was referred to the League of Nations, which sent a commission in 1937 and concluded that the Turks were in the majority. In 1939, the independent Republic of Hatay announced its decision to unite with Turkey. With the incorporation of Hatay the modern Turkish state reached its current borders.

As stated earlier, socio-political transformation has to follow economic growth in order to promote modernity, and foreign policy spontaneously gains special importance during the development of a national capitalist economy and industrialisation, which is also among the essential clusters of modernity. Thus, there is further scope to expand the proposed interdisciplinary approach to the role of foreign policy in the economic development of transitional states. The interdisciplinary theoretical framework emphasised that the political dimension of the transition to modernity cannot be separated from the economic, but priority was given to the former due to the main concern of the book, i.e. to analyse the role of foreign policy during the construction of political identity.

Nevertheless, the role of foreign policy on economic issues had been highlighted with reference to receiving Bolshevik financial aid and war materials, which played a crucial role in the early stages of the Turkish state building. One of the main reasons for this limited emphasis in this book was that economic development did not become a primary concern in Turkish politics until 1929.[11] In the

1920s, industrialisation did not really take off in the Turkish economy of which agriculture was the largest sector. The Law for the Encouragement of Industry (*Teşvik-i Sanayi Kanunu*) in 1927 was enacted to encourage the necessary private capital in the development of industry. However, the Turkish economy was also influenced by the world economic crisis and the years 1929–1932 became a period of searching for foreign loans. Although foreign investors were hesitant to enter Turkey, the Turkish government secured an American loan in 1930. The same year, the British–Turkish Treaty of Commerce and Navigation was signed. In 1931, 'statism' (*Devletçilik*) was adopted as the basis of a new economic policy, which was a combination of the state-led economy with the assistance of private capitalism for major developments – a kind of 'third way'.[12] Turkish statist policies were influenced by the five-year plan of the Soviet Union. A Soviet delegation visited Turkey and not only recommended the development of Turkish industry but also provided financial aid for the Turkish industrialisation programme. The first Turkish five-year plan was announced in 1933. US, British, French, German as well as Soviet loans enabled the Turkish government to develop its industry by the end of the 1930s.

Moreover, the theoretically informed analysis of Turkish history at the end of the Ottoman Empire could not have been applied to the Ankara government's foreign relations with its contemporary neighbouring states – Iran, Iraq and Syria – since the modern state system in the 'Middle East' as we know it today was not created yet by the colonial powers. The disintegration of the Ottoman Empire at the end of the First World War produced radical socio-economic and political changes throughout the region. It was first in Turkey and Iran that had common features during the creation of centralised state systems: 'Both were based on the ruins of dynastic empires which had been challenged by constitutional and reformist groups in the early 20th century, occupied by foreign troops and finally overthrown by regimes led by military officers who had seized power in alliance with nationalist forces in the early 1920s.'[13] However, the region was under the control of Britain at the end of the war. There were no direct relations between the Iranian, Iraqi and Syrian nationalists and the Turkish nationalists, and not only these relations but also their links with the Bolsheviks were supervised by the existing powers, mainly the British and French colonialism.[14] The Turkish nationalists did not have direct relations with the Arab successor states of the Ottoman Empire during the construction of the Turkish state and had to give priority to normalising relations with Britain (in Iraq) and France (in Syria).

Implications of the Turkish experience for the Arab world in the 21st century
There are two last, but not the least, historical lessons to be drawn from the findings of this book – those of Islam and of democracy. The Turkish transition to modernity had distinctive characteristics, among which was its role as a pioneer among Muslim societies. The Turkish experience in advancing an alternative form of modernity was important for other Muslims, but the relationship between Islam, modernity and secularism has only been mentioned here in passing. The Ottoman Empire was the last Islamic imperial state when it was

obliged to redefine itself as a 'multinational secular state' as a member of the Concert of Europe in 1856.[15] This participation compelled the Ottoman state to begin the process of emulative modernisation. 'Secularism and positivism' were the two important elements of this modernisation, which reached its institutional peak with the establishment of the Turkish nation-state in 1923.[16]

The progress of modernity in Europe was relatively organic and it was the Reformation that paved the way for Christian societies to develop further economically. 'In Muslim societies a similar reformation is long overdue, which would create the basis for the societies to move forward.'[17] The concept of political sovereignty also developed belatedly in Muslim societies, since in the Islamic faith the only sovereign is God.[18] Much of what characterises the Turkish transition in the eighteenth and nineteenth centuries was experienced by other Muslim societies in the nineteenth and twentieth centuries.[19] As a result, the Turks had to face the consequences of this transition earlier than other Muslims, meaning the need to modify an Islamic identity with a degree of secularism within a broad historical context.

As suggested earlier, the transition to modernity is partly the consequence of a continual dialogue between past and present. Meanwhile, the construction of modern nationhood on the ruins of communal identities inherited from the 'umma' (religious community) tradition has led to contradictions with the secular state identity, given the fact that the majority of Turkish people still describe themselves as Muslims, albeit in a modern and enlightened manner.[20]

Paradoxically, as the findings of this book highlight, Islam not only served as a source of national integrity against the non-Muslim subjects of the Ottoman Empire – the Armenians and the Greeks – but it was also utilised by the nationalist leaders in both domestic and foreign policies: first, to provide a basis for Turkish–Bolshevik co-operation in the East; and to disqualify the claims of Turkish communists and Islamists to provide a solution to the Turkish question.

The nationalist Kemalist regime, therefore, pragmatically used/abused Islamic propaganda in domestic and foreign affairs as the Young Turks (1908–1918) had done, but unlike their predecessors they tried to gradually remove Islam from the political discourse.[21] This was not an easy task given the fact that religion is the strongest means of resistance to radical change in any society. Any essentialist and orientalist understanding of Islam overlooks this important historical fact in the case of Turkey: during the transition from an empire to a nation-state Islam served as a source of national unity and it still continues to be one of the elements of Turkey's national identity.[22] One can certainly argue that the Turkish state did not renounce Islam, but kept it under constant review. Therefore, a peculiar mix of modernity, secularism and Islam has characterised an alternative form of modernity and the construction of a modern Turkish identity as Muslim and secular.[23]

It was argued that the Turkish state inherited an 'identity crisis' that emerged through the Ottoman Empire's integration into the European international system in the nineteenth century. The last chapter concluded that the declaration of the Turkish Republic on 29 October 1923 enabled Turkey to participate in the international society of nation-states, which provided an answer to the modern dilemma of its 'identity crisis' on the international level. However, these achievements were not interpreted as the completion of its transition to modernity. On the contrary, they were a beginning, and the uneven character of modernity brought new complex dimensions to the Turkish identity crisis by opening up gaps between the secular character of state and the Muslim identity of society.

In the Turkish context, modernity has been associated with Westernisation/ Europeanisation without paying enough attention to its link with democratisation.[24] The Turkish experience with the consolidation of democracy has differed from those of both the modern Western states and most developing countries. There had been a strong state tradition in Ottoman/Turkish history, and this caused problems for the Turkish transition to democracy. Turkey's democracy has been consolidated by the gradual inclusion of Islam into politics 'while constitutional and legal secularism have been kept intact'.[25] The rigid control of the public sphere by the state was the dominant character of Turkish politics between 1923 and 1946, although it softened gradually from the 1950s to the 1980s.[26]

The rise of Islamic fundamentalism and the Kurdish question in the 1990s can be interpreted as the result of the problematic nature of democratisation, and a reaction to the uneven development of secularism and modernity on the societal level.[27] However, the Turkish transition to modernity is, as Habermas described, 'an incomplete project' which had its origins at the beginning of nineteenth century, and it is still 'questioning its present'.[28] Hence, since 2002, the rise of political Islam in the context of the AKP's tenure in power can be seen as Turkey questioning its present. Nonetheless Turkey's engagement with modernity is not only unique to its own historical, socio-economic and political conditions, but also should not be seen as a blue-print for the Arab successor states of the Ottoman Empire. Its relations with the Soviet Union at the beginning of the twentieth century assisted Turkey in beginning its advance as a modern nation-state along this path, but Turkish–European relations via the European Union in the twenty-first century will probably be helpful in reaching its final destination, an alternative modernity of a Muslim society.

Notes

1 Philip G. Cerny, 'Foreign policy leadership and national integration', *British Journal of International Studies*, 5 (April 1979), pp. 59–60.

2 Michael Hill and Lian Kwen Fee, *The Politics of Nation Building and Citizenship in Singapore*, London, Routledge, 1995, p. 24.

3 Louis Henkin, 'The Role of Law and its Limitations', in Marc Williams, ed., *International Relations in the Twentieth Century: A Reader*, London, Macmillan, 1989, p. 189.

4 Jonathan Aves, 'National Security and Military Issues in the Transcaucasus: the Cases of Georgia, Azerbaijan, and Armenia', in Bruce Parrot, ed., *State-Building and Military Power in Russia and the New States of Eurasia*, London, M.E. Sharpe, 1995, p. 211.

5 Kemal H. Karpat, *The Politicization of Islam: Reconstructing Identity, State, Faith and Community in the Late Ottoman State*, Oxford, Oxford University Press, 2001, 339.

6 Kemal Karpat, 'Introduction to political and social thought in Turkey', in Kemal

H. Karpat, ed., *Political and Social Thought in the Contemporary Middle East*, New York, Praeger, 1982, p. 366.

7 Tim Jacoby, *Social Power and the Turkish State*, London, Routledge, 2004, p. 80.

8 Ayla Göl, 'A short summary of Turkish foreign policy: 1923–1939', *A.Ü. Siyasal Bilgiler Dergisi*, 48:1–4 (Ocak-Aralık 1993), pp. 57–71.

9 After solving the problems with Britain, Turkey also progressed in its relations with the West: a treaty of friendship was signed between Turkey and France in 1926 and a similar one with Italy in 1928. Turkey also showed its determination to be part of international society and its allegiance to adhere to the rule of international law. For instance, the Turkish government signed the Briand–Kellogg Pact, which renounced 'war as an instrument of national policy' in international relations in 1928. E.H. Carr, *Twenty Years' Crisis, 1919–1939: An Introduction to the Study of International Relations*, London, Papermac, 1995, p. 160. Furthermore, its faithful ally, the Soviet Union, facilitated Turkish membership in the League of Nations in 1932.

After 1932, Turkey made the establishment of regional stability a priority in its foreign policy. The Balkan Entente Treaty was signed between Turkey, Greece, Yugoslavia and Rumania in 1934, which aimed to guarantee each other's territorial integrity and independence against Bulgarian and Italian irredentism. When Italy attacked Ethiopia in 1935, Turkey and Greece proposed the Mediterranean Pact, which was signed by Turkey, Greece, Yugoslavia and Great Britain in 1936. Afterwards, Turkey turned to its eastern neighbours and signed the Sadabat Pact with Iraq, Iran and Afghanistan in 1937.

10 Kemal Ciftci, *Tarih, Kimlik ve Elestirel Kuram Baglaminda Turk Dis Politikasi*, Ankara, Siyasal Kitabevi, 2010, p. 236.

11 In Korkut Boratav's classification, the period 1923–1929 saw the re-structuring of the Turkish economy in accordance with the liberal economy; and industrialisation under the control of the state followed between the years 1930 and 1939. Since the Second World War, the Turkish economy has been integrated into the world economy with its particular problems, which continue to the present day. Boratav, Korkut, *Türkiye İktisat Tarihi: 1908–1985*, Istanbul, Gerçek Yayınevi, 1998, p. 7.

12 Statism was one of the basic principles of Kemalist ideology, which were laid down in the party programme of 1931. The other principles were republicanism, secularism, nationalism, populism and revolutionism.

13 Roger Owen, *State, Power and Politics in the Making of the Modern Middle East*, London, Routledge, 1992, p. 26.

14 Eliezer Tauber, 'Syrian and Iraqi nationalist attitudes to the Kemalist and Bolshevik movements', *Middle Eastern Studies*, 30:4 (October, 1994), p. 898.

15 Edward Ingram, 'Introduction: six variations on a theme', in Edward Ingram, ed., *National and International Politics in the Middle East: Essays in Honour of Elie Kedourie*, Frank Cass, 1986, p. 5.

16 Nilüfer Göle, 'Secularism and Islamism in Turkey: the making of elites and counter elites', *Middle East Journal*, 51:1 (Winter 1997), p. 48.

17 Javel Saeed, *Islam and Modernisation*, London, Praeger, 1994, p. 204.

18 Bassam Tibi, 'The simultaneity of the unsimultaneous: old tribes and imposed nation-states in the modern Middle East', in Philip S. Khoury and Joseph Kostiner, eds, *Tribes and State Formation in the Middle East*, Berkeley, CA: University of California Press, 1990, p. 145.

19 Wilfred C. Smith, *Islam in Modern History*, Princeton, NJ: Princeton University Press, 1957, p. 162.

20 *Ibid.*, p.176.
21 Feroz Ahmad, 'Politics and Islam in Modern Turkey', *Middle Eastern Studies*, 27:1 (1991), p.3.
22 Ali L. Karaosmanoğlu, 'Turkey: Between the Middle East and the Western Europe', in Kemal H. Karpat, ed., *Turkish Foreign Policy: Recent Developments*, Madison, Wisconsin, 1996, p.20.
23 In the Turkish context, secularism become a modernist ideology which, as Gellner described, 'became a "didactic secularism": moralistic and pedagogical, teaching and imposing a modern way of life'. Ernest Gellner, *Muslim Society*, Cambridge, Cambridge University Press, 1981, p.68; Ayla Göl, 'The identity of Turkey: Muslim and secular', *Third World Quarterly*, 30:4, 2009, p.795.
24 E. Fuat Keyman, 'Globalisation, modernity and democracy: in search of a viable domestic polity for a sustainable Turkish foreign policy', *New Perspectives on Turkey*, 40 (2009), p.7.
25 Metin Heper, 'Islam and democracy in Turkey: toward a reconciliation?', *Middle East Journal*, 51:1 (Winter, 1997), p.33.
26 Göle, 'Secularism and Islamism in Turkey', p.49.
27 Another indirect consequence of the Turkish transition to modernity has been that of progress on gender issues. The penetration of secularism into daily life brought about the emancipation of women from religious practices and the participation of women in public life. Women in a Muslim society were depicted for the first time as the builders of a secular modern way of life both in the private and the public spheres. 'Ironically, women have played a central role in the rise of Islamism as well; the veiling of women in the 1980s and 1990s has indicated the re-Islamisation of personal relations, public spaces, and daily practices'. Ibid., p.51.
28 Jürgen Habermas, 'Modernity – an incomplete project', in Thomas Docherty, ed., *Postmodernism: A Reader*, New York, Harvester, 1993; Dilip Parameshwar Gaonkar, 'On Alternative Modernities', *Public Culture*, 11:1 (1999), p.13.

Appendices

Appendix 1 Chronology: Turkey and the South Caucasus, 1918–1921

1918

3 March	Brest-Litovsk Armistice
14 April	Ottoman forces occupy Batum
22 April	Transcaucasian Federation declared
26–28 May	Georgia, Armenia, Azerbaijan declare independence
4 June	Batum Agreement between Ottoman Empire and Transcaucasian republics
30 October	Ottoman Empire signs Armistice of Mudros
1 November	CUP leaders leave Turkey
14 November	First local congress at Kars
17 November	Turks leave South Caucasus; British land at Baku
24 December	British forces occupy Batum

1919

1 February	Turks leave Kars, Ardahan, and Batum
March	Armenian Delegation's territorial claims to six Vilayets of Ottoman Empire at Paris Peace Conference
30 April	Mustafa Kemal appointed Inspector of IXth Army
10 May	Kazım Karabekir becomes Commander of XVth Army
15 May	Greek forces occupy İzmir
19 May	Mustafa Kemal in Samsun
28 May	Declaration of Act of a United Armenia (Russian and Turkish) by Armenian government
30 May	Organisation of first Turkish national military force (*Kuvayi Milliye*) at Ödemiş
22–23 June	*Amasya Tamimi* by Turkish nationalists
8–9 July	Mustafa Kemal resigns from Ottoman Army
23 July–7 August	Erzurum Congress
4–11 September	Sivas Congress

September	Discussion of American Mandate in Armenia at Paris Peace Conference
24 September	Harbord Commission in Erzurum
27 December	Turkish nationalists in Ankara

1920

15 January	Georgia, Azerbaijan, Armenia *de facto* recognised by the Allies
28 January	Turkish National Pact
16 March	Istanbul occupied by the Allies
18 April	San Remo Agreement on the Armenian Question
23 April	Grand National Assembly opened in Ankara
26 April	President Wilson's appointment as arbitrator for the Armenian borders
28 April	Azerbaijan Soviet Socialist Republic declared
11 May	First Turkish delegation leaves for Moscow
27 May	Mustafa Suphi, the Turkish communist, in Baku
1 June	Armenian Mandate in Armenia rejected by US Senate
3 June	Chicherin's letter to Mustafa Kemal
10 August	Treaty of Sèvres and Bolshevik–Armenian Agreement
19 August	Ankara government rejects Treaty of Sèvres
24 August	Turkish–Soviet Friendship Agreement's first draft signed
1–7 September	First Eastern Peoples' Congress in Baku
28 September	Kazım Karabekir advances towards South Caucasus; occupies Sarıkamış
30 October	Turkish forces occupy Kars
7 November	Turkish forces occupy Gümrü
2 December	Armenian Soviet Socialist Republic declared
3 December	Treaty of Alexandropol (Gümrü)

1921

10 January	First İnönü victory
29 January	Death of Mustafa Suphi and first Turkish communists
8 February	Soviet Ambassador Mdivani in Ankara
23 February	The London Conference
25 February	Georgian Soviet Socialist Republic declared
1 March	Turkish–Afghan Agreement in Moscow
16 March	Treaty of Moscow
19 March	Turkish forces evacuate Batum
12 August	Turkish victory at Sakarya
13 October	Kars Agreements in the South Caucasus

Appendix 2 List of the local congresses in Turkish history, 1918–1920*

(1) Islamic Council in Kars, 5 November 1918
(2) First Kars Congress, 14 November 1918
(3) Grand Congress of Islam Council in Kars, 30 November 1918–2
     December 1918
(4) First Ardahan Congress, 3–5 January 1919
(5) Second Ardahan Congress, 7–9 January 1919
(6) Grand Congress in Kars, 17–18 January 1919
(7) First Trabzon Congress, 23 February 1919
(8) Grand Congress in İzmir, 17–19 March 1919
(9) Second Trabzon Congress, 22 May 1919
(10) First Balıkesir Congress, 27 June 1919–12 July 1919
(11) Erzurum Congress, 23 July–7 August 1919
(12) Second Balıkesir Congress, 26–30 July 1919
(13) First Nazilli Congress, 6–8 August 1919
(14) Alaşehir Congress, 16–25 August 1919
(15) Muğla Congress, 18 August 1919
(16) Sivas Congress, 4–12 September 1919
(17) Third Balıkesir Congress, 16–27 September 1919
(18) Second Nazilli Congress, 19–20 or 23–24 September 1919
(19) Third Nazilli Congress, 6 October 1919
(20) First Edirne Congress, 16 October 1919
(21) Muğla Congress, 20–31 October 1919
(22) Fourth Balıkesir Congress, 19–29 November 1919
(23) Second Edirne Congress, 15 January 1920
(24) Congress of Oltu Islamic Progress Party, 21 February 1920
(25) Fifth Balıkesir Congress, 10–23 March 1920
(26) Lüleburgaz Congress, 31 March–2 April 1920
(27) Third (Grand) Edirne Congress, 9–14 May 1920
(28) Afyon Congress, 2 August 1920
(29) First Pozantı Congress, 5 August 1920
(30) Second Pozantı Congress, 8 October 1920

Note

* *Source*: Bülent Tanör, *Türkiye'de Kongre İktidarları (1918–1920)*, Istanbul, Yapı Kredi
   Yayınları, 1998, p. 114.

Appendix 3 The National Pact, 28 January 1920*

The Ottoman *Meclis-i Mebusan* in Istanbul, of which most members were pro-nationalist, declared the Turkish 'National Pact' that confirmed the principles of the Sivas Congress. The clauses of the pact were as follows:

(1) The destiny of the portions of Ottoman territory under foreign occupation and peopled by an Arab majority at the time of the signing of the armistice on 30 October 1918 should be determined by a plebiscite of all inhabitants. All such territories inhabited by an Ottoman Muslim majority, united in religion, race and inspirations, are imbued with feelings of mutual respect, concern and devotion, and form an indivisible whole.

(2) We accept a new plebiscite in the case of the three sancaks [Kars, Ardahan and Batum], which had by general vote decided to join the mother country when they were first freed [from Russian occupation].

(3) The juridical status of western Thrace, which has been made dependent upon the peace treaty to be signed with Turkey, must also be determined in accordance with a free vote of the inhabitants.

(4) The city of Istanbul, which is the seat of the Islamic Caliphate and of the Ottoman Sultanate and government, as well as the Sea of Marmara must be protected from every danger. So long as this principle is observed, whatever decision arrived at jointly by us and other states concerning the use for trade and communication of the Straits of the Black Sea and the Mediterranean shall be honoured.

(5) The rights of minorities as agreed on in the treaties concluded between the Allied powers and their enemies and certain of their associates shall be confirmed and assured by us on condition that Muslim minorities in neighbouring countries will benefit from the same rights.

(6) Like every country, in order to secure a more effective and well-ordered administration that will enable us to develop our political, judicial and financial affairs, we also need complete independence and sovereignty as a fundamental condition of our life and continued existence. Therefore we oppose restrictions that are harmful to our political, judicial and financial development. The conditions of the settlement of our [foreign] debts shall be determined likewise, in a manner not contrary to these principles.

Note

* *Source:* Stanford J. Shaw and Ezel Kural Shaw, *History of the Ottoman Empire and Modern Turkey; Vol.II: Reform, Revolution and Republic, The Rise of Modern Turkey,* Cambridge, Cambridge University Press, 1995, p. 348.
See the original document both in Ottoman and modern Turkish in *Atatürk'ün Milli Dış Politikası (Cumhuriyet Dönemine Ait 100 Belge: 1919–1923),* Vol.I, Ankara, T.C. Kültür Bakanlığı Yayınları, 1994, pp. 131–133, Doc. 13.

Appendix 4 List of cabinets and their chief ministers in Istanbul and Ankara, 1918–1923*

The names of the grand viziers and foreign ministers and the periods of their cabinets in <u>Istanbul</u> were as follows:

(1) Ahmet Izzet Pasha (14 October–11 November 1918)
  Memmet Nabi Bey: Minister for Foreign Affairs
(2) Second Ahmet Tevfik Pasha (11 November 1918–12 January 1919)
  Mustafa Reşit Pasha: Minister for Foreign Affairs
(3) Third Ahmet Tevfik Pasha (13 January–23 February 1919)
  Mustafa Reşit Pasha: Minister for Foreign Affairs
(4) Fourth Ahmet Tevfik Pasha (24 February–3 March 1919)
  Yusuf Franko Pasha: Minister for Foreign Affairs
(5) First Damat Ferit Pasha (4 March 1919–15/16 May 1919)
  Damat Ferit Pasha: Minister for Foreign Affairs
(6) Second Damat Ferit Pasha (19 May–20 July 1919)
  Damat Ferit Pasha, Safa Bey: Minister for Foreign Affairs
(7) Third Damat Ferit Pasha (21 July–1 October 1919)
  Damat Ferit Pasha: Minister for Foreign Affairs
(8) Ali Rıza Pasha (2 October 1919–3 March 1920)
  Mustafa Reşit Pasha, Safa Bey: Minister for Foreign Affairs
(9) Salih Hulusi Pasha (8 March–2 April 1920)
  Safa Bey: Minister for Foreign Affairs
(10) Fourth Damat Ferit Pasha (5 April–30 July 1920)
  Damat Ferit Pasha: Minister for Foreign Affairs
(11) Fifth Damat Ferit Pasha (31 July–17 October 1920)
  Damat Ferit Pasha: Minister for Foreign Affairs
(12) Fifth Ahmet Tevfik Pasha (20 October–4 November 1920)
  Ahmet İzzet Pasha: Minister for Foreign Affairs

The cabinets and their chief ministers in <u>Ankara</u> were as follows:

(1) Mustafa Kemal Pasha [Atatürk] (25 April–3 May 1920)
  Bekir Sami Bey [Kunduh]: Minister for Foreign Affairs
(2) First Fevzi Pasha [Çakmak](3 May 1920–19 May 1921)
  Bekir Sami Bey, Yusuf Kemal Bey [Tengirşek]: Minister for Foreign Affairs
(3) Second Fevzi Pasha (19 May 1921–12 July 1922)
  Yusuf Kemal Bey: Minister for Foreign Affairs
(4) Hüseyin Rauf Bey [Orbay] (12 July 1922–4 August 1923)
  Yusuf Kemal Bey, İsmet Pasha [İnönü]: Minister for Foreign Affairs

(5)   First Ali Fethi Bey [Okyar] (14 August–27 October 1923)
        Ismet Pasha, Minister for Foreign Affairs

Note

*   *Source*: H. Adnan Önelçin, *Nutuk'un (Söylev'in) İçinden*, Istanbul, Yüce Yayınları, 1981,
    pp. 291–307.

Appendix 5 The clauses of the Treaty of Sèvres, 10 August 1920*

The Treaty of Sèvres was signed between Britain, France, Italy, Japan,
Armenia, Belgium, Greece, the Hedjaz, Poland, Portugal, Romania, the Serbo-
Croat-Slovene state and Czecho-Slovakia on the one part and Turkey on the
other on 10 August 1920. The clauses of the treaty can be briefly summarised as
follows:

After the covenant of the League of Nations in Part I (Articles 1 to 26) the frontiers of Turkey were determined in Part II (Articles 27 to 35).
In Part III, the Political clauses were discussed (Articles 36 to 139). The Ottoman
Empire was left as only a rump state in northern Asia with Istanbul as its capital
(Article 36). There would be international control of the Straits with demilitarisation of the adjacent lands, but Istanbul would remain under nominal Ottoman
control (Article 37 to 61). Kurdistan to the north of the province of Mosul was
left within the Ottoman Empire, but was to receive autonomy and the right to
appeal for independence to the League of Nations within a year. The territory
known as Kurdistan, east of the Euphrates, was to gain autonomy with the right
to opt for independence within a year if the Kurds wished (Articles 62 to 64).
The city of İzmir and its environs were put under Greek administration for a
period of five years, after which what was left of the population would be allowed
to request permanent incorporation into the Greek state if it wished (Articles 65
to 83). Greece, in addition to western Thrace (which it had just acquired from
Bulgaria), received eastern Thrace, including Edirne, right up to the Çatalca line,
only 40 kilometres from the Ottoman capital (Articles 84 to 87). An independent Armenian state was recognised in Eastern Anatolia, with its boundaries to
be determined by arbitration on the part of President Wilson (Articles 88 to 93).
The Arab provinces were detached from the empire, as decided already at San
Remo. France established mandates in Syria and Lebanon and a sphere of influ-
ence in southern Anatolia. Britain established mandates in Palestine, southern
Syria (now called Transjordan) and Mesopotamia (Iraq), including the oil-rich
province of Mosul (Articles 94 to 97). Hedjaz became a free and independent
state (Articles 98 to 100). Turkey recognised the Protectorate proclaimed over
Egypt by Great Britain in 1918 and the British rights over Sudan and Cyprus
(Articles 101 to 117). Morocco and Tunis were left under French protection
(Articles 118 to 120). Italy received the south eastern part of Asia Minor as a

sphere of influence when the Aegean Islands were given to Italy (Articles 121 to 122).

The rest of the treaty dealt with different issues within thirteen parts; there were 433 articles in total.
Part IV: Protection of Minorities (Articles140 to 151); Part V: Military, naval and air clauses (Articles152 to 207); Part VI: Prisoners of war and graves (Articles 208 to 225);
Part VII: Penalties (Articles 226 to 230); Part VIII: Financial Clauses (Articles 231 to 260); Part IX: Economic clauses (Articles 261 to 317); Part X: Aerial navigation (Articles 318 to 327); Part XI: Ports, waterways and railways (Articles 328 to 373); Part XII: Labour (Articles 374 to 414); Part XIII: Miscellaneous provisions (Articles 415 to 433).

Note

* *Source*: Seha L. Meray and Osman Olcay, *Osmanlı İmparatorluğunun Çöküş Belgeleri: (Mondros Bırakışması, Sevr Andlaşması, İlgili Belgeler)*, Ankara, Siyasal Bilgiler Fakültesi Yayınları, 1977, pp.45-185; The English version of this document is to be found in the treaty series of Parliamentary Papers. *Parliamentary Papers*, Vol. LI, Treaty Series No. 11 (1920), Cmd. 964, pp.1-99.

Index

Lightning Source UK Ltd.
Milton Keynes UK
UKOW02f1319110417
298878UK00005B/171/P